The CORETTA SCOTT KING AWARDS

1970–2014

ALA Editions purchases fund advocacy, awareness,
and accreditation programs for library professionals worldwide.

The CORETTA SCOTT KING AWARDS
1970–2014

Fifth Edition
45th Anniversary

Edited by Carole J. McCollough and Adelaide Poniatowski Phelps

The Coretta Scott King Book Awards Committee
Ethnic and Multicultural Information Exchange Round Table

An imprint of the American Library Association
CHICAGO 2015

CAROLE J. McCOLLOUGH, PhD, is a retired professor of library science from Wayne State University in Detroit. Currently, she conducts workshops and in-service programs and provides consulting services throughout Michigan and Ohio. She is a past chair of the Coretta Scott King Task Force and current board member of the Children's Defense Fund's Langston Hughes Library and of the Southfield (Michigan) Public Library.

ADELAIDE PONIATOWSKI PHELPS has a master's degree in library and information science from Wayne State University in Detroit and a second master's degree in English literature from Oakland University in Rochester, Michigan. She is a past coordinator of the Educational Resources Lab in the School of Education and Human Services at Oakland University and a past lecturer in children's literature there for the reading department. In addition, she served two terms on the Coretta Scott King Book Award Jury (2007–2008).

Cover art © Simon & Schuster Books for Young Readers, 2012. From *I, Too, Am America* by Langston Hughes, illustrated by Bryan Collier. Reprinted with permission from Simon & Schuster Children's Publishing.

Photograph of Leo Dillon by Chester Higgins Jr., chesterhiggins.com. Photograph of Fredrick L. McKissack Sr., shown with his wife Patricia C. McKissack, by John McKissack.

© 2015 by the American Library Association

Printed in the United States of America

19 18 17 16 15   5 4 3 2 1

Extensive effort has gone into ensuring the reliability of the information in this book; however, the publisher makes no warranty, express or implied, with respect to the material contained herein.

ISBN: 978-0-8389-3610-8 (paper).

Library of Congress Cataloging-in-Publication Data

The Coretta Scott King Awards, 1970-2014. — Fifth edition, 45th anniversary / edited by Carole J. McCollough and Adelaide Poniatowski Phelps, The Coretta Scott King Book Awards Committee, Ethnic and Multicultural Information Exchange Round Table.
    pages cm
Includes bibliographical references and indexes.
ISBN 978-0-8389-3610-8 (print : alk. paper) 1. Coretta Scott King Award. 2. American literature—African American authors—Bibliography. 3. American literature—African American authors—Awards. 4. Children's literature, American—Bibliography. 5. Children's literature, American—Awards. 6. African Americans in literature—Bibliography. 7. Children—Books and reading—United States. I. McCollough, Carole J., editor. II. Phelps, Adelaide Poniatowski, editor. III. Ethnic and Multicultural Information Exchange Round Table. Coretta Scott King Book Awards Committee.
Z1037.A2C67 2015
016.8108'0928208996073—dc23

2014023986

Book design by Kim Thornton in the Znikomit, Vista Sans, and Chaparral typefaces.

♾ This paper meets the requirements of ANSI/NISO Z39.48–1992 (Permanence of Paper).

Dedicated to the memory of

Leo Dillon
1933–2012

Fredrick L. McKissack
1939–2013

Walter Dean Myers
1937–2014

Contents

Preface by Jonda C. McNair ix
Acknowledgments xi
History xiii

Author Awards ... 1

Profile: Gabrielle Douglas ... 57

Illustrator Awards ... 59
Illustrations from award-winning books follow page 136

Selected Biographies ... 89

Contributors ... 123
Coretta Scott King Award–Winning Authors, 1970–2014 ... 127
Coretta Scott King Author Award and Honor Books by Title ... 131
Coretta Scott King Award–Winning Illustrators, 1974–2014 ... 135
Coretta Scott King Illustrator Award and Honor Books by Title ... 137

Subject Index 141
General Index 151

Additional content can be found at alaeditions.org/webextras

Preface

SINCE ITS INCEPTION IN 1969, THE CORETTA SCOTT KING AWARD HAS INCREASED THE VISIBILITY of children's literature about the black experience and accentuated the work of numerous African American authors and illustrators. For many of these artists the Coretta Scott King Award has served as a means by which to introduce them to the larger children's literature world—something that will benefit all readers, including children and adults. The John Steptoe New Talent Award has provided an outlet specifically for up-and-coming African American authors and illustrators to establish themselves and sustain their careers in the field of children's literature.

This fifth edition of *The Coretta Scott King Awards* features reviews of all award and honor books selected during the five years since the last edition was published, as well as biographies of awardees and full-color images from select titles. Grade-level indicators are also included with the reviews to assist educators and librarians in successfully matching texts to readers. In addition, nonfiction books are noted with an asterisk for those seeking out this particular genre. The index (by author, title, illustrator, and subject) makes it easy to navigate the book and quickly access information. Many thanks to the members of the Coretta Scott King Book Awards Committee for writing reviews of titles, to the OLOS staff at the American Library Association, and to the coeditors of this volume, Carole J. McCollough and Adelaide Poniatowski Phelps, for their dedication and hard work.

JONDA C. McNAIR
Chair, Coretta Scott King Book Awards Committee, 2012–2015

Acknowledgments

WE GRATEFULLY ACKNOWLEDGE THE SOUTHFIELD PUBLIC LIBRARY IN SOUTHFIELD, MICHIGAN, and Oakland University's Educational Resources Lab (ERL) for providing space for research and access to their collections. An extra word of thanks to Michelle Harrell Washington, MLIS, director, Office for Diversity, Office for Literacy and Outreach Services, and Jamie Santoro, acquisitions editor, ALA Editions, for their weekly conference calls and their confidence and support that kept us on track. In addition, Adelaide would like to acknowledge her husband, Tom, for his understanding of the time commitment required and recognition of the value of the work that the CSK committee does. Carole specifically would like to acknowledge her dog, Bella, for enduring her frequent absences for editing and research.

CAROLE J. McCOLLOUGH
AND ADELAIDE PONIATOWSKI PHELPS

History

THE CORETTA SCOTT KING BOOK AWARD AND ITS ASSOCIATION WITH ALA ORIGINATED IN 1969. It came as the result of a discussion between two librarians, Glyndon Flynt Greer and Mabel McKissick, and the publisher John Carroll. The impetus flowed from the observation that no African American author or illustrator had ever been honored by the prestigious Newbery and Caldecott awards, established in 1922 and 1938, respectively, and sponsored by what was then the ALA Children's Service Division. It was thought that the establishment of a special award would bring attention to the fine work produced by African American authors and illustrators in books for children and young people. The first award was presented during the New Jersey Library Association meeting in May 1970. The first winner was the late Lillie Patterson, who was honored for her young readers edition of the life of Martin Luther King Jr., written shortly after his assassination. Over the next twelve years, without official recognition from the executive board of ALA, the presentations continued, and in 1974 an illustrator award category was added. The first to receive that award was George Ford, for the illustrations in Sharon Mathis's biography *Ray Charles*.

In 1982, through the efforts of E. J. Josey, an ALA councilor, the awards committee, chaired by Effie Lee Morris, was named the Coretta Scott King Task Force and became a part of the ALA Social Responsibilities Round Table (SRRT). This congenial union remained in place until the ALA midwinter meeting in January 2004 in San Diego. Under the leadership of chairperson Fran Ware and past chairs Carole McCollough and Barbara Jones Clark, the task force's affiliation was changed from the Social Responsibilities Round Table to the Ethnic and Multicultural Information Exchange Round Table (EMIERT)—the rationale being that the goals and missions of the task force were more closely aligned with those of EMIERT. All was done with the approval and blessings of the action council of SRRT. The Coretta Scott King Task Force expressed appreciation to SRRT for its twenty-four years of working together.

In a continuous process of growth and visionary expansion, the task force functions under well-constructed bylaws. Included in this organizational pattern is the clear definition of the makeup, length of terms, and responsibilities of the seven-member awards jury. Also included are established criteria for the selection of the award-winning titles:

> Thematically the material (text or illustration) must speak to some aspect of African American culture, with an awareness of Martin Luther King Jr.'s sense of the brotherhood of all cultures.

The author or illustrator must be African American.

The content (illustration or text) must be of high literary or visual quality, with a theme that has the potential for long-term, meaningful significance.

Only books published the year preceding a jury's period of deliberation are eligible for consideration.

Books must be published in the United States.

The winner of the Coretta Scott King/John Steptoe New Talent Award must meet the same standards as winners of the other awards, but eligibility is limited to works of those who have had no more than three books published.

Since 1972, the awards have been presented at a gala breakfast. The breakfast, held during the ALA annual conference, is marked by ever-increasing attendance. Each winner in art and text receives an honorarium, the value of which continues to grow. The honorarium for the winners has been a gift from the Johnson Publishing Company since the award's inception in 1970. The winners also receive a plaque and a set of encyclopedias, one from Encyclopedia Britannica and the other from World Book, Inc. In keeping with the times, the encyclopedias are now on discs. In 1995, the first Genesis Award for new talent was presented. This award, which was later officially renamed the Coretta Scott King/John Steptoe New Talent Award, recognizes a writer or illustrator whose early potential speaks of things to come. The first recipient, Sharon M. Draper, the author of *Tears of a Tiger*, went on to become a Coretta Scott King award winner in 1998 for her novel *Forged by Fire*. She continues to be recognized not only for novels about contemporary young adults (*November Blues* received a Coretta Scott King author honor in 2008) but also for her monumental, thoroughly researched historical novel *Copper Sun*, which won the Coretta Scott King author award in 2007.

Since 1984, among the special highlights at each breakfast is the presence of children, the ones to whom the books are designed to speak. These young guests, sponsored by generous donors, come from the geographical area of ALA's annual conference. For some of the young people attending the breakfast there is a moment of special individual recognition. Each year, starting in 1999, Disney/Jump at the Sun has sponsored an essay contest for students who live in the area of the conference. From papers written by elementary and middle school students, judges choose the best paper about a preselected book. The audience is always delighted with the poise with which the young winners read their essays and graciously thank the award sponsors and the Coretta Scott King Book Awards Committee for their special opportunity and the scholarship check. Other support comes from the publishing houses of the winning titles. Each young guest goes home with a selection from the winning and honor books for his/her personal collection. The publishers further collaborate on the design and production of the study guides created by each awards jury. The guides are distributed at the breakfast and are available through the ALA Office of Library Outreach Services (OLOS) as long as the supply lasts.

As the Coretta Scott King Book Awards Committee looked forward to the commemoration of its fortieth anniversary, the members celebrated the life of its last surviving founder, Mabel McKissick, whose early works ended in 2009 after her twenty-seven years as a school librarian in Connecticut and elsewhere. 2009 was also the time to remember the late Basil Phillips, photographic editor for *Ebony* magazine. Phillips was instrumental in establishing the author honorarium through the largesse of John Johnson, founder of Johnson Publishing. The memory of our stalwart leaders will be a permanent part of the Coretta Scott King Book Awards history.

Coretta Scott King award-winning books can be recognized by a seal designed in 1974 by the internationally known artist Lev Mills, who at the time was artist-in-residence at Atlanta University. The elements of this official seal convey the principles to which Martin Luther King Jr. was dedicated. Within a circle, which represents continuity, sits a child reading a book. The five religious symbols below the image of the child represent non-sectarianism: star and crescent (Islam), om (Hinduism), cross (Christianity), Star of David (Judaism), yin-yang (Taoism). The seal also includes a dove of peace and a superimposed pyramid, a tribute to human strength and to the strength of Atlanta University, where the award was headquartered at the time the seal was designed.

The original seals for the winners were printed in bronze, which represented the earth tones of Mother Africa, and the seals for the honor books were printed in tones of silver. In the late 1990s, without a change in the design, the seals were produced in a more environmentally friendly format—a black background with character details superimposed in bronze for winners or in pewter for honor books. The seal for the Coretta Scott King/John Steptoe New Talent Award is detailed in green, a color symbolic of new beginnings.

Among the many highlights in the history of the Coretta Scott King Book Awards is Legends, Folklore, and Real Life Stories: The Coretta Scott King Award Books, a special exhibit of illustrations from award winners mounted by the Art Institute of Chicago from July 2000 to February 2001. In addition, educational programs and workshops were conducted by some of the illustrators whose works were on display.

During the tenure of chair Barbara Jones Clark, the task force launched a national awareness campaign to acquaint a wider audience with the role the Coretta Scott King Book Awards play in showcasing the valuable and informative works of African American authors and illustrators. The late Virginia Hamilton served as honorary chairperson of the committee that spearheaded this endeavor in 1998. In 2008–2009, chair Deborah Taylor, working with author and editor Andrea Pinkney, widened the visibility of the Coretta Scott King Book Awards by launching a broad-based Fortieth Anniversary Public Awareness Program, which showcased a handsome broadside by award-winning artist Kadir Nelson and a celebratory poem by Arnold Adoff.

The first edition of *The Coretta Scott King Awards* was published in 1994. It presented the history of the award, biographical sketches of winners and honor recipients, annotations of each title, and handsome reproductions of illustrations from award winners published from 1974 to 1994. Following the same format, the second edition was published in 1999, the third in 2004, the fourth edition in 2009, and now the fifth edition in 2014. Each new edition is updated to make the material more relevant and more useful to a wider audience. With an attitude of always looking forward and broadening the vision of the Coretta Scott King Committee, in 2010 a new award category was added. In appreciation and remembrance of the late Virginia Hamilton, the Coretta Scott King–Virginia Hamilton Award for Lifetime Achievement was established. Over each three-year cycle an author, illustrator, and librarian in the field will be recognized for their body of work. Each recipient will receive an honorarium, a medal emblazoned with his/her name, and a photograph of the late "word master" Virginia Hamilton. The first recipients were author Walter Dean Myers, illustrator Ashley Bryan, and librarian Henrietta M. Smith.

The Coretta Scott King Book Awards Committee is indebted to Henrietta M. Smith for her many contributions, including as editor of the first four editions of *The Coretta Scott King Awards* and as author of the history. We begin a new era with a discussion guide commissioned by ALA, published in 2014, and written and edited by Carole J. McCollough and Adelaide Poniatowski Phelps: *Coretta Scott King Award Books Discussion Guide: Pathways to Democracy*.

Author Awards
1970–2014

An * indicates nonfiction

2014 Winner

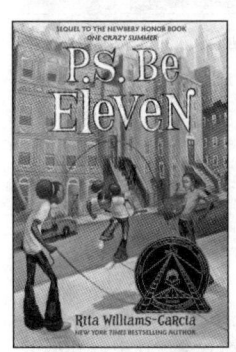

WILLIAMS-GARCIA, RITA.
P.S. Be Eleven. Amistad/HarperCollins, 2013. Gr. 4–6.

Sisters Delphine, Vonetta, and Fern are back from their life-changing summer in Oakland with their mother, Nzila, in this new adventure that follows up on Williams-Garcia's award-winning *One Crazy Summer*. It's the late 1960s in Bedford-Stuyvesant and a lot is going on there and in the country. The Gaither girls return to some changes, the biggest of which is that their father now has a girlfriend, Miss Marva Hendrix. The civil rights movement is on everyone's mind, the Vietnam War is raging . . . and the Jackson 5 are coming to town! These are exciting and challenging personal times as Delphine negotiates the changes in her family and begins to lose her leadership role with her sisters. Woven through the narrative are letters between Delphine and Nzila, which allow the readers a front-row seat on their developing relationship. Each letter from Nzila responds to Delphine's questions and challenges honestly, but ends with the snappy "be eleven" when she feels her daughter pushes too hard. Nzila's wisdom comes through in these letters and, in the end, she drops the warning and trusts her eldest daughter. Though this story is made richer by reading *One Crazy Summer*, the story stands on its own two strong feet, just like Delphine is learning to do. —*Robin Smith*

From **P.S. Be Eleven**

For me, the sixth-grade dance meant trying to match steps with boys I'd slugged. Boys I'd said "Your mama" to in the school yard because they'd said it to me first in a battle of the Dozens. For me, and me alone, it meant waiting to be asked to dance when no one would ask because they'd have to look way up at me and now I was even taller than when I'd left for Oakland.
—*Rita Williams-Garcia*

2014 Honors

LEWIS, JOHN, ANDREW AYDIN, AND NATE POWELL.
March: Book One. Top Shelf Productions, 2013. Gr. 4–10. *

Congressman John Lewis (GA), one of the legendary and iconic figures from the civil rights movement, uses the graphic novel format to recount his personal story in *March: Book One*. From growing up on a farm in Alabama to participating in the sit-ins and freedom rides across the South, this recollection of life for African Americans in the mid-1960s is compelling. The book begins with the inauguration of President Barack Obama on January 20, 2009. As the congressman prepares to leave his office on Capitol Hill to attend this historical event, he is visited by a mother and her two sons who begin to ask the congressman questions that take him "back down memory lane." As in his life, Lewis shares his humorous side as he recalls his early days of preaching to the chickens; not to be overshadowed by the more serious events of being beaten and attacked by dogs for standing up for his civil rights. The retelling of his story in a graphic novel format makes this history lesson not only more effective, but more accessible. This descriptive autobiographical account grips the reader as you realize that the image of them spitting in his face actually happened. The Nate Powell artwork, combined with Lewis's text, vividly tells the story. Congressman Lewis credits a 1958 comic book, *Martin Luther King and the Montgomery Story*, as the reason he decided to share his own telling of this time period in a modern-day comic book format that allows the story of the civil rights movement to travel through different generations. —*Rose Dawson*

From **March: Book One**

This is an UNLAWFUL ASSEMBLY! YOUR MARCH IS NOT CONDUCIVE TO THE PUBLIC SAFETY—YOU ARE ORDERED TO DISPERSE AND GO BACK TO YOUR CHURCH OR TO YOUR HOMES!

YOU HAVE TWO MINUTES TO TURN AROUND AND GO BACK TO YOUR CHURCH.

— *John Lewis, Andrew Aydin, and Nate Powell*

MYERS, WALTER DEAN. *Darius & Twig.* Amistad/HarperCollins, 2013. Gr. 8–12.

Two friends—one African American, one Dominican—navigate their young lives in Harlem amidst a jumble of obstacles, including race, violence, family expectations, and personal choice. Darius is the dreamer and the writer of the pair; he rises over the streets of Harlem in his daydreams as Fury, a peregrine falcon who soars and strikes out while Darius cannot. Twig, a star runner, uses his gift of speed to free him from his family's expectations and the bullying by peers who won't accept his dream. Darius and Twig fiercely defend their ambitions for a better life through their friendship, all the while living in a climate where even the slightest misstep could send either of them down the wrong path and shatter the hopes for the future they so strongly hold.

Myers captures the realities of life in Harlem in this short novel that focuses on two believable contemporary characters. He offers a glimpse into the achievable dreams of today's youth—bringing forth a much-needed perspective in contrast to the stereotypes abundant in media reports today. He documents the bravery of two young men from different backgrounds coming together in a strong friendship made even stronger by their differences and in spite of the prejudices that surround them. Myers also offers a perspective of the negative associations inherent in the sports industry, and the dangers our youth face in seemingly positive opportunities. The distinctive teen voices of Darius and Twig make the novel an admirable and important inclusion to young adult fiction. As always, Myers populates this novel with characters that we might know, teens who live in the real world, and, who in the case of Darius and Twig, find their way with sensitivity, friendship, and even grace. —*Sue Sherif*

From **Darius & Twig**

Fury sits on my wrist, and I can feel the power of his talons as he grips the thick leather glove. I am breathing hard but he barely moves, only rocking slightly as he anticipates the hunt. I reach for the string that covers his mask, and taking the other string in my teeth, I loosen it. He turns his head quickly and sees it is me.

—*Walter Dean Myers*

GRIMES, NIKKI. *Words with Wings.* Word Song/Boyd's Mills, 2013. Gr. 4–10.

Grimes's spare, concise poetry masterfully conveys the emotions and inner life of a young girl coping with important life changes—divorcing parents, a new school, moving away from her best friend. Daydreaming becomes her refuge. In portraying Gabriella's daydreams, Grimes celebrates the power of words and the importance of imagination. The poems also fill in the "back story" that explains why Gaby has withdrawn so heavily into daydreaming, and the importance of an understanding new teacher who finds a way to creatively support Gaby and invite the whole class to harness their daydreams in a productive way.

The poems not only convey the storyline, they do so with vivid imagery and the skillful use of other poetic devices. The poems themselves are well crafted. Grimes uses a variety of poetic forms, including haiku and shape poems. She also makes effective use of poetic devices such as alliteration and assonance. Her poems are clear and accessible to a youthful audience. Some lines are memorable, such as the following haiku: Mom names me for a /creature with wings. Then wonders /what makes my thoughts fly. The poems also paint a realistic portrait of a girl gaining confidence in her own power to be resilient in the face of adversity. —*Rudine Sims Bishop*

From **Words with Wings**

Some words
sit still on the page
holding a story steady.

Those words never get me into trouble.
But other words have wings
that wake my daydreams.
They fly in, silent as sunrise,
tickle my imagination,
and carry my thoughts away.
I can't help
but buckle up
for the ride!

—*Nikki Grimes*

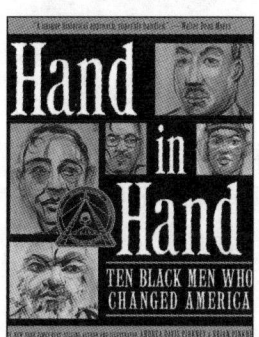

2013 Winner

PINKNEY, ANDREA DAVIS. *Hand in Hand: Ten Black Men Who Changed America.* Illustrated by Brian Pinkney. New York: Jump at the Sun Books, 2012. Gr. 5–8. *

Hand in Hand: Ten Black Men Who Changed America highlights the legacy of ten brave men who saw a need for change in the lives of black Americans. Each in his own courageous way dared to make a difference. The history is told chronologically from colonial times to the twenty-first century. With the author's unique writing style, each individual is introduced with narration describing how the use of his HANDS was instrumental in reaching his goal in the fight for justice. A full-page watercolor image of the individual, a contribution from the palette of artist Brian Pinkney, follows the narration. The biographical sketch gives a chronological report of each man's life from childhood until his goal was reached. Those whose stories are included are: Benjamin Banneker, Frederick Douglass, Booker T. Washington, W. E. B. Du Bois, A. Philip Randolph, Thurgood Marshall, Jackie Robinson, Malcolm X, Martin Luther King, Jr., and Barack H. Obama II. —*Cora P. Dunkley*

From **Hand in Hand: Ten Black Men Who Changed America**

These are the stories of ten bold men
who built a chain called hand in hand.
Each a link in this mighty strand:
Reaching
Pulling
Believing
Achieving
Working toward freedom
Hand in hand.

—*Andrea Davis Pinkney*

2013 Honors

WOODSON, JACQUELINE. *Each Kindness.* Illustrated by E. B. Lewis. Nancy Paulsen Books, 2012. Gr. K–3.

One winter's day Ms. Albert introduces her class to Maya, a new student who is assigned the desk next to Chloe. After spending the winter ignoring Maya's overtures of friendship, Chloe learns the meaning of kindness and the regrets that come from not being kind.

A wonderful updating of Eleanor Estes's *The Hundred Dresses*, *Each Kindness* is an outstanding example of a "purposeful" book in the hands of a skilled writer. Woodson lets the story unfold without mentally stopping the narrative to point to the lesson. Instead, she trusts that the child reader will understand it. The story is enhanced by E. B. Lewis's illustrations that add to the power of the narrative. Chloe comes to understand her varying emotions from pouty face to regrets in the light of Ms. Albert's lesson on kindness. A strong story for classroom sharing that illuminates the power of each kindness. —*Therese Bigelow*

From **Each Kindness**

Our teacher Ms. Albert said,
Say good morning to our new student.
But most of us were silent.
The only empty seat was next to me.
That's where our teacher put Maya.
And on that first day, Maya turned to me and smiled.
But I didn't smile back.
I moved my chair, myself and my books
a little farther away from her.
When she looked my way, I turned to the window
and stared out at the snow.
And every day after that,
when Maya came into the classroom,
I looked away and didn't smile back.

—*Jacqueline Woodson*

NELSON, VAUNDA MICHEAUX. *No Crystal Stair: A Documentary Novel of the Life and Work of Lewis Michaux, Harlem Bookseller.* Carolrhoda, 2012. Gr. 8–12.

Some of the language in this fictionalized history may shock contemporary readers ("Negro," "colored," and so on), and that's as it should be in this realistic portrait of black American life in the early to mid-1900s. The story begins in 1906 in Newport News, Virginia, when Lewis was about ten. His wry humor comes through when he learns a lesson about Jesus helping those who make an effort, although not quite the way his mother intended. Readers "mature" along with Lewis as he grows up before coming in to his own as the "Harlem Bookseller," proprietor of the National Memorial African Bookstore, an institution that was much more than a store. This groundbreaking enterprise focused on black literature, readers, and writers, and offered a community hub for people interested in current affairs, particularly civil rights.

Varying points of view keep the first-person narrative interesting, some voices are those of real historical figures, including Lewis himself, his brothers, Nikki Giovanni, and others; some are fictional. An index helps identify what is factual. Archival images—again, some factual, some not—of newspaper articles, advertisements, FBI reports, photos of the store and prominent people who visited it are interspersed throughout these narratives and add flavor to the period, as do black-and-white spot sketches.

This account doesn't sugarcoat what life was like for its subject, Lewis Michaux, and many other Americans at that time; yet, it is an inspiring and uplifting history lesson, even better for being couched in such a gripping read. —*Diane Foote*

From **No Crystal Stair**

I am interested in going into the book business and approach Carter G. Woodson for guidance. His stellar reputation in scholarly circles and connection with the *Negro History Journal* led me to his doorstep. "I'm a historian. I'm a writer. I am not a seller of books," Mr. Woodson said when I met him. "The man you need to interview about Negro book sales is Michaux in New York."

Woodson was right. Lewis Michaux knows about books . . . and selling. And he shared his knowledge with enthusiasm. A trifle self-impressed but a fascinating man, and his National Memorial African Bookstore is a literary treasure.

—*Vaunda Micheaux Nelson*

2012 Winner

NELSON, KADIR. *Heart and Soul: The Story of America and African Americans.* HarperCollins, 2011. Gr. 3–7. *

Kadir Nelson's *Heart and Soul* is true to its title. In words and illustrations, it tells the story of Americans and African Americans through the voice of a narrator whose forefathers were brought to this foreign soil against their will. The text balances the ugliness of slavery against the contributions of African Americans in the building of this great nation, proving their endurance and perseverance while striving to become first-class citizens. Nelson's dramatic oil paintings show the slow, but steady changes made in this country, all embodied in a riveting story of survival, freedom, and equality. Included in the story are references to Dr. Martin Luther King's "I Have a Dream" speech at the 1963 March on Washington, the 1964 signing of the Civil Rights Act, and the 1965 Voting Rights Act. The vibrant colors in the paintings that open each chapter depict some of the actual freedom-based events in the history of this country. The final illustration—a pair of wrinkled hands holding a patriotically designed pin saying, "I voted"—may be the hands of the narrator who had the opportunity to vote for the first African American President of the United States, Barack Obama. —*Cora P. Dunkley*

From **Heart and Soul**

Life on the frontier was rough. In most parts there weren't any trees, so folks had to build their homes out of mud bricks and cow pies. For fresh water they had to dig wells. They grew their vegetables and hunted for food. Every day on those flat prairies was a fight to survive, but fighting to live as a free person out there was always better than living under the whip on a southern plantation.

—*Kadir Nelson*

2012 Honors

GREENFIELD, ELOISE. *The Great Migration: Journey to the North.* Illustrated by Jan Spivey Gilchrist. Amistad/HarperCollins, 2011. Gr. 3–5.

Collage illustrations with a grainy, archival look pair beautifully with these evocative poems. Maps, old photos, and woodblock prints blend to provide readers with an abundance of images to pore over while reading or listening to the poetry. The third spread of the poem entitled "The Trip" shows a picture of a steam train going past a cornfield. Perceptive readers will notice the images of people camouflaged among the cornstalks. The emotions of the travelers clearly reflect what they are feeling. In "Goodbyes Man" the man is shown with his head down, arms folded; the accompanying poem tells us "Saying goodbye to the land / puts a pain on my heart."

It's tempting for those of us on this side of history to assume everyone was happy to move to escape the unjust social order so prominent in the American South in the early 1900s; but in truth, the people who did so took great risks in leaving everything they knew behind, for an unsure outcome. "Question" poses aptly each traveler's worry: "Will I make a good life / for my family, / for myself?"

Young readers would benefit from some contextual knowledge before dipping into these narratives; some of the details are appropriately appalling to contemporary kids, such as the "Woman," who is rightfully angry, declaring "I can't wait to get away. / I never want to see this town again" as she is pictured against a backdrop of Jim Crow signs. An author's note at the beginning helps provide some historical information; Greenfield's poems and Gilchrist's art follow to effectively personalize this significant historical era. —*Diane Foote*

From *The Great Migration: Journey to the North*

> They hear the whistle blow.
> It blows again, not so far away.
> They see the train coming closer
> and closer, and then it stops. They gather
> on the platform, hold out their tickets,
> climb aboard. "All aboard!"
> the conductor calls. It's time.
> They're moving slowly,
> then faster, some think too fast,
> some think not fast enough,
> toward a world they don't yet know.
> —*Eloise Greenfield*

McKISSACK, PATRICIA C. *Never Forgotten.* Illustrated by Leo and Diane Dillon. Schwartz and Wade, 2011. Gr. 4–8.

Winner of the Coretta Scott King Author Honor Award, master storyteller Patricia McKissack creates a provocative, heartwrenching saga that portrays the anguish of slavery, especially that of the parents who had their children taken from them. Told in verse, this cycle of poems combines history, folklore, and mysticism to deliver a message of hope and of the importance of family.

In West Africa in 1725, Musafa is born to Dinga, a talented and respected seventh generation blacksmith. When Musafa's mother dies in childbirth, his father uses his gift of magic to personify the four elements of nature—fire, earth, wind, and water—to assist in his son's upbringing. By a twist of fate, when Musafa is enjoying the pleasures of freedom, he is captured by foreigners and ends up as a slave in South Carolina. With the help of the Mother Elements, who travel across the ocean to uncover his whereabouts, Dinga is informed that his son is alive and using the skills he was taught as a young boy. He finds comfort in this knowledge. Dramatic, stylized acrylic and watercolor illustrations perfectly frame the story and add to the sense of magical realism. —*Debby Gold*

From *Never Forgotten*

> Musafa,
> Sold.
> See him no more.
> Hear him no more.
> Shum Da Da We Da Shum Da Da We Da.
> —*Patricia C. McKissack*

2011 Winner

WILLIAMS-GARCIA, RITA. *One Crazy Summer.* Amistad/HarperCollins, 2010. Gr. 3–7.

Historical fiction at its best, *One Crazy Summer* brings the summer of 1968 into brilliant focus through the lives of Delphine and her two sisters, Vonetta and Fern. They learn to live for the summer in a new place with a mother they barely know. Flying to Oakland, where the girls have to avoid making a spectacle of themselves while they keep count of the black people on the plane and in the airport, is just the first part of their summer of growth. The girls react to their new life with confidence and skepticism: who are these men in berets who visit their mother, Cecile? Why does everyone else call her Sister Nzila? What is this Black Panther day camp? Why does their mother expect them to fend for themselves? How can they stay true to their father's and grandmother's instruction and still find their own way? Characters are fully and honestly developed, making these three sisters some of the most memorable in children's literature. Delphine tells the story, full of love and humor and strength, and the young reader is left to revel in the world of 1968. Pair with *The Rock and the River* by Kekla Magoon (CSK Steptoe Winner, 2010) for a first introduction to the complexities of the Black Panther Party. —*Robin Smith*

From *One Crazy Summer*

Sister Mukumbu announced, "Today we're going to be like the earth, spinning around and affecting many. Today we're going to think about our part in the revolution." Vonetta's hand shot up. I kicked her under

the table, but she was determined to have everyone look at her, which meant having everyone look at us. I forgot all about Hirohito and was afraid of what Vonetta would say next: and sure enough, Vonetta said, "We didn't come for the revolution. We came for breakfast." Then Fern added "And to meet our mother in Oakland."
—Rita Williams-Garcia

2011 Honors

MYERS, WALTER DEAN. *Lockdown*. Harper Teen/Amistad, 2010. Gr. 7–10.

In *Lockdown* Walter Dean Myers continues his tradition of portraying the struggles of urban youth. Like the characters in *Monster* (1999) and *Dope Sick* (2009), Reese is not completely innocent but is caught up in a system marked by poverty and discrimination. Reese's story takes place in a juvenile detention facility and in typical Myers fashion the context is not sugarcoated or romanticized in any way. While this novel is graphic in its portrayal of violence and use of language, Reese is a realistic character who readers will find likable. The relationship he establishes with Mr. Hooft adds a unique component to this story. While completing work release in a nursing home Reese forges a relationship with this elderly man who offers insight into Reese's struggle despite very different life experiences. This intergenerational relationship pushes Reese to question racism, both in the present and the past, and reflect on his own choices. Throughout Reese's story, readers are invited to debate big questions and moral dilemmas. Should Reese help a younger detainee who is being bullied? Is there any way to hold the guards accountable for their corruption? How can Reese simultaneously stay connected to his community and family (particularly his little sister) while staying safe and out of trouble? Of course, Myers does not provide easy answers. For readers who will experience this book as a window, Reese's story offers insight and honesty. For readers who will experience the story as a mirror, Reese's story offers authenticity and compassion. —*Lesley Colabucci*

From **Lockdown**

She was kidding around with me and I liked it. At Progress nobody kidded around with you. Even when you were talking to your friends it could change in a minute. You said the wrong thing and somebody would get mad and swing at you, or they were having a bad day and you didn't know it, or their medication wasn't working. You could never tell.
—Walter Dean Myers

RHODES, JEWELL PARKER. *Ninth Ward*. Little, Brown, 2010. Gr. 5–8.

Mystical story elements and a realistic narrative paint a compelling picture of Hurricane Katrina's aftermath, from the perspective of a young girl left to survive the storm with her "Mama Ya-Ya" in their Ninth Ward neighborhood. Mama Ya-Ya, with the "sight," and 12-year-old Lanesha both know, like everyone else, that a storm is coming. Only Mama Ya-Ya knows that the storm itself isn't the biggest threat. The subsequent failure of the levees is what doomed the Ninth Ward; Mama Ya-Ya's eerie, vague premonitions effectively evoke the apprehension she feels.

Lanesha's plight is moving and potentially tragic, but readers don't pity her; her bond with Mama Ya-Ya, who has taken her in after her mother dies in childbirth and her biological family rejects her, is too strong for pity. Legitimate anger is warranted when Lanesha's wealthier family members do not remember her birthday and do not come to help when the population is told to evacuate.

Horrifying details aren't spared here. One friend goes to the Superdome and is separated from his family; others leave the city; still others are never heard from again, and just as happened in real life, it's unknown whether they lived or died.

Lanesha's ability to see ghosts and interpret signs (as taught by Mama Ya-Ya) fit well in a story set in New Orleans, a city known for the practice of varying religions and spiritualities. In another setting, such mystical elements may seem jarring, but here the blend seems appropriate, bringing the time and place of Lanesha's story alive.
—*Diane Foote*

From **Ninth Ward**

The TV flashes pictures "The highways are bumper-to-bumper," says a male reporter. "When gas runs out, they just get out and walk. See, that family there. Hitchhiking. Thousands of folks are trying to leave New Orleans." Another picture. "even though it's a mandatory evacuation, the mayor is allowing those who don't have the money to leave to spend the night in the Superdome." I lean forward, trying to see if I can see TaShon or Ginia in the sea of people on the screen.
—Jewell Parker Rhodes

NERI, GREG. *Yummy: The Last Days of a Southside Shorty.* Illustrated by Randy DuBurke. Lee and Low, 2010. Gr. 8–12. *

Who was "Yummy" and why at eleven years of age did he end up a gang leader responsible for the death of fourteen-year-old Shavon Dean? Was he a victim of his circumstances or a cold-blooded killer who got what he deserved? Based on facts, Robert "Yummy" Sandifer, a boy who loved sweets, grew up on Chicago's South Side where being a gang member was the only way to survive. Told through the eyes of a fictional observer, Yummy accidentally kills his neighbor and for three days becomes a fugitive from the law with very little hope for survival. This powerful and stirring graphic novel will haunt the reader as it grapples with difficult questions of right and wrong that have no easy answers. Bold, evocative black-and-white drawings complement this gritty, award-winning saga that needs to be told. —*Debra Gold*

From **Yummy: The Last Days of a Southside Shorty**

You ready to take the black disciples nation pledge? I guess so . . . better guess again. I wanna be a black disciple! All right then, little man, let's do it. Hold up your right hand. Your other right hand.

—Greg Neri

2011 John Steptoe Award for New Talent

BOND, VICTORIA, AND T. R. SIMON. *Zora and Me.* Candlewick Press, 2010. Gr. 5–8.

This book is a fictionalized account of the childhood of Zora Neale Hurston, the renowned Harlem Renaissance writer. Carrie Brown, Zora's best friend, is the enthusiastic narrator of the incidents that happened during the summer before they began fourth grade. The girls have an adventure that comes together like a fantastical detective story with king alligators, a strange murder, and family mysteries. The events take place in Florida during the early 1900s in their small town of Eatonville. It is a close-knit community of African Americans who are somewhat insulated from the segregation and racism of that time period.

When the men of the town gather to watch the fate of a young man who was foolish enough to try to wrestle Ghost, the king of the gators, only the two girls were eyewitnesses. One evening that incident piqued Zora's imagination as she sees Mr. Pendir, who appears to have a gator head and a man's body. Carrie and their friend Teddy are Zora's partners as they investigate the frightening events that seem related to this magical shape-changing man. When an elderly woman falls near the swimming hole and a man is murdered near their town, they are sure Mr. Pendir is involved.

The story reads like a folktale of strange creatures and brave children who challenge them. The character, Gold, who passes for white, is rare in children's books and some young readers will need to talk with an adult about it. The authors create a realistic scene of how the girls talk to Gold and other adults when they try to understand the confusing idea. One of the strengths of this novel is the support of adults who interact with the children. At the end of the book the authors have included a biography and timeline of Zora Neale Hurston's life. This is a unique story that offers children a captivating glimpse of African American history. —*Martha Ruff*

From **Zora and Me**

I saw it. That night at the Blue Sink, I saw Mr. Pendir with a gator snout plain as I see you right now. It can't be no accident that Old Lady Bronson—a woman who's never been sick a day in her life—fainted and fell, and Mr. Pendir only a few hundred yards away!

—Victoria Bond and T.R. Simon

2010 Winner

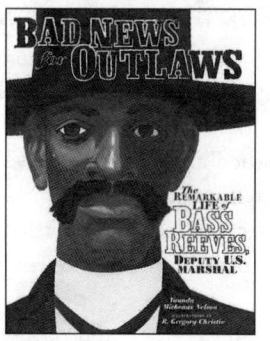

NELSON, VAUNDA MICHEAUX. *Bad News for Outlaws: The Remarkable Life of Bass Reeves, Deputy U.S. Marshal.* Illustrated by R. Gregory Christie. Carolrhoda, 2009. Gr. 3–5. *

Stunning oil paintings and fluid storytelling come together in a rip-roaring tale of heroism, bravery, and adventure in the late 1800s. Born into slavery in Texas, Bass Reeves fled his owner during the Civil War and lived with Indians, learning all he needed to know to become a deputy U.S. marshal. This well-researched biography reads like great fiction, complete with the tone and rhythm of a tall tale. Bass was a straight-shooting, honest marshal for 32 years, arresting more than 3,000 outlaws with only 14 deaths. Christie's paintings capture the personality of the no-nonsense, clever, and respectable Bass. His eyes shift while he plans his captures, surprises the bad guys, and arrests his own son. One special illustration shows Bass aiming his gun at the outlaw Jim Webb, who has just put a bullet through the marshal's cowboy hat. Never flinching from the realities of slavery, lynching, and racism, Nelson and Christie tell the story of a strong black man who defied the odds and became a legend. Modern children need to know his story and this fine biography is the perfect place to start. Generous endnotes include a bibliography and fascinating author's note. —*Robin Smith*

From *Bad News for Outlaws*

Jim Webb's luck was running muddy when Bass Reeves rode into town. Webb had stayed one jump ahead of the lawman for two years. He wasn't about to be caught now. Packing both rifle and revolver, the desperado leaped out a window of Bywaters' store. He made a break for his horse, but Reeves cut him off.

—*Vaunda Micheaux Nelson*

2010 Honor

DAVIS, TANITA S. *Mare's War.* Knopf, 2009. Gr. 6–10.

Road trip! One summer sisters Octavia and Tali are forced to ride across country with their grandmother to the family reunion. It is not a trip to be enjoyed but endured. Their grandmother, Mare, as she wants to be called, is an atypical grandmother and she smokes. Octavia and Tali have "baggage," too—they like to complain and are disagreeable. Somehow, when Mare opens up to them about her life, the trip becomes an adventure. Octavia and Tali didn't know their grandmother had run away from home and joined the Army as a teenager. So begins the trip—along the way, the sisters become less self-absorbed and argumentative. Mare's experiences in World War II mesmerize the girls. Previously untold stories of African American military women, and their own family history, transform the road trip into a meaningful life lesson.

Told in alternating voices and times—then and now—Davis's smooth transition from the past to the present keeps pace with the changing scenery and the sisters as Mare's life unfolds. Octavia and Tali's teenage attitude, behavior, and voice are very real. Their reactions evolve in this part of the journey as they become more sensitive to the world outside of their own friends and interests. Teens will recognize either themselves or someone they know in the characters and the story. —*Eunice Anderson*

From *Mare's War*

What happens if I forget how to use my mask? If I get that gas in my lungs, it will kill me dead. I hear about folk who didn't duck fast enough when those grenades came in and got their hands and arms and legs blown clean off. I can't go to France. I can't go where they're throwing them grenades. I can't go and leave Fern. I can't. I can't.

—*Tanita S. Davis*

2010 John Steptoe Award for New Talent

MAGOON, KEKLA. *The Rock and the River.* Aladdin/Simon & Schuster, 2009. Gr. 6–8.

Participating in demonstrations, marches, and other nonviolent tactics has almost taken over the life of thirteen-year-old Samuel Childs, who is the son of a well-known African American civil rights leader in Chicago. From the opening scenes, Sam struggles with his father's strict discipline, a sheltered home life, and society's racial injustices. On the other hand, he loves and admires his seventeen-year-old brother, Steven (known as Stick), who has begun to rebel against their parents' middle class lifestyle by joining the Black Panther Party. Amid his family's conflict, Sam wants to do ordinary teenage things like spend time with his classmate Maxie Brown and ask her to be his girlfriend.

When Bucky, one of Stick's friends, is beaten and falsely arrested by the police, the community erupts in militant protest. Not only is Sam a witness to the police brutality, he also has discovered a handgun that his brother hid in their bedroom. Sam feels helpless and unable to do anything about this miscarriage of justice. On the day of Bucky's trial, Mr. Childs organizes a peaceful demonstration, with Stick and the Black Panthers present. Sam is torn between using his father's method of nonviolence and his brother's tactics of hard-hitting action. Will he be a stable rock or follow the river's path of motion and change?

This dynamic coming-of-age story recreates the tensions of the 1960s civil rights movement and the emotions of the young activists of that era. The author skillfully weaves in historic events like the 1963 March on Washington and the assassination of Dr. Martin Luther King, Jr. The inclusion of the Black Panther Party is a part of African American history that is missing in children's fiction. While the organization's militant stance is well known by many, their social programs like free breakfast and health care are often overlooked. At the end of the book the author includes an historical overview of the civil rights movement and the Black Panther Party. —*Martha Ruff*

From **The Rock and the River**

"Explain what happened tonight," she said. "Pick up your head and look at me." "Yes, mama." I breathed deeply and looked in her eyes. I couldn't lie to her. She knew. Somehow, she already knew. "I went to a political education class."

"What were you thinking?" Father's granite demand placed the last straw on the load I was carrying.

I spun toward him. "What do you want from me?" I shouted.

Father's stunned expression sucked the fight out of me. I'd never talked back to him. Never. He gazed at me with slacked incredulity. I had shocked him into silence, and that was saying something.

—*Kekla Magoon*

2009 Winner

NELSON, KADIR. *We Are the Ship: The Story of Negro League Baseball.* Jump at the Sun/Hyperion Books for Children, 2008. Gr. 3–8. *

"Seems like we've been playing baseball for a mighty long time. At least as long as we've been free" begins the story of a remarkable group of men dedicated to a sport that did everything in its power to exclude them. Kadir Nelson steps into the role of storyteller and team member in this mesmerizing narrative of the African American community's passion for and dedication to baseball. This treasure is divided into nine innings, each of which is devoted to a different aspect of the history of Negro League Baseball. The final chapter, "Extra Innings," chronicles the demise of the great institution. The story begins in the mid-1860s, traveling forward to 1920, when Andrew "Rube" Foster, "an old-time trick pitcher," arrived on the scene. He came from Texas to organize what became the Negro National League. This section discusses not only well-known players like Josh Gibson and Satchel Paige but also lesser-known players like George "Mule" Suttles and Norman "Turkey" Stearns. Inning by inning, Nelson deftly recalls the hardships of traveling through a racist South and the thrill of the crowd when the fast-moving "bunt-and-run" play, an invention credited to Foster, proved successful. A bibliography, endnotes, and index verify the work's authenticity, but it is Nelson's talent as a wordsmith that brings this story to life for baseball lovers and history buffs of all ages.

From **We Are the Ship**

People ask all the time if we are bitter because we weren't given the chance to play baseball in the major leagues for all of those years. Some of us are, but most of us aren't. Most Negroes back then had to work in factories, wash windows, or work some man's plantation, and they didn't get paid much for it. We were fortunate men. We got to play baseball for a living, something we would have done if we hadn't gotten paid for it. When you can do what you love to do and get paid for it, it's a wonderful thing.

— *Kadir Nelson*

2009 Honors

SMITH, HOPE ANITA. *Keeping the Night Watch.* Illustrated by E. B. Lewis. Henry Holt, 2008. Gr. 6–8.

This narrative poem continues the saga begun in *The Way a Door Closes* (2003), as family members deal with Father, who returns home as abruptly as he left. Daughter Zuri views his return with both joy and fear, feelings that manifest themselves when she names her pillow dog "Stay." Bryon joins his father in a pickup game of hoops as if he'd never been gone; Momma goes about the house "wearing a painted smile on her face"; and C.J. is filled with anger, having lost his position as man of the house: "I'm a pot with the lid on / I keep all my mad inside." Yet, with the changing seasons, the household changes. C.J., in a fragile truce with his father, experiences the pangs of young love; readers are introduced to the quieting presence of Maya: "Preacher claims I'm a thief because I steal glances at her and store them in my head." Smith's moving prose poem about a family in turmoil does not lull readers with an all's-well ending, but there's a faint light at the end—a message of hope for young people who may be in a similar situation.

From **Keeping the Night Watch**

I take my Daddy's hand and I start to dance
with him
around the room.
We laugh
hard
and the water that flows from our eyes
flows into one big river,

but we are not afraid . . .
We keep our eyes on Him.
We dance on our tears.

From "Dance with Me" —Hope Anita Smith

THOMAS, JOYCE CAROL. *The Blacker the Berry: Poems.* Illustrated by Floyd Cooper. HarperCollins, 2008. Gr. K–3.

Black as a single color has been lauded in prose and poetry across time: "Black is the color of my true love's hair"; "Yet do I marvel at this thing, / To make a poet black and bid him sing." Joyce Carol Thomas expands black into a kaleidoscope of colors in poems that speak to children of every shade. A message of rejoicing comes from a "biscuit brown" child, and a salute to "raspberry black" recognizes Native Americans, here "from the first seed." Floyd Cooper's energetic illustrations capture the exuberance of the young people who rejoice in their color birthright. Thomas is highly deserving of the Coretta Scott King honor for her tribute to the beauty of "all the colors of the race," a positive message that speaks to readers everywhere.

*From **The Blacker the Berry***

We are color struck
The way an artist strikes
His canvas with his brush of many hues

Look closely at these mirrors
these palettes of skin
Each color is rich
in its own right . . .
We come in all shades

From "Color Struck" —Joyce Carol Thomas

WEATHERFORD, CAROLE BOSTON. *Becoming Billie Holiday.* Illustrated by Floyd Cooper. Wordsong/Boyds Mills Press, 2008. Gr. 6–9. *

Born in Philadelphia in 1915 to a teenage mother, the child who became Billie Holiday experienced poverty, discrimination, heartbreak, and parental neglect. Yet by the time she was twenty-five, she was a legend in the world of music. Billie quit school in the fifth grade, while she was living in Baltimore. To earn money she took all kinds of jobs, which some have said ranged from being a maid to being a prostitute. She felt that she had been on her own throughout her childhood. As a teenager, she realized she had a good singing voice and made her way to Harlem. She started singing in small clubs, but by the age of sixteen she had become well known enough to sing with famous bands led by musicians such as Teddy Wilson, Artie Shaw, and Duke Ellington. Carole Boston Weatherford, who has always thought of Holiday as her muse, tells the singer's story in a fictionalized verse memoir, creatively using the titles of Holiday's songs to head her ninety-seven poems. Holiday's longing for love and attention becomes clear, and her personality shines through as readers learn about her troubles in school, her feelings about music, her mother, her absent father, and the various places where she lived. They will also get a glimpse of other famous people who were important in her life: she traveled with Count Basie and appeared in a movie with Duke Ellington and in a play with Paul Robeson. Through this imaginative book, written as if spoken in Holiday's own voice, readers get a personal sense of the singer, from childhood to about age twenty-five. The final poem, titled "Coda: Strange Fruit," is an acknowledgment of Holiday's signature song, "Strange Fruit."

*From **Becoming Billie Holiday***

No one taught me to sing just behind the beat,
to tease listeners with my tempo,
to glide above the band, flit between
musicians like a canary finally free.
No one trained me to blow like a horn,
to milk a measure by bending the melody,
to breathe a universe in a single note,
and end a song in a different key . . .
That came natural, baby. That all came natural.

From "I Gotta Right to Sing the Blues"
—Carole Boston Weatherford

2008 Winner

CURTIS, CHRISTOPHER PAUL. *Elijah of Buxton.* Scholastic, 2007. Gr. 3–6.

The town of Buxton, located a few miles from the Detroit River in Canada, was a community founded as a destination for slaves who traveled the Underground Railroad to freedom. Elijah was the first child born free in Buxton. Although being the first freeborn child was significant enough, Elijah was best known for upchucking on Frederick Douglass! This happened when Douglass, the abolitionist, made one of his historic visits to Buxton. Twelve-year-old Elijah, known in his family for his tender heart and spirit, was frequently described as "fra-gile." In spite of this failing, Elijah was skilled at fishing without hook or line, capturing his prey by beaning them with stones chucked from the bank. This ability would serve him well in a life-threatening situation.

With his familiar style of extracting humor from the lives of young boys, author Curtis delivers again. Elijah and his friend Cooter are eager to participate when they see their teacher's planned lecture subject on the blackboard: "familiarity breeds contempt." Through an innocent but unknowingly careful dissecting of each word, and all the context clues they can muster, they decide that the teacher will be speaking about a "family breeding contest," and they don't want to miss a minute.

With each recovery from hilarious laughter, the reader sees both the scars of slavery and the ways in which the opportunity to live free are revealed in the lives and character of the residents of Buxton. Work ethics, sense of community, and the unrelenting efforts to raise the funds to buy the freedom of those left in bondage are ever present. Excitement and suspense are heightened when Zephariah, a man who calls himself Preacher, convinces Mr. Leroy, Elijah's friend and sometime employer, to let him go to Detroit to barter the freedom of Leroy's wife and children. Elijah's pa tries to warn Mr. Leroy about those rattlin-snake words, words that warn you you're about to get bit, but Mr. Leroy will not hear of it. In a real page-turner, the reader is taken on a midnight whirlwind of lies, suspense, grim examples of servitude, and dangerous situations. Needless to say, "fra-gile" Elijah is right in the middle. A mixture of pain and pleasure, Elijah of Buxton is a coming-of-age historical read about a time and place where few writers have ventured.

From **Elijah of Buxton**

Whenever new-free folk come to live in Buxton, we ring the bell twenty times for each one of 'em. Ten times to ring out their old lives and ten more to ring in their new ones, their free lives. Then, we ask the new-free folks to, one by one, climb the ladder of the steeple and rub the bell with their left hand. Most times when you're doing something important you're supposed to use your right hand, but we ask 'em to use their left hand 'cause it's closest to their hearts.

—*Christopher Paul Curtis*

2008 Honors

DRAPER, SHARON M. *November Blues*. Atheneum, 2007. Gr. 9–12.

There were three things of which November was sure: Josh was dead; Josh was her "baby daddy"; and she, November, was pregnant. What she did not know was how she would tell her mother, what she would do with a baby, or what would happen to her plans for college on scholarship. In a normal school setting filled with dances, football games, teachers with a wide range of personalities, and the vagaries of teenage friendships, Draper tells a poignant story of one thoughtless moment and its effect not only on the protagonist but also on all who are in this circle. November's mother moves between anger, disappointment, and motherly concern. Josh's parents have designs on adopting the baby, decrying November as an unfit mother. Jericho, Josh's cousin, a talented musician and best friend, pledges to be November's ardent supporter. In addition, in his grief over the loss of his cousin, Jericho puts down his trumpet and joins the football team, convincing himself that he need only "sweat and run tackle!"

With an awareness of the questions her intended audience may want to ask, Draper uses a quietly informative writing style to share the complexities of having a baby—not only the physical concerns before, during, and after but also the seemingly endless financial responsibilities, the physical care, and the effects on all concerned. Be aware that Draper offers no easy answers. Still, with all of November's problems, the book is not without moments of high drama, humor, and laughable boy-girl scenarios. *November Blues* is listed as a companion to *The Battle of Jericho*, but with its strength and focus it can truly stand alone.

From **November Blues**

"That's some nice music you're playing," Olivia said as she relaxed into the sofa cushions. "I like the blues." She closed her eyes.

November nodded, "I used to think it was dumb, old-timey music. Maybe you gotta deal with some stuff before you can really feel the blues." She looked at Olivia, and the two girls exchanged knowing glances.

—*Sharon M. Draper*

SMITH, CHARLES R., JR. *Twelve Rounds to Glory: The Story of Muhammad Ali.* Illustrated by Bryan Collier. Candlewick Press, 2007. Gr. 5–9. *

In twelve chapters, lavishly illustrated with powerful and moving watercolors by Bryan Collier, Smith's epic-style poem, influenced by the rhythms of rap, takes the reader and listener into the story of Muhammad Ali's life, his values and public persona. These aspects are emphasized even as readers go to ringside at Ali's matches with Sonny Liston, George Foreman, Joe Frazier, Ken Norton, and Leon Spinks. Smith's polished poetry reflects his admiration for his subject—not only for his prowess in boxing, graphically described, but also for his personal expressions of black pride. We read of Ali's fight against discrimination and segregation. We see not just the pugilist but a sincere man advocating peace, standing fast with his pacifist credo when he refuses induction into the U.S. Army. As he faces the loss of his world championship title and banishment from the ring, we hear him saying no to war and reinforcing his dedication to the tenets of his Islamic religion and faith in Allah. Smith captures Ali's voice teasing and taunting his opponents, using his well-known penchant for poetry to express himself. Smith addresses Ali, often using the word "you":

> Arriving in Rome
> you put on a display
> of a swift and strong style
> that defined Cassius Clay:
> lightning-quick feet
> dancing in the ring
> and flurries of fists
> that swarmed like bee stings.

Phrases in large black print and different fonts decorate the pages and emphasize chapter titles, important points, Ali's words, and descriptions: "slipping and sliding and bobbing and hiding, left to right, right to left, dodging leathered lightning," "Cassius Clay . . . reborn as Muhammad Ali," "burning from a faith on display throughout your life," "'Eat your words! Eat your words! I am the king! I'm the king of the world!'" Later chapters cover Ali's personal life, his four marriages and eight children, the diagnosis of Parkinson's disease, and that unforgettable moment when he carries the torch to light the cauldron at the 1996 Atlanta Olympic Games. A lengthy, informative time line of Ali's life through 2005 completes a gripping presentation of a heroic figure.

From **Twelve Rounds to Glory**

> Round TWELVE—Muhammad on the Mountain
> Holding the Olympic torch
> with a warrior spirit,
> you reignited memories
> of the champ who never quit
> in the ring,
> in life,
> using substance and style,
> now a gentle gladiator
> with a sparkling smile,
> you lit the Olympic cauldron
> glowing golden in the night
> and became a supernova
> bathed in beautiful light.
> —Charles R. Smith Jr.

2008 John Steptoe Award for New Talent

FRAZIER, SUNDEE T. *Brendan Buckley's Universe and Everything in It.* Delacorte, 2007. Gr. 3–5.

Meet Brendan Buckley, lively ten-year-old, maybe a budding scientist, striving to please the master in his tae kwon do class, sharing mischief with his buddy, Khalfani, and missing his late grandfather, Clem. Life seems just about okay until Brendan stops at a rock exhibit in the mall. He is talking to the exhibitor when with sudden swiftness his grandmother Gladys pulls him abruptly away, just as the "rock" man was about to sell him a calcite. Yet another strange thing—the name on the man's card was the same as his mother's maiden name: DuBose. Could there be a connection between Gladys's actions, the name of the gentleman who happened to be white, and his mother's reaction when Brendan arrives home? Undaunted by the silence at home, Brendan and Khalfani do some detective work, find a way to Mr. DuBose's home, and finally get to the bottom of the behavior on everyone's part. The end of the story is skillfully crafted. There is no sudden "happily ever after" in the family relationships, but the reader is left knowing that things will turn out all right in this cross-generational, multicultural tale.

From **Brendan Buckley's Universe and Everything in It**

> I flipped back a couple of pages and found the reason I'd opened the book in the first place. I checked off the question "What am I?"

Here is What I Found Out: I am a scientist, a mineral collector, a sometimes Noble Tae Kwon Do warrior, a friend, a son, a grandson, someone who belongs to both black and white people, a mixture like a rock, my color, but—much more—myself.

—Sundee T. Frazier

2007 Winner

DRAPER, SHARON M. *Copper Sun.* Atheneum, 2006. Gr. 9–12.

Day broke like any other day in Amari's African village, but before the sun went down her life had tragically changed forever. Slavers looted the village, killed or captured the villagers, and led others on a tormented journey in the dark hold of a slave ship. Fifteen-year-old Amari is eventually sold to a plantation owner as a birthday present for his sixteen-year-old son Clay. In this setting, Draper relates Amari's story of life-threatening activities on the plantation, her degradation as Clay's sex object, the cold-blooded murder of an innocent newborn, and the often disquieting relationship between Amari and Polly, an indentured servant. The opportunity to escape encourages Amari, Polly, and a little child, Tidbit, to seek the road to freedom—promised *if* they can reach the safe haven of Fort Mose, in St. Augustine, Florida.

Classified as fiction, this page-turner is based on impeccable research of the lives of those who were captured as slaves in eighteenth-century America. Throughout the burdensome, physically and emotionally painful life she led as a slave, Amari never lost her dream of once again being free.

Draper captures in often poetic prose what the hapless captives feel and see: there was "sorrow, raw and palpable, like spoiled meat"; "huge live oak trees lined each side of the road, dangling with beards of Spanish moss . . . looked like old men, bent over and exhausted from the heat."

From *Copper Sun*

A large woman came and sat down next to her and offered her a small piece of her own portion. Amari took it gratefully.

"Crying won't help, child," she told her. "This place is slimy with tears."

Amari was surprised to hear the woman speak in her own Ewe language. She wiped her eyes and said in barely a whisper, "I feel like a broken drum—hollow, crushed, unable to make a sound."

"You must learn to make music once more."

. . .

"So why should I endure this? Why did you not let me just die in there?" Amari cried out.

"Because I see a power in you." Afi lifted her shackled wrist and reached over to touch Amari. "You know, certain people are chosen to survive. I don't know why, but you are one of those who must remember the past and tell those yet unborn. You must live."

—Sharon M. Draper

2007 Honor

GRIMES, NIKKI. *The Road to Paris.* G. P. Putnam's Sons, 2006. Gr. 4–8.

Paris and her brother Malcolm have endured a tough childhood. Escaping from the latest in a string of abusive situations, they are now living with their grandmother in a small apartment. They only want peace and safety. Unfortunately, security is something the grandmother can't provide. The caseworker separates the siblings, sending Malcolm to an unknown destination and Paris to a foster family in upstate New York. The Lincolns, with two boys of their own and another foster daughter, aren't perfect, but quietly they show Paris the patience and generosity she so desperately needs. The inbred community racism doesn't dominate Paris's life. She has already felt the sting of racism; a biracial child, she was abandoned by her white father. What concerns her now is whether to give her alcoholic mother a second chance. The support of other children and singing in the church choir help Paris develop trust, find a belief in God, and eventually discover her home inside herself.

Faith is a real part of Paris's growing ability to handle her life confidently, yet author Grimes is never evangelistic. Her quiet portrayal doesn't leave out the prejudice or hurt, but the tender poignancy of Paris's internal voice powerfully reveals the strength of a child discovering herself, flourishing, and learning to use her gifts.

From *The Road to Paris*

Paris sat swinging her legs, pouting—until she heard the first chords of the organ. The sound sent an electric spark up one pew and down the next, and Paris forgot all about being cold. The melody flowed into her body like liquid sunshine, warming her as it traveled from the tips of her ears to the tips of her toes. Paris never knew that such a sound existed.

"Are you okay?" asked Mr. Lincoln. Paris, her lips slightly parted, nodded and went on listening. She didn't know how to explain it, but as the music played, she felt herself waking up inside.

—*Nikki Grimes*

2007 John Steptoe Award for New Talent

JONES, TRACI L. *Standing against the Wind.* Farrar, Straus, & Giroux, 2006. Gr. 6–9.

In this first novel, protagonist Patrice, a thirteen-year-old, is suddenly moved from the security of her grandmother's home in rural Georgia to the bustling city of Chicago. When her mother is sent to jail, Patrice finds shelter in a small apartment with her mother's sister and her three young cousins. While coping with being responsible for chores around the home, holding afternoon school for her cousins, and struggling to maintain her grades, young Patrice finds she must also deal with the constant harassment of neighborhood gangs and youthful drug dealers. Then Monty, living in the same building, comes to her rescue—the beginning of an abiding friendship. As the school year moves on, Patrice is informed that her grades make her eligible for a prestigious scholarship. There is only one hitch. The application must be signed by her mother, in jail many miles away. With Monty at her side, a determined Patrice stands up against many seemingly insurmountable obstacles as she strives to reach her goal. Gradually, the relationship between Patrice and Monty grows. Monty admires Patrice's academic abilities and is encouraged to improve his own study habits. At the same time, his personal ingenuity is instrumental in securing Patrice's scholarship. Tense moments, tender moments, and moments of adult encouragement combine to make *Standing against the Wind* a real page-turner, worthy of the 2007 Coretta Scott King/John Steptoe New Talent Award.

From **Standing against the Wind**

"Your watch. It was such a nice watch. I can't believe you sold it."

But to Patrice it was a really big deal. He had taken the one thing of value that he owned and sold it for her.

…

Patrice looked at him. And for the third time that day, she kissed him.

—*Traci L. Jones*

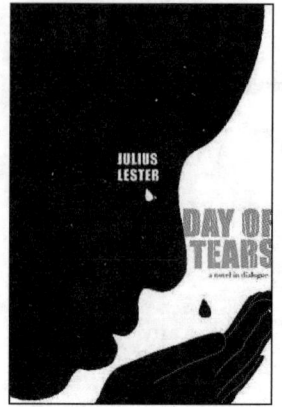

2006 Winner

LESTER, JULIUS. *Day of Tears: A Novel in Dialogue.* Jump at the Sun/Hyperion Books for Children, 2005. Gr. 9–12.

Lester's fictionalized account of the largest slave auction in U.S. history, held in 1859 in Savannah, Georgia, makes immediate and personal the horror of the event. In a powerfully dramatic format, the voices of enslaved Africans and their masters move between monologues and conversations. Lester's sparing words always seem vividly to illuminate each character. Begging to be staged, this work makes clear the moral dilemmas inherent in the slave auction. The inhumanity of the process is strengthened by characters who speak years down the line, giving a broad perspective and bringing a kind of closure to the happenings. The challenge to affirm our humanity in this most inhumane situation is reflected in the somber words and setting: the rain comes down like fiery sorrow, rain like needles on your skin or rain as hard as regret. As the character Mattie says, "This ain't rain. This is God's tears."

From **Day of Tears**

Mattie: I look at the slave-seller sitting beside Master Butler. There's a toothpick sticking out of the left corner of his mouth. He takes a sip of coffee without moving that toothpick out of the way. He eats with that toothpick bobbing up and down. I wish he'd stop looking at Emma like she's a hog and he's trying to figure how many pork chops and slabs of bacon he can get out of her.

—*Julius Lester*

2006 Honors

BOLDEN, TONYA. *Maritcha: A Nineteenth-Century American Girl.* Harry N. Abrams, 2005. Gr. 4–7. *

Maritcha Lyons was born to free black parents who owned their own boardinghouse in New York City. Her family enjoyed leisurely, fun-filled outings and the company of many famous friends and guests, including Frederick Douglass. Maritcha's parents acquired a piano for her and paid for lessons to keep her spirits up while she recovered from illness. However, with all this seeming affluence, Maritcha was well aware of the difficulties faced by blacks. "'At anti-slavery meetings and conferences, mother was almost invariably present,' Maritcha remembered, 'not to agitate but to learn her duty.'" This duty was being an ace operator for the Underground Railroad. But the lifestyle Maritcha and her family enjoyed could not keep them from their own difficulties. They lost everything in the New York City draft riots of 1863. A mob torched their home and the family was forced to flee. Eventually they relocated in Providence, Rhode Island, where Maritcha became the first black person to graduate from the all-white Providence High School.

Author Bolden, using enhancing reproductions from Maritcha Lyons's unpublished memoir, has crafted a handsome biography, replete with contemporaneous illustrations. It is a well-documented narrative with source notes, bibliography, and illustration and text credits.

From **Maritcha**

She took part in school activities, such as playing the piano for the choral club. But Maritcha kept her guard up. "The iron had entered my soul. I never forgot that I had to sue for a privilege which any but a colored girl could have without asking."

—Tonya Bolden

GRIMES, NIKKI. *Dark Sons.* Jump at the Sun/Hyperion Books for Children, 2005. Gr. 5–8.

Grimes's novel in verse is a portrait of two young men who both feel betrayed by their fathers. Each father—one in ancient biblical times, one in a contemporary setting—has moved on to start a new family with "another woman." The biblical Ishmael and Sam, born in Brooklyn, New York, wonder if God has forsaken them and the mother who cares for them. Grimes's poetic word pictures of two damaged young men, told in alternating voices, are both heartbreaking and healing. As the stories parallel each other (a slight change in print marking the separation), a reader might ask, Are there no new stories under the sun? Introducing a story from a religious tradition to contemporary audiences of multicultural traditions, Grimes skillfully makes the leap from the past to the present in a way that is entirely credible.

From **Dark Sons**

When I am angriest,
His is the hand
that calms me,
the one that rests
on my shoulder invisibly,
pressing patience
into my very bones,
letting me know
it is all right
to breathe.

from "Silent Solace"

Moody as midnight,
I pound minor keys
on electric piano.
I am here to lose myself
in the music,
to jam with Jesus—
the only one
who hasn't let me down
so far.

from "Band Practice"

—Nikki Grimes

NELSON, MARILYN. *A Wreath for Emmett Till.* Illustrated by Philippe Lardy. Houghton Mifflin, 2005. Gr. 9–12. *

Emmett Louis Till was a lively fourteen-year-old African American boy who was lynched in August 1955 near Money, Mississippi, for allegedly whistling at a white woman. His mother, Mamie Till, held an open-casket funeral, for all to witness the horror of her son's death. A photograph of his mangled body, published in *Jet* magazine, shocked and galvanized people throughout the country. This lynching became a catalyst for the civil rights movement of the late 1950s and '60s.

A Wreath for Emmett Till is Nelson's sensitive and poetic response to "innocence slaughtered by the hands of hate," mourning Till's loss and hinting at the life he might have had. In the back matter, the author explains the allusions and the symbolism of the flowers in the wreath, which expand the dimensions of the poetry without literally depicting the lynching: *A Wreath for Emmett Till* is structured as a "heroic crown of sonnets," fifteen linked sonnets in which the last line of one, slightly paraphrased, becomes the first line of the next, until the final entry combines the first lines of the preceding sonnets to become the fifteenth. "The strict form became a kind of insulation, a way of protecting myself from the intense pain of the subject matter. . . . I wrote this poem with my heart in my mouth and tears in my eyes." Members of the Coretta Scott King awards jury surely must have read the piece with the same emotion and respect for Nelson's creative ability when they selected *A Wreath for Emmett Till* as a 2006 author honor book.

From **A Wreath for Emmett Till**

A running boy, five men in close pursuit.
One dark, five pale faces in the moonlight.
Noise, silence, back-slaps. One match, five cigars.

Emmett Till's name still catches in the throat.
...
We can speak now, or bear unforgettable shame.
Rosemary for remembrance, Shakespeare wrote.
—Marilyn Nelson

2006 John Steptoe Award for New Talent

ADOFF, JAIME. *Jimi & Me.* Jump at the Sun/Hyperion Books for Children, 2005. Gr. 6–8.

Keith James, the narrator of Adoff's free-verse novel, is thirteen years old when his father, a music producer and fan of Jimi Hendrix's music, is shot by thugs during the robbery of a local deli. Aspiring to become a singer and guitarist, Keith finds escape from his feelings of loss, resentment, and guilt by focusing on the music of his father's idol. Dad and Jimi were like brothers who never knew each other: black hippies with big souls and even bigger smiles.

Shocked to find that her husband has left them with huge debts, Keith's mother is forced to move with Keith from Brooklyn to the house of Keith's paternal aunt in a small, largely white, Ohio town. Here Keith's loss is compounded by his mother's increasing withdrawal and the prejudice he faces because of his biracial "caramel brown Frap-pu-ccino face—BIG, bushy 'fro." Most distressing is the revelation that Keith's father had another woman and a son, three years older than Keith, named Jimi. "Everything is different now. / Even Hendrix songs don't sound the same, / all because of that name. / His voice reminding me of the pain." Feeling as though his father has died a second time, Keith arranges to meet this half brother, who has been disabled in a fall, for which his father had blamed himself. Jimi confronts the possibility of reconciliation in the face of betrayal.

Adoff's pulsing narrative, which he has characterized as "poetic-prose," captures with perfection Keith's anguish. The author's experience as a musician finds expression, not only in his knowledgeable description of music and the music business but in the rhythmic music of the book's effective language.

From *Jimi & Me*

> two weeks
> since I met Jimi and I'm tryin'
> my best.
> Some days it all makes sense.
> Some days

it just hurts.
I feel hate towards dad,
but at least I know he tried.
He wasn't a bad guy.
He wasn't all good either.
But
he was my dad.
I try to keep telling myself that.
—Jaime Adoff

2005 Winner

MORRISON, TONI. *Remember: The Journey to School Integration.* Illustrated with photographs. Houghton Mifflin, 2004. Gr. 6–8. *

Archival photographs, strikingly reproduced in sepia tones, illustrate the era of school integration in Morrison's first historical work for young readers. Opening with images of segregated schools, the work documents the impact of the Supreme Court's decision that segregated educational facilities are "inherently unequal." It depicts integrated classrooms where southern schools complied with the ruling, the ugly resistance the decision too frequently evoked, and the brave children who faced vicious harassment to change our society. Later images show the wide-ranging effects of the decision as the movement spread to integrate restaurants, theaters, buses, and other public facilities. Throughout Morrison reminds today's readers, "the path was not entered, the gate was not opened, the road was not taken only for those brave enough to walk it. It was for you as well. In every way, this is your story."

In the brief text accompanying the photographs, Morrison imagines thoughts that might have been in the minds of the young people in the various photographs. At the end of the book, thumbnail reproductions of the photographs expand the actual situation each records.

From *Remember*

Because remembering is the mind's first step toward understanding, this book is designed to take you on a journey through a time in American life when there was as much hate as there was love; as much anger as there was hope; as many heroes as cowards.
—Toni Morrison

2005 Honors

FLAKE, SHARON G. *Who Am I Without Him? Short Stories about Girls and the Boys in Their Lives.* Jump at the Sun/Hyperion Books for Children, 2004. Gr. 6–12.

Urban African American youth search for romance, friendship, and ultimately love as Flake's ten stories explore the roles boys and men play in the lives of girls. The titles of many of the stories reach out to capture the reader: "So I Ain't No Good Girl"; "The Ugly One"; "Don't Be Disrespecting Me"; "Wanted: A Thug." Respect, race, class, beauty, parental roles, and self-awareness are among the issues delivered in voices that capture the authentic lyric, cadence, and beat of contemporary black teenspeak. The topics of these stories range from problem solving to humor, heartache, abuse, advice good and bad, crossing borders, and true love. It all adds up to a collection that reflects the variety of ways in which the African American youth of today see themselves.

From *Who Am I Without Him?*:

People say things about me. Bad things. Momma says I give 'em reason to. That if I would just be a good girl—like the girls who wait for the bus with me in the mornings—then things wouldn't go so hard for me. But I don't wanna be like them girls: so plain and pitiful, boys don't even look their way or ask their names.

I wanna be me. Ain't nothing wrong with that. Is it?

From "So I Ain't No Good Girl" —Sharon G. Flake

MOSES, SHELIA P. *The Legend of Buddy Bush.* Margaret K. McElderry, 2004. Gr. 6–9.

Uncle Buddy is family kin but not actual blood kin to twelve-year-old Pattie Mae. Pattie Mae admires him for his Harlem ways and is glad to have him back full-time when he returns to the old slave house, Pattie Mae's home in rural Rich Square, North Carolina. The story is set around a terrifying event that happened in 1947. Though fictionalized, it is an intimate account of an incident that made national news. Pattie Mae observes and gradually begins to understand the racism around her and the dangers that affected her beloved family from such an unjust world. Pattie Mae has strong connections with family members who have gone north, but her mother and grandparents rule her world. Although she has observed many petty instances of unfairness, it rocks her when she witnesses the incident: an insulted white woman distorts an encounter into "attempted rape." Uncle Buddy is arrested and nearly lynched by members of the Ku Klux Klan.

Moses's writing style creates a narrative that veers between down-home folksy vernacular and an almost poetic cadence that often sings. In the intimacy of an imperfect family struggling to maintain their pride in a segregated world no matter what, the legend of Buddy Bush grows, revealing an endurance and resiliency that exact not only a heavy toll but also the admiration of more than just Pattie Mae.

From *The Legend of Buddy Bush*

Hey, baby, I'm fine. Ole Man Taylor let you off earlier today?"

"Yes, Grandma, he did."

"You wash up and get you someteat." I do as I'm told, and check on Grandpa, who is sleeping. My mind must be playing tricks on me because the sound I suddenly hear coming from the road is women folks singing. I rush to the front door and Lord I am in shock.

Sure enough, it is the women from church. The women from the choir.

All of them.

Walking.

Walking and singing.

"Jesus, what in the world is they doing?" Grandma says as she stands up.

They are all dressing in white and Miss Cora Mae Jones, who ain't related to us, is leading the choir.

"Hush, somebody calling my name," she sing on and on.

By the time they get to the doorstep, Grandma is singing, too. I join in as Grandma shouts for joy.

—Shelia P. Moses

NELSON, MARILYN. *Fortune's Bones: The Manumission Requiem.* Front Street, 2004. Gr. 6–12. *

In 1933, the skeletal remains of Fortune, an enslaved African American man who died in 1798, were donated to the Mattatuck Museum of Waterbury, Connecticut. Prior to 1996, the museum was unsure of the identity of the skeleton. It was later learned that Fortune and five members of his family were owned by a Dr. Preserved Porter. It was determined that after Fortune's death his bones were rendered and displayed by Dr. Porter and also used for anatomical study. With the discovery of new information about Dr. Porter and Fortune, the museum commissioned Nelson, poet laureate of Connecticut, to create a literary work to serve as part of a community healing. Conceived in the aftermath of the September 11, 2001, terrorist attack on the United States, this lyrical eulogy is based on Fortune's life, his family, the Porter family, and the Waterbury community. Nelson's six haunting poems (particularly haunting is the selection describing Fortune's wife having to dust his bones, since Dr. Porter's wife feared to do so) are a requiem and a celebration of life and what may be thought of as Fortune's ultimate freedom.

From **Fortune's Bones**

Not My Bones

I was not this body,
I was not these bones.
This skeleton was just my
temporary home.
Elementary molecules converged for a breath,
then danced on beyond upon my individual death.
And I am not my body,
I am not my body.

—Marilyn Nelson

2005 John Steptoe Award for New Talent

HATHAWAY, BARBARA. *Missy Violet and Me.* Houghton Mifflin, 2004. Gr. 3–5.

Little does eleven-year-old Viney realize how much she will learn when she's sent to spend the summer with Missy Violet, Richmond County's prominent midwife. Her curiosity leads her to discover the mysterious contents of the midwifery medicine bag, and while assisting Missy Violet, she learns the rigors of "catching" a newborn baby. Her stubborn persistence leads to a heroic climax in this concise, fast-paced novel spiced with humor and built on well-researched facts.

From **Missy Violet and Me**

I'd handled myself like a big girl, like somebody with backbone. I wasn't the same silly little girl who thought babies came out of tree stumps and cabbage patches. I was a midwife's helper, and I knew a few things about "catchin" babies.

—Barbara Hathaway

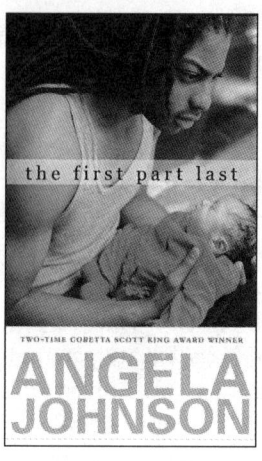

2004 Winner

JOHNSON, ANGELA. *The First Part Last.* Simon & Schuster Books for Young Readers, 2003. Gr. 6–12.

Feather is Bobby's baby daughter. Her arrival means that at sixteen, Bobby has to find a way to balance his own needs and those of his infant daughter in the necessary absence of the baby's mother. Johnson's masterful depiction of Bobby's situation reveals sadness and love as alternating chapters move the reader between the then and the now in the course of events. Only gradually (with well-paced tension) does the reader discover the complex truth of Bobby's love for his girlfriend, Nia, the baby's mother. That love is the foundation of all he does. *The First Part Last* introduces a different aspect of the life of the protagonist, Bobby, whom some readers met in Johnson's earlier award-winning novel *Heaven*. In a fluid writing style, where every single word contributes to the whole, and with an almost deceptive simplicity, Johnson creates a poignant, sometime humorous, always sensitive story of a young person who has to become a man sooner than expected. With quiet insistence, readers see a child become a parent, making a new life out of a loss and conquering pain and sorrow with a subtle essence of joy. The details of Bobby's daily struggle to balance many opposing forces result in a powerful portrayal of a sensitive and nurturing young man caught in a rare but realistic dilemma.

From **The First Part Last**

But I figure if the world were really right, humans would live life backward and for the first part last. They'd be all knowing in the beginning and innocent in the end. Then everyone could end their life on their momma or daddy's stomach in a warm room, waiting for the soft morning light.

—Angela Johnson

2004 Honors

DRAPER, SHARON M. *The Battle of Jericho*. Atheneum, 2003. Gr. 7–10.

High school junior Jericho Prescott is thrilled to receive an invitation to pledge for the Warriors of Distinction, his school's most prestigious service club, even when the pledging process seems unexpectedly demanding—a Warrior of Distinction is not afraid to lower himself for his brother, does not show fear, celebrates obedience, and never breaks the code of silence. For the first time, Jericho no longer feels like an outsider, and he has the attention of attractive, popular Arielle.

When the pledge masters demand that he miss a long-awaited music contest that could win him a scholarship to Juilliard, Jericho is ready to sacrifice his joy in playing the trumpet for acceptance by his peers. As the hazing rituals become increasingly disturbing, however, Jericho begins to question the price of belonging. Tragically, the hazing reaches its climax with the "Leap of Faith," as Jericho's beloved cousin, Josh, jumps to his death. Draper's engrossing, disturbing novel challenges young readers to think about how one measures self-worth and loyalty, and about the possibility of refusing to bow to peer pressure. The novel ends "as Josh did, in silence," but the issues it raises will continue to echo in the minds of its readers.

From *The Battle of Jericho*

> Jericho felt excited and anxious to begin whatever awaited.... He wasn't sure if he felt like curling into a ball and sleeping for a week, or exploding like a grenade and destroying something. All he knew was that whatever they asked him to do, he was ready to do it.
>
> —*Sharon M. Draper*

McKISSACK, PATRICIA C., AND FREDRICK L. McKISSACK. *Days of Jubilee: The End of Slavery in the United States*. Scholastic, 2003. Gr. 6–8. *

The tumultuous period following the Civil War and the end of legal slavery for African Americans is the focus of this well-researched text. Using slave narratives as their primary source, the McKissacks have reconstructed the facts and stories of this critical period in American history. Showcased is the impact of events on the lives of real people, some as famous as Abraham Lincoln, others more obscure. The efforts the enslaved made to ensure their own freedom are an important part of this dramatic story. The authors address complicated issues such as the role of blacks in the Confederate army. The readable text presents the difficulties of the times as well as the hopes and jubilation of the newly freed. Illustrations of the period and direct quotations from those involved provide a particular immediacy to the narrative. A time line, a bibliography, and an index are helpful additions.

From *Days of Jubilee*

> Freedom meant different things to different people and they responded accordingly. For one woman, naming her child without her master's permission was freedom. Others felt freedom meant they could go wherever they wanted, whenever they wanted. Large groups of the freed migrated west and many men became cowboys, or signed on as Pullman car porters when the Transcontinental Railroad was completed.
>
> —*Patricia C. McKissack and Fredrick L. McKissack*

WOODSON, JACQUELINE. *Locomotion*. G. P. Putnam's Sons, 2003. Gr. 3–6.

In a novel of sixty poems, fifth grader Lonnie Collins gradually reveals his grief and refinds his joy in living. The grief is the result of a tragic fire that four years earlier killed his loving parents. The fire also separated him from his dear sister, Lili, who was adopted by a different family. The healing process begins with his caring foster mother and his teacher, Ms. Marcus, who introduces him to the beauty of poetry. The very process of writing in verse helps Lonnie to observe, think, mourn, remember, and finally to smile again. Set in contemporary Brooklyn, *Locomotion* is a lyrical yet realistic depiction of urban school life. In Woodson's capable hands, it is also a compelling and accessible story of a boy who can "write the word 'HOPE'" on his hand.

From *Locomotion*

> Ms Marcus
> says
> line breaks help
> us figure out
> what matters
> to the poet
> Don't jumble your ideas
> Ms Marcus says
> Every line
> should count
>
> —*Jacqueline Woodson*

2004 John Steptoe Award for New Talent

SMITH, HOPE ANITA. *The Way a Door Closes.* Henry Holt, 2003. Gr. 3–5.

In this debut novel written in poetic prose, thirteen-year-old C.J. tells the poignant story of a family that learns to cope when the proud and recently unemployed father just walks out, closing the door behind him. In spite of neighborhood predictions that the father will never return, the youngster continues to hold on to the hope that his father will return. Thirty-four poems speak with a voice of pain, loss, the power of love, and ultimate triumph when the family is once again united.

From *The Way a Door Closes*

> Schoolyard Sermon
> My best friend, Preacher,
> is being just that.
> His sermon today is on fathers . . .
> "Dads are light.
> They have no roots.
> One strong wind, and they're
> gone . . .
> History . . .
> they don't come back." . . .
> "My dad is coming back,"
> I announce . . .
> "Man," he says, "that only happens
> once in a blue moon."
> I smile as I head to my next class
> and I say,
> more to myself than to Preacher,
> "But it happens."
>
> —Hope Anita Smith

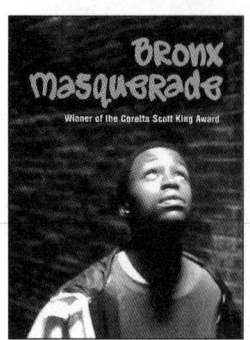

2003 Winner

GRIMES, NIKKI. *Bronx Masquerade.* Dial, 2002. Gr. 6–8.

Bronx Masquerade is a masterful blend of poetry and prose. The result is a composite of the lives of contemporary teenagers taking on life in the twenty-first century. When Mr. Ward gives his racially mixed class the assignment to write a poem, the reader can almost hear the groans. Nonetheless, the resulting pieces give insight into the problems, concerns, tribulations, and ambitions of their writers, and through the writers' eyes, readers can see themselves or someone they know. Gloria's youthful journey is complicated by her having a baby out of wedlock; Raynard is dyslexic; Leslie is always angry until she learns that a fellow student, Porscha, is also struggling with the changes that come with the loss of a parent. The reader meets the student who is gay and the student who is almost a dropout. Indeed, the reader meets everyman. The realistic scenarios in this tightly written novel invite readers to take a look at this slice of life and to take comfort in a text whose conclusion, although it does not solve everything, shows each character accepting the challenge of overcoming his or her problems. The format attests to the power of poetry to succinctly express a well-deep range of thought and emotions.

From *Bronx Masquerade*

> There's something about reading poetry. It's almost like acting . . . it's like you become somebody else and you can say anything, as long as it's a poem. Then, when you're finished, you just disappear into the dark and sit down, and you're back to being your own self.
>
> —Nikki Grimes

2003 Honors

GRIMES, NIKKI. *Talkin' About Bessie: The Story of Aviator Elizabeth Coleman.* Illustrated by E. B. Lewis. Orchard, 2002. Gr. 2–5. *

From the moment of her birth, Bessie's daddy knew that she was someone special. In Nikki Grimes's creative narration, the reader learns that Bessie's life was indeed special. Intellectually gifted, determined, and self-assured, Bessie Coleman became not only the first African American aviatrix but also an internationally known stunt pilot. She drew crowds of awestruck spectators to watch her daring performances. Written in lyrical prose, Coleman's life story unfolds in a series of vignettes, each from the perspective of a person with whom Bessie had some type of association. Her mother, though not formally educated herself, realized Bessie's ability to learn and made whatever sacrifice was necessary to get her daughter an education. In an era of racial prejudice and segregation, Bessie displayed her self-assurance. The white woman to whom Bessie delivered laundry wondered what made her "different": "this Colored girl would be standin' lookin' me straight in the eye, like we were just any two people . . . You know, like we were equals!"

In spite of the language barrier, Coleman went to France for the flight training that she could not as a "colored" person get in America. In that vignette, Grimes's masterful writing skill shines as she describes with dramatically quiet prose a tragic training accident:

> . . . Wedges of earth and sky flashed by too fast
> for memory as the plane hurtled, then slammed
> to the ground with student and teacher on board.
> . . . Bessie gasped, knowing how easily she could be
> the one in flames . . .

The innovative use of multiple voices (family, instructors, sponsors, etc.) in this factually based fictional biography provides insight into the life of a woman whose activities as a pilot extended far beyond mere headline-grabbing performances. The story sends a message of inspiration to all who learn her history. Bessie Coleman's achievements as a role model, an aviatrix, and a stunt pilot are orchestrated in a handsome blend of words and illustrations. Nikki Grimes's convincing writing prompted one young fan to remark, "I haven't made up my mind about being a pilot, but Bessie made me know I could be anything."

From *Talkin' About Bessie*

Lord spoke kindly of the eagles and dove, but he also loved the raven: a strong mysterious black bird of high intelligence is she; a creature slighted by many, but cared for by God—that was Bessie.

—*Nikki Grimes*

WOODS, BRENDA. *The Red Rose Box*. G. P. Putnam's Sons, 2002. Gr. 5–8.

Leah and her younger sister Ruth live in quiet Sulphur, Louisiana. They cannot imagine life thousands of miles away in California until their aunt Olivia sends train tickets for the girls to make the trip. The sisters find life in California much different from the segregated experiences they knew at home. Leah finds new opportunities so special that she cannot imagine anyone choosing to live in the Jim Crow South. When tragedy strikes the family, Leah and Ruth return to Los Angeles to make it their permanent home. Now the "wonderful" experiences are bittersweet, making Leah question if she can ever overcome the loss of her family. Perhaps the contents of the Red Rose Box may help. Brenda Woods's evocative novel successfully explores the complex emotions involved in leaving the past behind.

From *The Red Rose Box*

It felt like a million miles from Sulphur and crayfish, cotton fields and hand-me-down clothes, a one-room school house, segregation and Jim Crow. But I knew one thing. I knew that I would gladly give up this new comfort and freedom to be in my mama's arms, to feel the tenderness in my daddy's touch one more time.

—*Brenda Woods*

2003 John Steptoe Award for New Talent

MCDONALD, JANET. *Chill Wind*. Frances Foster Books/ Farrar, Straus, & Giroux, 2002. Gr. 7–12.

Bold and brash Aisha Ingram is a nineteen-year-old mother of two young children. A high school dropout with no plans for the future, she is at a crossroads for she has come to the end of the five-year limit on receiving public assistance. This "project girl" sees no future in the workfare option of cleaning graffiti from public spaces or in patrolling New York City's subway system as a member of a youth force. Who would have imagined that Aisha would have a golden opportunity to shine as a plus-size, roller-skating spokesmodel! BIGMODELS called, and the House of Rap 'n Roll, an urban roller rink, has Aisha in the house and on the payroll.

From *Chill Wind*

Raven's words came back again: "They kick you off welfare after five years." What was she going to do? With no diploma, no skills, and two kids, Aisha Ingram's chilled life had suddenly gotten a little too chilly.

—*Janet McDonald*

2002 Winner

TAYLOR, MILDRED D.
The Land. Phyllis Fogelman Books/Penguin Putnam, 2001. Gr. 8–12.

The Land chronicles the struggles and triumphs of Paul Edward Logan, the son of a white slave owner and an enslaved African Indian woman. Taylor offers a gripping and painful story of a young man's awakening to racial injustice. This riveting account takes place in Mississippi during Reconstruction and follows Paul Edward's growth to manhood. The unending injustices of that place and time, when race defined everything, are told through a narrative that is never whitewashed or turned into melodrama. Paul Edward's ability to cope is stretched to staggering degrees, but with the support of friends and through his own unending labor he makes his way toward the ultimate goal, a piece of land that represents paradise. A prequel to *Roll of Thunder, Hear My Cry* and other novels about the Logan family, this powerful family memoir is also a love story, a suspense thriller, and a meticulously detailed work of historical fiction. It is an unparalleled tour de force by one of children's literature's most prestigious writers.

From **The Land**

I watched him go, then sat down on a stump, closed my eyes and tried to take hold of my Fury. Ever since I had left my daddy's house, I had been learning and relearning that harsh lesson my daddy whipped into me when I was fourteen. It was a white man's world and I had to survive in it.

—Mildred D. Taylor

2002 Honors

FLAKE, SHARON G. *Money Hungry.* Jump at the Sun/Hyperion Books for Children, 2001. Gr. 6–8.

Thirteen-year-old Raspberry Hill is money hungry. In order to protect herself and her mother from being homeless again, living on the street and eating at soup kitchens, she finds ways to make money. She sells pencils and candy to her fellow students, washes cars, and cleans houses, stashing the money she makes away in her bedroom. Although her friends call her greedy because she makes money off them, Raspberry is not deterred. She is determined to provide some sense of stability for her mother. Through a series of circumstances, life takes a downturn for Raspberry. She lends her friend Janae $200 of her hard-earned money without knowing why Janae needs it, her mother's application for housing under Section 8 is denied, and Janae's grandmother wrongfully accuses Raspberry of stealing her money. Then, frustrated by these events, Raspberry's mother throws what money they have left out the window.

Told in the first person, Raspberry's story involves the reader with likable characters like Odd Job, a man who washes cars at intersections, and invites the reader to reflect on such social issues as the effects of poverty, absentee parents, and one aspect of life in the projects. It is also an upbeat story full of hope and spirit. A real sense of community shines through the book, replete with believable people dealing with life's ups and downs and acknowledging the importance of friends and family.

From **Money Hungry**

Even now, Momma's always dreaming about the future. But you can't cash dreams in at the bank or buy bread or pay rent with 'em. You need hard cold cash for that. So every penny I get, I save.... Cause if you got money, people can't take stuff from you—not your house or your ride, not your family. They can't do nothing much to you, if you got a bankroll backing you up.

—Sharon G. Flake

NELSON, MARILYN. *Carver: A Life in Poems.* Front Street, 2001. Gr. 6–9.

Marilyn Nelson's 59 poems tell the life story of the famed scientist, inventor, musician, and artist George Washington Carver. The story is told through the voices of people who knew him as well as through his own voice. For example, one poem is by a man sent by Carver's owner to find Carver and his mother after slave catchers had abducted them. Another piece is by Susan Carver, a white woman who, with her husband, "owned" and raised young George. There are selections from teachers in the schools where he studied, from his own students, from admirers, and even from detractors. The total gives a living picture of an admirable human being. Selections describe Carver's life from his birth to a slave woman in Diamond Grove, Missouri, and his childhood with Moses and Sam

Carver, to his travels and work in parts of the Midwest, where he began his education. Poetic entries describe his life's work teaching at Tuskegee Institute and his continuing search for the many uses of the peanut and the sweet potato. There are vignettes that bring to life Carver's devastation at the death of Booker T. Washington and his reaction at receiving a diamond ring as a gift from the automobile magnate Henry Ford. (Carver kept the ring in a box along with his collection of minerals.)

Handsome archival black-and-white photographs enhance the elegantly displayed text. Time line notes at the bottom of selected pages place events in Carver's life within the context of world history. The reader comes away not only with an appreciation of Carver and his life but also with an admiration for the wonderful power of poetry in general and of Nelson's poetry in particular.

From *Carver: A Life in Poems*

> Four a.m. in the Woods
> Darkness softens
> tissue of mist between trees.
> One by one the day's
> unaccountable voices come out
> like twilight fireflies, like stars.
> The perceiving self sits
> with his back against rough bark,
> casting ten thousand questions into the future.
> As shadows take shape, the curtains part
> for the length of time it takes to gasp,
> and behold, the purpose of his
> life dawns on him.
>
> —Marilyn Nelson

2001 Winner

WOODSON, JACQUELINE. *Miracle's Boys*. G. P. Putnam's Sons, 2000. Gr. 6–10.

Miracle's Boys is the story of three brothers, Ty'ree, Charlie, and Lafayette, and their struggle to stay together as a family after the death of their mother. The family's struggles actually began two years earlier with the death of the father. He drowned while saving a jogger and her dog who had fallen into an icy lake. Milagro (the mother's name in Spanish) worked hard to raise her boys. Although she could not give them many material things, she was able to pass on her strong values and a love of learning. After her death, Milagro's belief in the importance of family becomes evident when Ty'ree turns down a college scholarship to remain at home, work, and take care of his brothers—even refusing help from another family. Middle brother Charlie loses his way temporarily, has brushes with the law, deserts the family, associates with the wrong crowd, and ends up spending time in a juvenile facility. Ty'ree does not give up on Charlie, and the young prodigal eventually returns to the family unit. Also, ultimately, youngest brother Lafayette comes to terms with Charlie's accusation that he caused his mother's death. Milagro, despite her death, proves to be a powerful presence in the lives of her sons—a presence felt throughout the entire narrative. It is her spirit that keeps the boys together and helps them to overcome the destructive lure of the streets. The young men face hardships but demonstrate the resilience of the human spirit and the power of family love to help family members survive even the toughest circumstances. Ty'ree, Charlie, and Lafayette come to life through Woodson's elegant prose and skill at presenting three authentic young voices.

From *Miracle's Boys*

> Newcharlie moved the plastic bag away from his eyes so he could get a better look. He hadn't seen these pictures probably in years. I'd hidden them from him, afraid he'd burn them up too. But now I held them out so he could see, not afraid anymore. It was like the pictures were chiseled in my brain. "You tried to kill the memory of her," I said. "But she's too deep inside of us."
>
> —Jacqueline Woodson

2001 Honor

PINKNEY, ANDREA DAVIS. *Let It Shine! Stories of Black Women Freedom Fighters*. Illustrated by Stephen Alcorn. Gulliver Books/Harcourt, 2000. Gr. 5–8.

Andrea Davis Pinkney offers brief, powerful portraits of ten African American women who fought for freedom. "These women fought for many freedoms—freedom from sexism, oppression, the fear of being silenced." Some of her subjects, such as Biddy Mason, Dorothy Irene Height, Ella Josephine Baker, and Fannie Lou Hamer, may not be familiar to young readers. Others, including Sojourner Truth, Harriet Tubman, and Rosa Parks, are better known. Pinkney's tellings, however, with their rich imagery and original, rhythmic, often colloquial language, bring fresh insights and perspectives. She writes of Sojourner Truth, for example: "Sojourner traveled often on nothing more than her size-twelve feet throughout the United States preaching fairness and liberty. If there was a rock in the road, Sojourner made it her pulpit." The author describes the uncomfortable weekly train trip during which Ida Wells-Barnett was forced, as a black woman, to ride in the smoking car: "Whew, that smoking car sure smelled nasty. . . . The smoke was as thick as intolerance."

Each of these freedom fighters acted to change her own life and to improve the world for others. With their colorful language and telling details, the depictions of brave, determined women, illustrated with Stephen Alcorn's stunning allegorical pictures, make up a beautiful and inspiring volume.

From *Let It Shine!*

Now, anybody knows that wishing and doing are two different things. And Mary McLeod Bethune wasn't just one of those sapheaded daydreamers. She was a doer. All she needed was a mustard seed of inspiration.

—*Andrea Davis Pinkney*

2000 Winner

CURTIS, CHRISTOPHER PAUL. *Bud, Not Buddy*. Delacorte, 1999. Gr. 4–6.

Christopher Paul Curtis's second novel, *Bud, Not Buddy*, is the first book to win both the Coretta Scott King Book Award and the Newbery Medal. It is the story of ten-year-old Bud Caldwell's quest to find his father. It is 1936, the height of the Great Depression. Bud's mother died when he was six years old. Running away from a cruel foster family, Bud carries in his cardboard suitcase fliers his mother had collected advertising bass player Herman Calloway and the Dusky Devastators of the Great Depression. Buoyed by memories of his mother's love and his own "Rules and Things for Having a Funner Life and Making a Better Liar of Yourself," Bud sets out to find Calloway, whom he mistakenly assumes to be his father. Bud is a beguiling narrator, whose voice conveys his naive yet street-smart character. Curtis peoples his book with other memorable characters, including Calloway and Lefty Lewis, who are based on Curtis's own grandfathers. On the way to finding the truth about his family, Bud and the reader confront the realities of Depression-era life: soup kitchens, Hoovervilles and their wanton destruction by Pinkerton agents and police, labor strife, and the racism that makes it dangerous for Bud to travel Michigan highways alone at night. He also encounters kindness from strangers. By the time Bud learns that he is actually the son of Calloway's estranged daughter, the reader will have enjoyed adventure, social commentary, laugh-aloud humor, and the redemptive power of forgiveness.

From *Bud, Not Buddy*

Rules and Things Number 83: If a Adult Tells You Not to Worry, and You Weren't Worried Before, You Better Hurry and Start 'Cause You're Already Running Late.

—*Christopher Paul Curtis*

2000 Honors

ENGLISH, KAREN. *Francie*. Farrar, Straus, & Giroux, 1999. Gr. 7–10.

In a fast-paced story set in Alabama, Francie is the best student in her school. It is a time after World War II and before the turmoil of the civil rights era. Francie and her mother work hard at the local black boardinghouse as they wait for word from her father. He has gone to Chicago to work. When Francie is not working or attending school, she is reading. Her teacher recognizes her special skills and asks the young student to tutor sixteen-year-old Jesse, who has never learned to read well. The friendship that develops during the course of the tutoring causes Francie to make a difficult decision. Following a racial incident, Francie hides Jesse from the wrath of an unjust sheriff, placing her entire family in grave danger. Karen English has crafted a compelling story with a rich sense of tension, time, and space and well-developed characters who truly come to life.

From *Francie*

By the time I had taken him through the sounds of the consonants so that he could remember them, I'd changed my mind. Jesse Pruitt wasn't no dummy and I was going to teach him to read. The idea gave me butterflies in my stomach.

—*Karen English*

McKISSACK, PATRICIA C., AND FREDRICK L. McKISSACK. *Black Hands, White Sails: The Story of African-American Whalers*. Scholastic, 1999. Gr. 6–12.

The history of whaling in the Americas and around the globe is an exciting and captivating story of strong, fearless, ruthless, and often lawless men. Patricia and Fredrick

McKissack have written an intriguing account of the roles that African American sailors played in the whaling industry, skillfully interspersed with information about the risks and rigors of life aboard ship.

It was axiomatic that "southern whalers and others with an aversion to living and working with black sailors" soon learned that when hurricane winds were blowing or their boat was attached to a raging sperm whale, it didn't matter what color the hands were that handled the sails or pulled the oars. The rules were clear. All men had to work together if they were to survive. This reality is what earned blacks respect, or at least tolerance, even though they were not always accepted.

Short, readable chapters present basic information about ships, whales, and whaling. Roughly organized by geographical regions, the lives and deeds of black sea captains and whalers, known and unknown, famous and infamous, are chronicled, along with the more commonly known adventures of white seamen. Readers will be interested in learning the parts played by the abolitionist Frederick Douglass and the ingenious Paul Cuffe, to mention just two. Photographs, diary entries, traditional sea shanties, folk sayings, and superstitions make *Black Hands, White Sails* a fascinating reading experience for all ages.

MYERS, WALTER DEAN. *Monster.* HarperCollins, 1999. Gr. 9–12.

How does an ordinary kid, an OK student with a developing interest in film, living with two parents struggling to raise two sons in an urban community, find himself jailed and labeled as another of those "monsters from the ghetto"? What relationship does this ordinary kid have with the justice system? He is, after all, only a kid who most of the time focuses on ways of using film to document his surroundings and on negotiating to coexist with ever more demanding street gangs.

The skillful pen of master writer Walter Dean Myers provides a highly readable and interesting teen novel that has immediate reader appeal. The book takes the form of a film script written by the main character, Steve Harmon, who also uses the script format to calm the fear he is experiencing. Jailed and accused of being an accomplice to murder, Steve tries to divert his anxiety by analyzing the situation as an outsider. The story unfolds with short filmmaker's instructions: cut to/long shot/close-up, etc. Reaction shots and director's notes are seamlessly intertwined with the story of a real robbery and murder committed by local gang members.

The reader is never quite sure which of the adults in Steve's world, including his defense attorney, believe and support his plea of innocence. He receives clear and unwavering support only from his mother.

The design of this book, including the changing typefaces, is critical to the device of having the central character tell the story in the third person, as if he were an arm's-length observer. The theme of putting a face on crime is subtly juxtaposed with the realities of the justice system and the vagaries of honesty and integrity among thieves.

1999 Winner

JOHNSON, ANGELA. *Heaven.* Simon & Schuster Books for Young Readers, 1998. Gr. 6–10.

Fourteen-year-old Marley is living a warm and happy life in the small town of Heaven, Ohio, surrounded by family and friends in an almost idyllic community while enjoying a connection to the outside world through letters from her uncle Jack. Then, quite by accident, Marley learns that her parents are really her aunt and uncle, that "Uncle Jack" is really her father, and that her mother died when she was a baby. Shattered by this discovery, Marley closes herself off from family love and affection and begins to question every thought and belief that she had previously valued. The friends and family she once held dear no longer seem to offer her strength and support, and life becomes empty and unsure. As Marley sees it, only the wide-open spaces, the farmland and the fields, seem unchanged by what she has learned—and it is in those open spaces that she seeks comfort. Eventually Marley begins to understand that all families have secrets, that she can accept truths about herself without coming apart, and that real "heaven" is where love is unwavering and unconditional.

Angela Johnson's compelling first-person narrative is a finely tuned vehicle for an engaging protagonist who speaks with refreshing candor. The author's fluid writing is an invitation to the reader to reach a deeper appreciation for the universal search for self-identity.

1999 Honors

GRIMES, NIKKI. *Jazmin's Notebook.* Dial, 1998. Gr. 9–12.

Jazmin Shelby is a bright, inquisitive fourteen-year-old who writes her feelings and observations in a journal that provides special insight to the readers of this novel. Jazmin is a girl who had a strong family beginning that has since come apart. Her father, now dead, insisted on the z in the spelling of her name to reflect his love for jazz. Her mother is in the hospital, suffering from a mental illness. As the story opens Jazmin finally has a home with her older sister, CeCe. She goes through the normal teenage anxieties: worries about her appearance and fears about the future. She also handles attraction to a handsome boy who takes her interest as an invitation to rape. Most troubling of all, however, is her inability to accept her mother's illness and limitations. Jazmin's writing and her growing maturity finally give her the courage to visit her mother in the hospital, where she gains new hope from the changes she can observe.

A stunning combination of poetry and prose brings a special dimension to this coming-of-age novel. It is written with a sense of humor and a texture that will engage its readers.

HANSEN, JOYCE, AND GARY McGOWAN. *Breaking Ground, Breaking Silence: The Story of New York's African Burial Ground.* Henry Holt, 1998. Gr. 8–12. *

In 1991, the African Burial Ground in New York City was rediscovered, offering scholars and ultimately everyone a unique look at the lives of blacks in one section of colonial America. This volume offers young people a compelling look at the work of anthropologists, historians, and scholars as they piece together the elements of this long-hidden history. The authors use the physical evidence, documents, and narratives of the time to complete as much of the picture as is currently possible.

The combined talents of a team that brought scholarly research skills, an archaeological background, and outstanding writing abilities to the project have produced a historically accurate and readable text. In words and pictures, Joyce Hansen and Gary McGowan describe social conditions, ancestral traditions, and types of personal effects gleaned from the study of the remains of African Americans in a volume that closes yet another gap in the history of blacks in America.

JOHNSON, ANGELA. *The Other Side: Shorter Poems.* Orchard, 1998. Gr. 7–12. *

When writer Angela Johnson received word from her grandmother that Shorter, Alabama, was about to be razed to make room for a dog track, she made a literal and mental pilgrimage there. The result is this captivating collection of poems. Life in the small town of Shorter is crisply described by these concise pieces with a biographical overtone. Each poem stands on its own, but together they are evocative of another time with a clear sense of place and community. Johnson does not sentimentalize the past; rather, she celebrates the people who created families and communities despite the difficulties of the times. The realities of life in the rural South are never glossed over. The emotional tone of the poems varies from pathos to humor, reflecting the author's early life and coming of age in a loving, supportive community.

Through clever use of language, Johnson paints vivid pictures that allow readers to share her love and affection for her family and their small-town life. Family photographs add a further connection for readers.

1999 John Steptoe Award for New Talent

FLAKE, SHARON G. *The Skin I'm In.* Jump at the Sun/Hyperion Books for Children, 1998. Gr. 9–12.

Maleeka Madison begins seventh grade determined to fit in. She has grown weary of being teased by her classmates for her poorly constructed, homemade clothes and her physical appearance, particularly her dark skin. She decides to become part of the inner circle of Charlese, "the baddest thing in this school," even going so far as to change into Charlese's old clothes in the girls' bathroom. She endures cruel treatment from Charlese and her friends, still believing that is better than to be without friends. When she sees her new English teacher, Miss Saunders, she is shocked at her face, which "looks like someone threw a hot pot of something on it." Nonetheless, Miss Saunders appears confident and unruffled by the students' reactions. Miss Saunders recognizes a kindred spirit in Maleeka and encourages her writing skills even as Maleeka attempts to hide her strong academic abilities.

First-time novelist Flake has produced a thoughtful and timely story that explores peer pressure as well as the role that color plays in the body image of African American teens. Maleeka is a strong protagonist, struggling to become comfortable with who she is. The voices of the characters ring true, and school and community settings are presented with authenticity.

1998 Winner

DRAPER, SHARON M. *Forged by Fire.* Atheneum, 1997. Gr. 7–10.

Forged by Fire is a contemporary novel that unflinchingly comes to grips with many of the problems that beset the youth of today's society—broken homes, drugs, and child abuse—problems that are so much a part of a dysfunctional family.

Teenaged Gerald, whom some readers met in *Tears of a Tiger,* learns early in his troubled life that he must grow beyond his years if he is to survive and protect his younger sister, Angel. Gerald's and Angel's lives are stalked by tragedy: the death of Aunt Queen, the one person who truly showed them love; life with a substance-abusing and seemingly unaware mother; and the cruel acts of Jordan, their mother's boyfriend. Gerald finally takes matters into his own hands when he finds that Jordan is sexually molesting Angel. For some readers, the raging fire that brings Jordan to a tragic, but not entirely regrettable, end and nearly costs Angel her life may seem symbolic of the fire that rages in Gerald's spirit. It is the fire that in the end forges together this fragile family.

1998 Honors

HANSEN, JOYCE. *I Thought My Soul Would Rise and Fly: The Diary of Patsy, a Freed Girl.* Scholastic, 1997. Gr. 4–8.

The Coretta Scott King awards jury recognized *I Thought My Soul Would Rise and Fly* for extending the story of slavery into an arena seldom discussed in books for young readers.

Twelve-year-old Patsy, a slave in the Davis household in Mars Bluff, South Carolina, learns to read and write and secretly keeps a diary of the day-to-day occurrences in the "master's" family and the family of slaves he holds in bondage. Through her diary entries, individual personalities come alive: the slave Nancy, who claimed that "Missus was training her to be a fine ladies maid, not a cook"; Reverend McNeal, who started the organization that "helps men and women learn about government and voting"; the field hands, who fertilize the cotton fields with pine straw for the new planting next year; and Patsy herself, who reads from Goody Two Shoes and secretly passes her knowledge of words and letters to the other slaves. After the Emancipation Proclamation is announced, Patsy's diary dramatically reveals the trials, tribulations, quandaries, and uncertainties that ensued for the freed slaves. She also presents the changes the proclamation produced in the lives of the "masters" and "mistresses," whose indolence and dependency on others' labors were uprooted, and makes poignantly evident their lack of survival skills.

HASKINS, JAMES. *Bayard Rustin: Behind the Scenes of the Civil Rights Movement.* Hyperion Books for Children, 1997. Gr. 5–8. *

Bayard Rustin, born in 1912, was a civil rights activist and organizer whose pacifist beliefs and commitment to the principles of nonviolent action inspired Martin Luther King Jr. Because Rustin did much of his work behind the scenes, he may not be as well known as the other notable people with whom he worked in virtually every major initiative in the civil rights movement. James Haskins, in this eloquent and moving biography, brings Rustin's story of courage and commitment to the attention of a new generation of readers.

Raised by his grandparents in Pennsylvania, Rustin maintained that his Quaker grandmother was the greatest influence on his life. Citing an extensive bibliography, including primary source material, Haskins masterfully integrates the story of the civil rights movement in the United States with details of Rustin's personal and professional life, often using Rustin's own words. The quotations address incidents from Rustin's childhood and young adulthood, showing the development of his beliefs and commitment to issues of peace, equality, and justice.

Although Rustin served time in prison for refusing to join the military during World War II, had been a member of the Young Communist League, and was openly homosexual, his beliefs and organizational skills made him a dynamic leader in the civil rights movement. His talent in that area was most powerfully effective as he planned the procedures for the 1963 March on Washington, which led to the passage of the Civil Rights Act of 1964. Haskins creates a fascinating, respectful, and inspirational portrait of a man who left a lasting legacy in the struggle for equality and justice in the United States and throughout the world.

1997 Winner

MYERS, WALTER DEAN. *Slam!* Scholastic, 1996. Gr. 6–8.

From preschool through high school, both off and on the basketball court, Harlem-born Ice and Slam have been friends. Now seventeen-year-old Greg "Slam" Harris has transferred to a Bronx high school specializing in the arts. Both young men have NBA dreams and aspirations. Slam discovers that the students at his new school are serious young artists, and it becomes apparent that he must work hard to achieve good grades and personal satisfaction. It is also apparent that the basketball team, the perennially losing Panthers, could use a star player. What the Panthers don't need is a star with an attitude, especially one who is in continual conflict with the coach. In one school year Slam and Ice take separate paths. Slam embraces athletic and academic excellence while Ice accepts cash for drugs.

Myers's fast-paced novel develops a vivid flesh-and-blood portrait of young people in the Harlem community. For basketball fans, the description of moves on the court is hard to beat.

1997 Honor

McKISSACK, PATRICIA C., AND FREDRICK L. McKISSACK. *Rebels Against Slavery: American Slave Revolts.* Scholastic, 1996. Gr. 9–12. *

Patricia and Fredrick McKissack have written a most compelling narrative of those who resisted slavery in the Americas. *Rebels Against Slavery* includes the stories of individuals who bravely rebelled, runaway slaves who formed maroon communities, leaders who organized insurrections, conductors on the Underground Railroad, and those who became eloquent exponents of abolition. While the authors describe the contributions of all who fought slavery, their work emphasizes the role of African Americans. As the escaped slave and abolitionist Henry Garnet noted, "Others may be our allies, but the battle is ours." In these pages, the courage of slavery's opponents is brought to life. This book brings memories of a past that helped to map the future to a new generation. The authors stated,

As rebels for a righteous cause, they should be remembered for the terrible risks they knowingly took, the extraordinary determination they displayed and the important role they played in the abolition of slavery.

1997 John Steptoe Award for New Talent

SOUTHGATE, MARTHA. *Another Way to Dance.* Delacorte, 1996. Gr. 9–12.

Fourteen-year-old Vicki Harris imagines that someday she will have an opportunity to meet the dancer of her dreams, Mikhail Baryshnikov. This young ballerina is his greatest fan. She says, "I love him more than anything in the world." When Vicki is accepted into the prestigious summer program of the New York School of American Ballet, she is thrilled and frightened. The competition and racial tensions are easier to bear with her newfound friend and classmate, Stacey, the only other African American enrolled that summer. Summer also brings romance. Michael of Harlem may not be Mikhail of Latvia, but he, too, has dreams beyond those of flipping burgers. With New York City and the love of ballet as backdrops, Southgate gives a vivid picture of a thoughtful and talented young woman coming to terms with class, race, and cultural differences. She learns indeed that beyond the world of ballet, there is "another way to dance."

1996 Winner

HAMILTON, VIRGINIA. *Her Stories: African American Folktales, Fairy Tales, and True Tales.* Illustrated by Leo Dillon and Diane Dillon. Scholastic, 1995. Gr. 6–8.

In this aesthetically attractive volume Virginia Hamilton has gathered a collection of stories from African American culture in genres to fit just about everyone's literary tastes and has adapted them to her own inimitable "telling voice." As the title implies, the stories focus on African American women's stories. Notes at the end of each tale provide information on background, origin, and authenticity or historical significance. The repertoire includes familiar "girls and animals" stories such as "Little Girl and Buh Rabby" and one perhaps less familiar but thematically popular in many cultures, "Marie and Redfish." Fairy tales recall European and Asian versions of "Cinderella" and "The Talking Eggs." Readers will find that Hamilton's supernatural tales really do abound with "weird, mystical and magical elements . . . and odd and eerie events in the lives of female subjects." The true tales are touching biographical sketches of courageous women whose life stories were gleaned from documents collected under government projects in the 1920s and 1930s. In their carefully detailed illustrations, master artists Leo and Diane Dillon have captured the nuances of each story—from humorous to frightening to somber. *Her Stories* is a book to savor and to share.

1996 Honors

CURTIS, CHRISTOPHER PAUL. *The Watsons Go to Birmingham—1963.* Delacorte, 1995. Gr. 6–8.

Ten-year-old Kenny Watson narrates this funny and touching story of his family, "The Weird Watsons" of Flint, Michigan, as they are sometimes called. He relates comic stories of the escapades of his older brother, Byron, and the efforts of his strict but loving parents to keep the boys and their little sister, Joetta, out of trouble. Before long, however, Byron's pranks become more troubling, prompting Mom and Dad to plan a trip to Grandma's in Birmingham, Alabama. Here the story subtly shifts gears. As the family travels farther south, they find themselves headed for a place and time in history that will change them—and the country—forever: the civil rights movement.

Christopher Paul Curtis does a masterful job of weaving comedy and tragedy in this impressive first novel. He creates memorable and realistic characters that engage the reader from beginning to end. The author manages to present both a warm family story and a tragic episode of history in a style that makes both themes clear to the reader.

WILLIAMS-GARCIA, RITA. *Like Sisters on the Home Front.* Dutton, 1995. Gr. 8–12.

Gayle Whitaker is fourteen and pregnant, again. This time her mother escorts her to a women's clinic where she undergoes an abortion. The tough-talking Gayle is frightened. Mama is fed up and at the end of her rope. Drawing upon an African American tradition, Mama sends Gayle and her toddler son, Jose, down south to spend time with her minister uncle, his wife, and their daughter, the straight-laced cousin Cookie. In their quiet, antebellum home, the former site of a slaveholding plantation, Gayle meets the family matriarch, Great. This stately, near-death grandmother has a special fondness for the somewhat wayward and ignorant girl. Great sees in Gayle her own teenage behavior. It is Great who tells Gayle stories of the past that help Gayle to see that she indeed has a future.

Gayle appeared as a minor character in Williams-Garcia's first novel, *Blue Tights*. In this, her third novel, the author continues her compassionate and humorous portraits of New York City teenagers with flawed characters who are given opportunities for tremendous growth.

WOODSON, JACQUELINE. *From the Notebooks of Melanin Sun.* Scholastic, 1995. Gr. 9–12.

Thirteen-year-old Melanin Sun and his mother are extremely close; they have never needed anyone else. Even his name reflected their special bond: Melanin because that is what made him dark, and Sun because "his mom could see the sun shining through him." Things change between the two of them during the summer of Melanin's thirteenth year. Suddenly his mama has a new friend—a white woman named Kristin. Before too long his mother admits that Kristin is more than a friend—they are lovers. Just when Melanin is coming to grips with his own sexual feelings, he must sort out new feelings toward his mother. For a while it appears that the new truth about his mother will destroy his special relationship with her. In pain, Melanin lashes out at Mama, but eventually he decides that, despite his confusion, he needs her in his life and tries to make some connection with Kristin.

Jacqueline Woodson presents a powerful, trailblazing story, reaching across barriers of race and sexual orientation. She has created a strong, honest character in Melanin Sun, whose first-person narrative draws the reader into his innermost thoughts. Woodson reminds readers that no matter how painful, the possibility of love and understanding can be found in all human relationships.

1995 Winner

McKISSACK, PATRICIA C., AND FREDRICK L. McKISSACK. *Christmas in the Big House, Christmas in the Quarters.* Illustrated by John Thompson. Scholastic, 1994. Gr. 3–5.

Using details that are evidence of meticulous research and text that is presented through the voice of accomplished storytellers, the authors introduce readers to the life of the master of a plantation and his family as contrasted with the life of the slaves who work his Virginia plantation. In a story set during the last Christmas before the southern rebellion, the precursor of the Civil War, the book presents imaged-filled descriptions of traditions, superstitions, religious observances, songs, holiday menus, and games. The authors show the contrast between the gifts and decorations easily available to the master's family and those of the slaves, who ingeniously made their decorations from nature's bounty. Descriptions of the daily, seemingly endless tasks are interspersed with words from songs "'cause singing makes the time go faster."

Rumblings of unrest filter through the activities in the big house, and in the quarters there are secretive discussions among the slaves from neighboring plantations who were given passes for a short family reunion. The book closes with a portentous message:

> The way talk goin' I got a feeling we aine gon' need to run away. One day soon we gon' celebrate the Big Times in freedom.

John Thompson's dramatic paintings, the authors' historical notes, and a useful bibliography further enrich this moving story.

1995 Honors

HANSEN, JOYCE. *The Captive.* Scholastic, 1994. Gr. 9–12.

Through the voice of a master storyteller, twelve-year-old Kofi, the son of an African king, describes the way a joyful Ashanti celebration turns with unbelievable swiftness into a scene of treachery, murder, capture, and slavery.

> I became a captive.... I had lost my home, my family and even myself. I was a slave dressed in filthy loincloth. I could hardly remember what my beautiful robe looked like.

The narration covers the horrors of the slave ship, the indignity of the slave auction market, the rigorous work assigned to the young slaves, the strange and reserved relationship Kofi observes between his "master" and the master's wife. Kofi spends hours contemplating the strange movements and mumbling of words he later learns are elements of worship, and he ponders the dichotomy of those who would profess religion and still hold others in servitude.

Over the years, Kofi masters the English language and has an enthralling encounter with the able African American seaman Paul Cuffe. Eventually, as a freedman, Kofi visits Sierra Leone, marries his early love, Ama, and raises his family in America. The well-researched novel closes on this rich promise:

> I made a decision that I too [like his father, Kwame, and Paul Cuffe] would fight against slavery and open my heart and home to unfortunate men and women in bondage.... The trial of my life had not been in vain.

McKISSACK, PATRICIA C., AND FREDRICK McKISSACK JR. *Black Diamond: The Story of the Negro Baseball Leagues.* Scholastic, 1994. Gr. 8–12. *

This carefully researched volume not only tells the story of the Negro baseball leagues but also dispels some early myths about the "all-American" game in general. Documents were found that stated that as early as 1845 there were organized guidelines for playing the game and that the first all-star game was played before the Civil War. The main focus of the book, however, is on the story of the African American men who played the game even though rules established in 1867 eliminated the preponderance of blacks from playing with mainstream teams.

The history covers individual players, such as the noted Satchel Paige; the lesser-known but very important Moses Fleetwood Walker, nicknamed Fleet, who played for the American Association in Toledo, Ohio; and Sol White, a noted amateur ballplayer but more important a writer from whose records much history was learned. White, for instance, chronicled the history of the Cuban Giants (1887), the first professional all-black team, who in a time of racial prejudice, because of their team name, were able to play against white teams. White writes, "not one of them was white nor could they speak a word of Spanish," but calling themselves Cuban opened the door.

The McKissacks write of the hardships those stalwart and determined ballplayers suffered—the lack of eating or sleeping facilities on the road, the unwritten requirement that they often play the clown to draw fans to the games, and financial inequities—any one of which could have been a deterrent if not for the players' deep love of the game. The book includes profiles of many players, some of whom finally made the major leagues: Satchel Paige, Roy Campanella, and Jackie Robinson. (It is interesting to note here that the McKissacks include as a matter of interpretation that Jackie Robinson, according to research, may not have been the first black to sign a major league contract.) Also included are players who after years of rejection were finally entered in the Cooperstown Baseball Hall of Fame. A briefly annotated player roster gives readers a quick overview of the many personalities who sacrificed so much for a game they loved. Several black-and-white photographs give visibility to the men, their uniforms, their publicity material, and the camaraderie they shared.

WOODSON, JACQUELINE. *I Hadn't Meant to Tell You This.* Delacorte, 1994. Gr. 5–9.

Despite differences of race and class, Marie and Lena ignore the taunts of schoolmates and become best friends. Although Marie, from a middle-class African American family, seems to have little in common with poor, white Lena, the girls share a bond that means more than their differences: both girls have lost their mothers. As they share their deepest and most personal secrets, Marie is faced with a dilemma that can often confront good friends: can she help Lena more by betraying her confidence or should she keep her promise and remain silent?

Woodson's sensitive and skillful telling of this story places important issues before the reader: friendship across races, class differences, peer pressure, and family secrets. Woodson presents no easy answers but rather an honest portrait of the importance of seeking and finding understanding in all kinds of people.

1995 Genesis Award (later the John Steptoe Award for New Talent)

DRAPER, SHARON M. *Tears of a Tiger.* Atheneum, 1994. Gr. 9–12.

The opening words of this page-turner pull the reader into a gripping story of friendship, irrevocable injury, and death—a relentless story rife with contemporary reality. A newspaper headline screams:

> *Teen Basketball Star Killed in Fiery Crash*
>
> Andrew Jackson, the driver of the car and Robert Washington's best friend, finds his life forever changed by this avoidable accident. He closes himself off from a solicitous family, walks dazedly through school and studies, and avoids what seems to be useless help from a psychiatrist. And what of the others? Draper takes the reader into the heart and soul of everyone touched by this tragedy: B. J. Carson,

who did not drink but feels guilty because he did not try to stop the others on that fateful night; Keisha, the love interest who worries about Andy's depression; and Andy's little brother Monty, who does not understand Andy's screaming nightmares. Through careful character development, the reader sees how each person works through the tragedy to the very uncompromising conclusion when Andy, unable to forgive or forget, takes his own life. Powerful words and powerful questions are the benchmarks of this hard-hitting young adult novel. One can understand, if perhaps not accept, Andy's decision after reading his poetry:

> I cannot see the future
> And I cannot change the past
> But the present is so heavy
> I don't think I'll last.

1994 Winner

JOHNSON, ANGELA. *Toning the Sweep.* Orchard, 1993. Gr. 6–8.

Toning the Sweep, a cross-generational story, gloriously celebrates Grandma Ola's life even as that life, ravaged by cancer, is quietly slipping away. Fourteen-year-old Emily and her mother, Diane, have come to the desert to help Ola pack, bid farewell to her beloved desert, and move to spend the rest of her life with family in Cleveland. The sunshine yellow of Ola's house seems symbolic of the joy and warmth that overshadows the impending sense of loss.

Using a camcorder, Emily videotapes Ola with each of her friends. She records their laughter and the repetition of oft-told stories of people long gone. She makes a memory of their tragedies, dreams, and hopes so many times gone unfulfilled. The camera records the reason for her mother's quiet anger against the Ola whom Emily loves and brings a stronger understanding to their mother-daughter relationship. As Emily listens to Ruth and David and to Aunt Martha and all the other aunts, she becomes aware of the philosophical approach to life that makes them as relentlessly enduring as the Arizona desert they call home. And the human lives are not recorded in isolation. Emily photographs the lizards, the plants, and the trees that are the natural background of this arid place.

Readers will be intrigued to learn the poignant meaning of toning the sweep and its significance in the lives of Emily and her mother. Written in poetic prose and touched lightly with humor, this is an unforgettable story steeped with emotions that will linger with the reader long beyond the final page.

1994 Honors

MYERS, WALTER DEAN. *Malcolm X: By Any Means Necessary.* Illustrated with black-and-white photographs. Scholastic, 1993. Gr. 6–12. *

The dramatic opening chapter tells of Malcolm X's deceptively quiet confrontation with the police in Harlem and introduces readers to the multifaceted life of a man who left an indelible mark on contemporary American history. Myers provides an in-depth picture of the early years of Malcolm X, born Malcolm Little. He introduces Malcolm's father, an outspoken minister and civil rights leader in the Depression era. The author presents vivid pictures of Malcolm's poverty-stricken childhood after the death of his beloved father and of his mother's slow and tragic mental breakdown, which resulted in the disintegration of the Little family. Myers does not gloss over Malcolm Little's academic prowess and brilliant mind, which in his youth he often used to make a flashy but less than savory living. The author describes Malcolm Little's six years of imprisonment, during which he was introduced to the principles and philosophy of Islam—a turning point in the life of the man who became Malcolm X. And this astute author does not fail to explain to young readers the meaning of *X* as explained by Malcolm X's mentor, Muslim leader Elijah Muhammad. *X*, we learn, signifies the eradication of the surname a slave was given based on his or her master's name. It was symbolic of the irrevocable loss of the name given in Mother Africa.

The book includes sidelights of African American history relevant to the development of Malcolm X's personality, including the Marcus Garvey movement, the heroic work of the 54th Massachusetts Regiment of Civil War fame, the Anthony Burns slave case, and Malcolm X's interaction with Fidel Castro, among others.

With quiet compassion Myers discusses Malcolm X's gradual change from total hatred of the white man—and a disparaging view of Martin Luther King Jr.'s nonviolent approach to racial equality—to the realization that there is wisdom in being willing to accept people as individuals. This awakening came after his 1964 pilgrimage to Mecca. It marked the beginning of a negative change in the relationship between Malcolm X and Elijah Muhammad, one that many feel may have led to the outspoken Malcolm's assassination in 1965.

With consummate skill, Myers has written the story of a complex personality in tones that make his important life accessible to young adult readers. The book is further enriched with a bibliography that includes books and periodicals covering from the early 1930s to the present.

THOMAS, JOYCE CAROL. *Brown Honey in Broomwheat Tea.* Illustrated by Floyd Cooper. HarperCollins, 1993. Gr. 3–6.

The poems in this outstanding collection speak in many voices: a plea for acceptance in "Cherish Me"; cautionary wariness in the title piece, "Brown Honey in Broomwheat Tea"; and the strength that is an integral part of African American heritage in "Becoming the Tea."

> But like the steeping brew
> The longer I stand
> The stronger I stay.

Thomas's rhythmic patterns, image-filled language, and provocative themes evoke a wide range of emotions. Although perhaps particularly attuned to the African American heritage, the ideas are worthy of contemplation and reflection by readers regardless of their ethnic heritage.

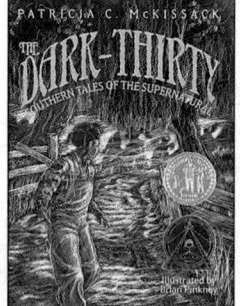

1993 Winner

McKISSACK, PATRICIA C. *The Dark–Thirty: Southern Tales of the Supernatural.* Illustrated by Brian Pinkney. Knopf, 1992. Gr. 6–8.

Patricia McKissack has written a collection of stories made for reading aloud or for telling "at that special time when it is neither day nor night and when shapes and shadows play tricks on the mind." There is a well-balanced mix of the humorous, the ghostly, and the supernatural among the ten entries. Readers will probably make individual choices among stories such as that of the Pullman porter who tried to avoid the 11:59, known as the death train, but answered its call on a gloomy night, and that of the slave who took a lesson from the wasps in making a wise decision to disobey his master. Or perhaps they will join in the fun of mastering the monster in the tale of the chicken coop. Each story is introduced with a historical note giving its foundation or origin. Brian Pinkney's scratchboard illustrations are a fitting complement to the mood of the stories.

1993 Honors

McKISSACK, PATRICIA C., AND FREDRICK L. McKISSACK. *Sojourner Truth: Ain't I a Woman?* Scholastic, 1992. Gr. 5–8. *

The McKissacks' stirring biography has captured the strength, the steadfastness, and the perseverance of a powerful woman determined to be free. There are engrossing details of Sojourner Truth's efforts to keep her family together, to save the life of her wayward son, Peter, and to escape from the deceit of two religious charlatans. Meticulous research documents events in Sojourner Truth's life as she traveled in places where others dared not go, speaking out against slavery and fighting for all women's rights at a time when this was the calling of only a select few—and mainly men. In a slavery dispute, for example, Sojourner Truth is recorded to be the first black woman to defeat a white man in a court of law. There was rapt attention when this imposing figure, over six feet tall, spoke with moving dignity. In answer to a minister's charge that God had intended them to be subservient because they were indeed the weaker sex, Truth responded:

> I have ploughed and I have planted. And I have gathered into barns, and no man could head me. . . . I have borne children and seen them sold into slavery when I cried out in a mother's grief none heard me but Jesus—and ain't I a woman.

This moving biography is enriched with interesting photographs and a very special section of brief biographical sketches of personalities, white and black, who were a part of Sojourner Truth's memorable life.

MYERS, WALTER DEAN. *Somewhere in the Darkness.* Scholastic, 1992. Gr. 7–12.

With a strikingly significant title, Myers sets the focus of this dramatic story. Somewhere in the darkness a father is trying to establish a relationship between himself and the son he abandoned at an early age. On a dark night Crab, just escaped from prison, shows up at his teenaged son's home. He abruptly tells guardian Mama Jean that he has come to claim his son. With this, Crab and Jimmy begin a cross-country trek during which Jimmy learns who his father is—an escapee, a con man, a womanizer, but still a man who wants to be a father to his son. Just before Crab's death there is a reconciliation and the poignancy of the moment when Jimmy realizes he has learned from Crab the kind of father he himself wants to be.

Jimmy thought about his having a child. It seemed so far off, like something that could never happen but somehow would. He thought about what he would do with the child if it were a boy. He wouldn't know much about getting money to buy food for him or what things to tell him to do except to be good and not get into trouble. But he would tell him all the secrets he knew, looking right into his eyes and telling him nothing but the truth so that every time they were together they would know things about each other. That way there would be a connection . . . something that would be there even when they weren't together. He would know . . . where their souls touched and where they didn't.

Somewhere in the Darkness speaks to all who are parents and to those who someday will be.

WALTER, MILDRED PITTS. *Mississippi Challenge.* Bradbury, 1992. Gr. 7–12. *

Mississippi Challenge is a documented study of a state whose historical treatment of African Americans is memorable for its cruelty and inhumanity. With candor, Walter traces freedom movements past and present and details the triumphs and failures of citizens who fought and died for justice: the sit-ins of the 1960s, the often fatal attempts at voter registration, and the inequalities in educational expenditures, which fostered the establishment of the freedom schools.

Blended into the text on contemporary affairs is a careful study of the early history of the state, the lives of some of the leaders, and little-known facts about nineteenth-century African American political leaders. This material helps youthful readers to link the past with the present.

Black-and-white photographs and personal interviews extend the information in this historically based reference. A scholarly bibliography provides reference sources for further research.

1992 Winner

MYERS, WALTER DEAN. *Now Is Your Time! The African American Struggle for Freedom.* HarperCollins, 1991. Gr. 4–8. *

In his first nonfiction book, Walter Dean Myers brings to audiences of all ages a memorable history of African Americans that spans over four centuries. The opening chapters share with readers an aspect of African history often omitted from most history texts—the time of high culture, noble rulers, great centers of learning, and scholars such as Ibrahima, whose knowledge brought students from all directions to learn from him. Scholarly research, personal interviews with the descendants of those captured and brought in chains to this country, and carefully selected photographs from historical collections are the foundation of a book that eloquently tells the story of African Americans who achieved in spite of hardships. Myers's prose is moving and convincing; the interviews add a sense of the contemporary. There seems to be a challenge to young readers in the very choice of the title *Now Is Your Time!* Like Myers, may those who share this masterpiece of American history move forward strengthened by the author's words of celebration:

> I claim the darkest moments of my people and celebrate their perseverance.
>
> I claim the joy and the light and the music and the genius and the muscle and the glory of these I write about . . . and of the legions who have passed this way without yet having their stories told.

1992 Honor

GREENFIELD, ELOISE. *Night on Neighborhood Street.* Illustrated by Jan Spivey Gilchrist. Dial, 1991. Gr. K–3.

From dusk to deep into the night these seventeen poems celebrate life in the neighborhood at that special time when the workday is done. Sleepovers, crying babies, church meetings, "Fambly Time," the child fearful of the dark, and kids playing on the street corner are all depicted. Gouache paintings highlighted with pastels accompany the poetry. Greenfield recognizes the many temptations toward wrongdoing that often accompany nighttime yet shows that the community can cope by uniting and offering "warmth and life" to undo the attractions of "The Seller" and others who want to harm its inhabitants. Powerful words offer comfort and solace to children with rhythms and images that soften the darkness's ability to frighten. Night becomes friend instead of nightmare.

1991 Winner

TAYLOR, MILDRED D. *The Road to Memphis.* Dial, 1990. Gr. 6–8.

Cassie Logan's personal courage serves her well during a dangerous trip she makes from Mississippi to Tennessee in 1941 with her brother Stacey and his friends in Stacey's new car. Out on the open highway, the four African American teenagers, far from the protection of their families and their community, face unknown hazards at every turn in the road. This gripping narrative re-creates the perilous tensions of that time and place, as Cassie crosses over an invisible boundary and suddenly finds herself traveling into the unfamiliar terrain of adulthood.

1991 Honors

HASKINS, JAMES. *Black Dance in America: A History through Its People.* Illustrated with photographs. HarperCollins, 1990. Gr. 6–12. *

Brief biographical passages about individual African American dancers are chronologically arranged and connected by descriptions of the dances they invented or refined, providing an accessible overview of this distinctive art form. Haskins also provides a social and historical context by showing the ways black dance influenced and was influenced by dance in general.

JOHNSON, ANGELA. *When I Am Old with You.* Illustrated by David Soman. Orchard, 1990. Gr. Pre-K–2.

In this warm, cross-generational story, the reader meets a child and his grandfather sharing hours of comfortable enjoyment. As they play cards, go fishing, enjoy a quiet picnic, or meet with friends at a lively party, the little boy muses that these are the things they will do together when he is as old as his grandfather. There is a moment of nostalgic sadness when the two are looking at the family album and each sheds tears for a different reason. One of the most endearing lines in the book occurs when the little boy, totally unaware of age differences, reflects on the idea that when he is old with his grandfather, they will sit, each in his own rocking chair, and "just talk about things." In word and picture, *When I Am Old with You* speaks with simple eloquence of the innocence of childhood.

1990 Winner

McKISSACK, PATRICIA C., AND FREDRICK L. McKISSACK. *A Long Hard Journey: The Story of the Pullman Porter.* Illustrated with photographs. Walker, 1989. Gr. 6–8. *

The authors combined in-depth research from primary and secondary sources to provide an uncompromising account of the history of African Americans who worked as porters aboard George Pullman's luxury sleeping cars. Whereas the first generation of porters were newly freed from enslavement and grateful for work, poor working conditions and mistreatment at the hands of management led succeeding generations to unite under the leadership of A. Philip Randolph in a struggle for better pay and fair treatment. Songs, stories, first-person accounts, and numerous black-and-white photographs accompany the narrative, which is unique in content.

1990 Honors

GREENFIELD, ELOISE. *Nathaniel Talking.* Illustrated by Jan Spivey Gilchrist. Black Butterfly Children's Books, 1988. Gr. K–3.

Nathaniel is nine years old and his voice is strong in this collection of eighteen poems accompanied by black-and-white illustrations. In the rhythms of blues and rap this young male voice comes through strong and buoyant. Emotions fill the corners of the poems as Nathaniel reflects and raps about his life. His pride and strength are grounded in his family and his troubles, which he faces with confidence.

Nathaniel springs to life, a vibrant, funny, clear-sighted human being.

HAMILTON, VIRGINIA. *The Bells of Christmas.* Illustrated by Lambert Davis. Harcourt Brace Jovanovich, 1989. Gr. K–6.

An elegant tribute to the childlike anticipation of family Christmas observances takes place in 1890 in the Bell family home located on the historic National Road near Springfield, Ohio. Told from the point of view of twelve-year-old Jason Bell, the story offers references to independence, to travel across time and space, and to the historical period. An invigorating sense of this loving African American family's continuity combines with a warm expression of uncommercialized holiday joy.

PATTERSON, LILLIE. *Martin Luther King, Jr., and the Freedom Movement.* Illustrated with photographs. Facts on File, 1989. Gr. 6–8. *

Expanding Martin Luther King Jr.'s image from that of a famous African American civil rights leader to that of the human rights leader who won the 1964 Nobel Peace Prize, Patterson's biography offers a reliable transition between juvenile and adult book accounts of the twentieth century freedom fighter. The biography is illustrated with black-and-white photographs, maps, and freedom songs, and includes an excellent annotated listing of further reading and a brief chronology.

1989 Winner

MYERS, WALTER DEAN. *Fallen Angels.* Scholastic, 1988. Gr. 9–12.

Using Vietnam for the setting and U.S. teenagers as most of the characters, this landmark novel offers a logical, easy-to-follow story about the often questionable logic of going to war. Seventeen-year-old Richie Perry is the African American protagonist whose medical papers don't catch up with him before he's shipped overseas. The war at home is revealed in letters the soldiers receive from friends and family; however, almost all of the episodes occur in the jungle during tedious hours of waiting, which are occasionally interrupted by minutes of sheer terror and chaos. Although author Myers never moralizes, a highly moral core is evident throughout this mesmerizing novel. Along with Richie Perry's humanity and bravery, the book's depiction of war's brutality will be remembered long after readers finish the book.

1989 Honors

BERRY, JAMES. *A Thief in the Village and Other Stories.* Orchard, 1987. Gr. 9–12.

The short stories in *A Thief in the Village* give the reader a picturesque glimpse into the day-to-day life of the people in a Jamaican village. The vignettes, which cover a range of emotions from sad to philosophical to humorous, sing with Berry's poetic prose. Among the children that Berry is celebrating, we meet Becky, who wants a bike so that she can ride with the Wheels-and-Brake Boys. Mum says girls don't do that, but with an all's-well-that-ends-well finish, Becky gets a bike and her widowed Mum gets a boyfriend. Then there is the pathos in the story of young Gustus, who, during a raging hurricane, nearly loses his life trying to save the banana tree that was marked as his personal birthright—he had hoped to make money from the sale of the fruit to buy shoes. His father did not understand this concern until Gustus's near fatal accident as he returns to his storm-torn home and is felled by the tree. In the title story, a sister and brother, Nenna and Man-Man, set up an all-night vigil to catch the thief who has been stealing their coconuts. *A Thief in the Village* is a charming look at the people who live and work in a tropical village that is not always a paradise.

HAMILTON, VIRGINIA. *Anthony Burns: The Defeat and Triumph of a Fugitive Slave.* Knopf, 1988. Gr. 6–12. *

Biography and historical fiction are interwoven in a carefully written account of Anthony Burns's 1854 Boston trial based on the controversial federal Fugitive Slave Act of 1793. Documented from primary sources, the biographical portions concerning Burns's imprisonment and trial are interspersed with innovative fictional segments reconstructing his youth as an enslaved child in Virginia. Source notes, a list of persons in the book, excerpts from the Fugitive Slave Act, and the author's comments further increase the value of this unusual illuminating book.

1988 Winner

TAYLOR, MILDRED D.
The Friendship. Illustrated by Max Ginsburg. Dial, 1987. Gr. 6–12.

In a powerful short story issued as a single volume, the four Logan children are witnesses to a frightening scene at the general store in Strawberry, Mississippi. When a respected elder in the African American community dares to call the white store owner by his first name, the elder is brutally attacked by a group of white men who are unaware of a decades-long friendship between the two. Mr. Tom Bee refuses to be cowed by the attack, however, and he continues to call out the name of the store owner even after he is lying on the ground, beaten and bleeding. Both literally and figuratively, this deeply moving story shows children a courageous model of active resistance to racism and oppression.

1988 Honors

DE VEAUX, ALEXIS. *An Enchanted Hair Tale.* Illustrated by Cheryl Hanna. Harper & Row, 1987. Gr. K–2.

Sudan's wonderful hair—"a fan daggle of locks and lions and lagoons"—sets him apart from other kids in his neighborhood, who tease him because he is different. Upset by their cruelty, he storms away and, far from home, stumbles upon a whole family of folks with enchanted hair who help him celebrate his differences. De Veaux's rhythmic text is full of winsome rhyme and alliteration. Her imagery brilliantly conveys the mystery and magic of Sudan's hair. The poem is enhanced and extended by Cheryl Hanna's captivating black-and-white pencil drawings.

LESTER, JULIUS. *The Tales of Uncle Remus: The Adventures of Brer Rabbit.* Introduction by Augusta Baker. Illustrated by Jerry Pinkney. Dial, 1987. Gr. 3–6.

A new Uncle Remus emerges from Lester's creative reshaping of forty-eight Brer Rabbit stories from African American traditions into modified, contemporary southern black English. Storytelling specialist Augusta Baker's introduction speaks of the importance for contemporary children to hear these tales; Lester's foreword advises telling or reading the tales in one's own language. Occasional black-and-white drawings complement the high-spirited tales, and four watercolors are reproduced in full color on double-page spreads.

1987 Winner

WALTER, MILDRED PITTS. *Justin and the Best Biscuits in the World.* Lothrop, Lee, & Shepard, 1986. Gr. 3–5.

After the death of his father, ten-year-old Justin finds himself living surrounded by women—his mother and his two sisters. There is constant conflict because Justin has very set ideas about what is and is not a man's work. His room is always a mess, washing dishes is not on his list of masculine chores, and if he ever tries to cook anything the kitchen becomes a disaster. But Grandfather Ward comes to the rescue when he takes Justin to his home, a prosperous ranch in Missouri, where Justin learns several lessons about what it takes to be a man. These lessons include how to make a bed, clean the kitchen, and make prize-winning biscuits. But for Justin and all the readers there is another reward: Walter shares a history of the contributions of black cowboys and, through the grandfather's narration of his family history, a lesson in the importance of knowing who you are and where you come from. One moving moment occurs when Justin learns that it is even all right for a man to cry. Grandfather explains his tears and shares a proverb: "The brave hide their fears but share their tears. Tears bathe the soul."

Walter has written a well-paced story with several levels of historical and social information.

1987 Honors

BRYAN, ASHLEY. *Lion and the Ostrich Chicks: And Other African Folk Tales.* Atheneum, 1986. Gr. 3–5.

Using his special talent for blending rhythmic word patterns with all the details of a well-told story, Bryan has adapted a diverse collection of African tales that beg to be read aloud. Through his research into the history and culture of several tribes, this author-illustrator found the roots of the stories in many geographical regions and, in his inimitable writing style, retold the tales for young readers. Complete scholar that he is, Bryan has included a bibliography listing his sources for all the stories in the book.

One cannot miss the folktale concept of the triumph of good over evil, whether it is in the title story, in which the lion tries to claim the ostrich chicks as his own, or in a telling of how the born-foolish boy outwits the trickster Ananse.

Bryan extends the text with his own art prints in sharp black-and-white figures or in illustrations using the earth colors of the land in which the tales are set. The Coretta Scott King awards jury enjoyed both the humor and the lessons in *Lion and the Ostrich Chicks.*

HANSEN, JOYCE. *Which Way Freedom?* Walker, 1986. Gr. 6–8.

You born a man, not a slave—that the thing to remember. You got to learn which way freedom be. "It here first," he said, touching his own creased forehead, "in your mind."

Some two hundred thousand African Americans fought in the Civil War. The figure is real and so large that it is impossible to incorporate all of those soldiers' stories into a single story. By creating one fictional representative of the two hundred thousand, Joyce Hansen brings this impersonal statistic to life.

We meet Obi as a nineteen- or twenty-year-old Union soldier, an escaped slave with a haunting memory of his mother's cries as years earlier he was torn from her arms and sold off to a different master. In a flashback, Obi relives the years he then spent as one of three young slaves on a small South Carolina tobacco farm. He was sustained during his youth by a vague plan to find his mother again on one of the Sea Islands and escape with her to Mexico. As his memories of her become cloudy, he relies on the old freed slave Buka to help him recall her appearance and remember the bitter tears that fell on deaf ears.

With the start of the Civil War, the pressures to harvest the tobacco crop increase, as do the beatings that Obi must endure. When Obi learns that the farm and its slaves are about to be sold, he enlists Buka's help to finally realize his dream of escape. On the plantation, Obi, Easter, and young Jason were always fast friends. Because of the danger they would face in their escape attempt, Obi and Easter are forced to leave young Jason behind as they follow Buka's plans for the journey. Easter and Obi finally part, each seeking a separate way to freedom.

The reader follows Obi's tense flight until the moment that opened the book, when Obi joined the advancing

Union army and was assigned to the Sixth U.S. Artillery of Colored Troops. For the first time he could call himself by the name he wanted, Obidiah Booker (*Obidiah* meaning "first born" and *Booker* for his faithful counselor and friend, Buka). Was this the way to freedom?

1986 Winner

HAMILTON, VIRGINIA. *The People Could Fly: American Black Folktales.* Illustrated by Leo Dillon and Diane Dillon. Knopf, 1985. Gr. 3–5.

The first comprehensive anthology of African American folklore selected and retold especially for children includes twenty-four exquisitely crafted, individually developed tales. Historical notes accompany each story, and the compilation as a whole is arranged in four categories: trickster tales, tall tales, ghost and devil tales, and stories of liberation and freedom. Hamilton handles information about the Joel Chandler Harris texts with dignity, placing those versions of the traditional tales into a historical context. Her impressive use of black English from several distinct cultures also distinguishes this excellent collection of folktales.

1986 Honors

HAMILTON, VIRGINIA. *Junius over Far.* Harper & Row, 1985. Gr. 6–8.

Junius feels a strong connection between himself and his grandfather, who has recently returned to his Caribbean island home. When his grandfather's letters are suddenly filled with obscure references to pirates and kidnapping, Junius convinces his father that they must rush to Grandfather's aid. Shifting points of view give readers insights into the thoughts and feelings of both the teenager and his grandfather, stressing the strength of this intergenerational African American family. Hamilton creates a rich ambience with a lyrical use of language filled with Caribbean cadences and rhythms.

WALTER, MILDRED PITTS. *Trouble's Child.* Lothrop, Lee, & Shepard, 1985. Gr. 6–8.

Set on Blue Island, off the coast of Louisiana, *Trouble's Child* paints a picture of life both simple and complex on the island. The narration shares superstitions, customs, folklore, traditions, and the communal sorrow of an isolated people. Martha, the protagonist, who was born during a storm and is therefore a "trouble child," longs to go to the mainland to study. Her grandmother, Titay, island matriarch and revered midwife, expects Martha to remain on the island and learn from her the secrets of healing herbs and signs. While the folks on the island watch for Martha to bring out her quilting pattern, a signal that she is ready to marry, the stalwart young woman's life is changed. Harold Saunders, an outsider washed ashore during a storm, and Ms. Boudreaux, her teacher, support Martha in her goal to go to school and study science so that she might more effectively help her people. This is an intriguing story, a mix of the old and the new, with a satisfying ending. Walter's use of the island dialect is readable, sensitive, and consistent.

1985 Winner

MYERS, WALTER DEAN. *Motown and Didi: A Love Story.* Viking, 1984. Gr. 9–12.

In a story of love, violence, despair, and hope, Myers describes the unlikely courtship of a homeless young man and an ambitious young woman confronting Harlem's drug culture. Didi's dream of attending college, getting a good job, and saving her family from poverty is shattered when she comes home to find her brother Tony high on dope. Motown lives alone in a condemned, abandoned building. His only treasures are the books he is reading at the suggestion of the Professor—his friend and mentor and the owner of the Spirit of Life bookshop. When Didi reports her brother's pusher to the police, the pusher orders that she be hurt. It is Motown who saves her from her attackers. Though she helps Motown find a small apartment, Didi resists the possibility of a romantic attachment because the quiet young man does not seem to fit her imagined future. And Motown's experiences with foster care have hardened him against needing anyone. The leisurely pace of their growing love sets the stage for the work's fast-moving conclusion. When Tony dies of an overdose, Didi begs Motown to kill the pusher who destroyed her brother. If Motown kills the dealer, he will destroy his own life as well, but this near tragedy is averted.

As the Professor and Didi rush toward the impending confrontation between Motown and the dealer, Myers asks, "What was Harlem? A place, a name, a gaudy easel of colors." It is a place where drugs kill while the police take payoffs. It is a place where the city administration responds to urban decay by demolishing buildings, leaving empty lots where people dump their garbage, and then disguising the results with painted tin window covers to make it look as though abandoned buildings are still occupied. But it is also a place where Motown and Didi find one another.

The Professor tells Motown, "We're all in the tribe from the moment that we're named until the moment that the last memory of our deeds is gone.... When you walk down the street and you see members of the tribe falling by the wayside, you are to understand that that's part of you falling over there." Myers has created a beautiful novel that raises the question of whether we as individuals and our nation as a society can recognize and respond to this implied challenge.

1985 Honors

BOYD, CANDY DAWSON. *Circle of Gold.* Apple/Scholastic, 1984. Gr. 4–8.

Mattie Benson is the central character in this school and family story. There is much more to the book than a recital of the trivial concerns of a group of sixth graders. In the endearing relationship between Mattie and her twin brother, Matthew, the reader sees the two children trying to cope with the death of their father and the disintegration of family life when their mother cannot deal with the loss. In Mattie's friend, Toni, one sees the value of having a reliable and steadfast friend. In Angel, whose name is indeed a misnomer, and in Charlene one observes the unhappiness and trouble that can result from misplaced loyalties. Through this cast of characters the reader experiences a theft uncovered, a mother's rehabilitation through therapy, and Mattie's discovery of her own self-worth. The circle of gold at one level is the pin Mattie wins for her mother in an essay contest. The larger circle of gold is the one Mattie discovers when she is convinced of the place she has in her mother's heart.

The gentle writing, the spoken and unspoken lessons, and the exploration of human relationships were highlights that the Coretta Scott King awards jury recognized in this talented writer's first novel.

HAMILTON, VIRGINIA. *A Little Love.* Philomel, 1984. Gr. 9–12.

Sheema has no memory of her parents: her mother died after Sheema's birth and her father disappeared soon afterward. Her maternal grandparents have raised her with love and great caring, but as she nears graduation from the vocational high school, Sheema feels the need to search for her father. Her knowledge that he's a sign painter who lives somewhere down south is enough to set her on a journey of exploration and discovery, so she and her boyfriend, Forrest, load up the station wagon and hit the road. An extraordinary story flows from the characterization of an ordinary teenager searching for her identity with the loving support of her friends and family.

1984 Winner

CLIFTON, LUCILLE. *Everett Anderson's Goodbye.* Illustrated by Ann Grifalconi. Holt, Rinehart, & Winston, 1983. Gr. K–2.

In *Everett Anderson's Goodbye,* Lucille Clifton expresses the magnitude of a death in a few gentle words of understanding and compassion. Clifton shares with very young readers the five stages of death, writing with a warmth and a simplicity that transcend any lengthy conversation, serious discussion, or maudlin sentimentality. When his good father dies, Everett begs, promises, questions, and fasts while his mother quietly supports him and lets him know she understands. Ann Grifalconi's expressive black-and-white sketches deepen the mood of this classic, with its memorable closing words:

> Whatever happens when people die, love doesn't stop and neither will I.

1984 Honors

HAMILTON, VIRGINIA. *The Magical Adventures of Pretty Pearl.* Harper & Row, 1983. Gr. 3–5.

When god-child Pretty Pearl announces to her older brothers, John Henry and John de Conqueror, that she would like to try life as a mortal child, they warn her about those humans and their "winning ways" before they send her down from Mount Kenya to try life in the American South during the Reconstruction era. In the midst of a long journey through the South with a cast of characters from African and African American folklore, Pearl comes upon a clandestine self-supporting community of free blacks whose only link to the outside world is trade with Cherokee and Shawnee Indians. Living among them, Pearl discovers that her brothers were right—she is so drawn to the humans that she must eventually choose between her own immortal power and her newly emerging identity within a struggling mortal community. In a compelling African American odyssey that draws from myth, legend, and history, Hamilton brilliantly explores the relationship between mortal struggle and immortal dreams.

HASKINS, JAMES. *Lena Horne.* Coward-McCann, 1983. Gr. 6–9.

Throughout her successful career as an actress and singer, Lena Horne fought against stereotyping, segregation, and racism by rejecting demeaning roles and by refusing to perform in clubs that treated African Americans unfairly. Her insistence on placing her strong principles over the call of fame and money sometimes cost her work and, in her early years in show business, often made her unpopular among both her peers and her audience. Haskins characterizes the highly visible entertainer as a tough, intelligent, and ambitious woman whose struggles for self-definition began in early childhood and continued throughout her lifetime.

THOMAS, JOYCE CAROL. *Bright Shadow.* Avon, 1983. Gr. 9–12.

Although the writing style is simple, often poetic, the plot of this brief novel is complex. There is a sense of mysticism and the spiritual, with characters beset by strained family relationships, insane cruelty, and death. Abyssinia, called Abby for short, is a sensitive young woman in love with Carl Lee—much to her father's consternation. Many believe that she has the power to "see" things, which gives an aura of suspense to parts of the story. With a sense of relief the reader finds in the conclusion that after moments of high drama, Abby and Carl Lee will have a life together. *Bright Shadow* is a challenge to the imagination and to the reader's ability to move at times outside the real world.

WALTER, MILDRED PITTS. *Because We Are.* Lothrop, Lee, & Shepard, 1983. Gr. 9–12.

Emma Walsh, an outstanding black student, is entangled in problems in the all-white school for which she was specially selected. She also finds that she does not fit in when she returns to all-black Manning High. During her senior year Emma has to deal with ostracism by her peers, a confrontation with a white teacher who shows only contempt for the Manning students, rocky relationships with her divorced parents, and the usual boyfriend-girlfriend complexities.

The intended audience will easily relate to many of the situations in this fast-paced story.

1983 Winner

HAMILTON, VIRGINIA. *Sweet Whispers, Brother Rush.* Philomel, 1982. Gr. 9–12.

Because her mother's work takes her far from home, fourteen-year-old Tree is often left in charge of the household and caring for her brother, Dabney. She accepts the uncertainty in her life until the day she encounters the ghost of her uncle, Brother Rush, through whom she can go back in time to her early childhood. By reliving key events in the past, Tree begins to ask questions about some of the things left unsaid in her family so that she can begin to understand herself in the broader context of her family's history. This outstanding time-fantasy deals with the complexity of human relationships, the strength of the African American family, and the importance of understanding and acknowledging one's roots.

1983 Honor

LESTER, JULIUS. *This Strange New Feeling.* Dial, 1982. Gr. 9–12.

This Strange New Feeling is a collection of three well-honed stories, each filled with drama, suspense, danger, and the creative ingenuity of slaves in an endless quest for freedom. In the first tale, Lester's lyrical prose includes touches of humor tinged with bitterness as he deftly chronicles the story of Ras and Sally, who help others escape by hiding them in bales of tobacco and finally find their own freedom in a northern city.

There is a saddening poignancy in the account of Maria, who in "Where the Sun Lives" enjoys a few years of freedom happily married to Forrest, a freeman. Forrest dies suddenly and deeply in debt. Maria is "confiscated" along with other properties that legally can be used to satisfy the lender's claims. Readers are moved by the sense of dignity with which Maria approaches the auction block and, through Lester's forceful prose, realize that it is only Maria's physical self that will be enslaved. Her spirit will be forever free because she knows "where the sun lives."

"A Christmas Love Story" is a dramatic account of an enslaved couple who make a daring escape to Philadelphia when the wife poses as a young white gentleman traveling north to receive medical attention. "He" is accompanied by his very dark-skinned servant, William. Tension mounts and danger lurks at every stop along the four-day journey to freedom. The incident closes with Ellen and William Craft (the couple) having to flee to England to escape the vengeance that was an integral part of President William Fillmore's Fugitive Slave Bill.

Lester includes research sources for each of the historically based events to which this master storyteller gives such stirring life.

1982 Winner

TAYLOR, MILDRED D. *Let the Circle Be Unbroken*. Dial, 1981. Gr. 9–12.

Continuing the story begun in *Song of the Trees* (1975) and *Roll of Thunder, Hear My Cry* (1976), Mildred D. Taylor creates a sequel of epic proportions as the Logans face the impact of a racist government policy that threatens their farm. They must draw on the mutual support and strength of the African American community to pull through in a time of crisis. As in previous volumes, protagonist Cassie's gradual maturation is reflected by her ever-enlarging world and ever-increasing understanding of the complexities of adulthood.

1982 Honors

CHILDRESS, ALICE. *Rainbow Jordan*. Coward, McCann, & Geoghegan, 1981. Gr. 6–12.

Women of four generations are portrayed as fourteen-year-old Rainbow attempts to find hope and promise in her life. Her mother was a child herself when she became a parent and is of little help to Rainbow. The mother's youth, inexperience, and lack of education have led to an unstable relationship between mother and child. Instead, Rainbow's involvement with other women of differing social and economic classes helps her to find out who she is with respect to demands from a foster parent, a social worker, a boyfriend, and others. Characterizations are splendid and authentic language is used skillfully.

HUNTER, KRISTIN. *Lou in the Limelight*. Scribner, 1981. Gr. 9–12.

Hunter's scathing chronicle of the music business is a sequel to her pioneering *Soul Brothers and Sister Lou*. The song "Lament for Jethro," about a friend killed in a police raid on Lou's brother's printing shop, has become a hit and Lou and the group have come to New York under the stewardship of their manager, Marty Ross. Marty, determined to break up the solidarity of the group by promoting Lou at the expense of the boys, has them singing in garish, uncomfortable costumes and keeps them in virtual servitude as they live in debt while he manipulates their accounts. They have become "slaves in star-spangled costumes."

The reader recoils at their exploitation, especially when Marty gives the key to Lou's room to a well-connected friend who attempts to rape her. In Las Vegas, another member of the group, Frank, is given a line of credit to encourage his gambling, and all the young people are given cocaine and other drugs until Lou comes to realize that nothing they are being given is free. Marty steals their copyrights by registering their songs in his own name, and the group is forced to work as an opening act for a white singer "with a pseudo-black style and enormous popularity—with white audiences." Then a promised movie deal brings the group to a pornographic film studio.

In the midst of their troubles, the group derives strength from Jethro's mother, Aunt Jerutha, who comes from home to care for them; from Ben Carroll, a U.S. attorney determined to expose whites in the music business who are taking advantage of black youth; from newly found friends who arrange for them to perform in African American communities in the South; and ultimately from the continuing love of family. And always there is the strength of the music:

Blues was art and blues was therapy; it took gloomy situations and worked on them, turned them around and inside out and upside down until you could live with them and even laugh at them.

Their harrowing experiences do not break the young singers. Hunter uses their journey as an opportunity for self-exploration, an opportunity for Lou to begin to define herself as an African American.

MEBANE, MARY E. *Mary: An Autobiography.* Viking, 1981. Gr. 9–12. *

This painfully honest story of growing up in the rural South in the 1930s and 1940s chronicles the struggles of a determined and talented young woman who always felt like an outsider, even within her own family. Young Mary's distinctive personal story is set against the detailed backdrop of the ordinary and familiar day-to-day life of an African American community in rural North Carolina.

1981 Winner

POITIER, SIDNEY. *This Life.* Knopf, 1980. Gr. 9–12. *

This Life is a candid, outspoken autobiography of the noted actor and film star Sidney Poitier. In describing his life both in America and in his native Bahamas, Poitier recounts events that evoke in the reader feelings of laughter, anger, disbelief, and respect. Previous to his birth, Poitier's parents had left Cat Island in the Bahamas to try to make a better living. It was their hope to get back to Cat Island before their baby's birth, but he was born prematurely and given little chance to survive. The infant's fight for survival seems symbolic of Poitier's entire life.

The writer describes some of the many challenges he faced before gaining public notice. The reader has to laugh at Poitier's attempt to earn a living by parking cars after he had learned how to drive by watching what true valets did. Many an accident was the result. He writes of participating in the total destruction of a restaurant in the Deep South when as members of the U.S. Army, some of whom happened to be African Americans, he and his comrades were refused service. He speaks of voice and speech training aimed at getting rid of his island accent. Poitier describes the labored, disappointment-filled steps from bit-part actor to Academy Award winner and the touch of emptiness he felt on that special Oscar night because both of his beloved parents were dead.

The book includes his activities offstage and off-screen, his marriages, his friendship and conflict with Harry Belafonte, and his work with the cause espoused by Martin Luther King Jr. *This Life* is an introspective study by a man who has lived widely and, although not always, well. For today's readers perhaps the most significant message lies in Poitier's observation that when today's parents (including himself) give their children everything, they rob them of learning to take responsibility for working for things both needed and wanted. *This Life* is a thoughtful yet well-paced study of one man's view of himself and the world around him.

1981 Honor

DE VEAUX, ALEXIS. *Don't Explain: A Song of Billie Holiday.* Harper & Row, 1980. Gr. 9–12. *

Alexis De Veaux's respect and admiration for the singer Billie Holiday reaches out from every page of this factual, poetically written biography. The author does not dismiss the erring ways of which the singer has been accused. Nor does she overlook the high-handed manner in which Holiday was treated by the law. The story tells of some happy days and some days of hope when Holiday's family migrated to Harlem, reaching for the "good life" in the North. As a fledgling blues singer, Holiday was likened to the late Bessie Smith, and the comparison didn't stop there, because Holiday also felt the sting of racism that allegedly led to Bessie Smith's death. De Veaux's descriptions of Holiday's bout with drugs and her mercurial career, which ended with the singer strapped to a bed in a prison hospital, are written with a haunting beauty that ensures that readers will remember the Billie Holiday story with a combination of anger for what might questionably be called justice and tears for talent too soon lost.

1980 Winner

MYERS, WALTER DEAN. *The Young Landlords.* Viking, 1979. Gr. 6–8.

When a group of Harlem teenagers complain to the landlord about the condition of a tenement on their block, he sells it to them for one dollar so that they themselves can take responsibility for its repair and upkeep. With a great deal of warmth and humor, Myers offers young readers an appealing story about a group of ordinary kids who find out firsthand that, although there are no easy solutions to tough problems, the first step toward making the world a better place to live is to work together.

1980 Honors

GORDY, BERRY, SR. *Movin' Up: Pop Gordy Tells His Story.* Introduction by Alex Haley. Harper & Row, 1979. Gr. 8–12. *

The father of the founder of Motown Records tells his own life story, beginning with his childhood in Georgia, when his father always took him along on business transactions because he recognized the boy's shrewd mind for figures. Gordy's business skills sharpened as he grew older and continued working on the family farm. When the sale of timber stumps from his land netted him $2,600, Gordy wisely decided to travel north to Detroit to cash the check rather than to raise the suspicions of unscrupulous white neighbors. He soon sent for the rest of his family to join him, and within a few months he had saved enough money to open a grocery store. All eight of his children worked in the store, and each one grew to be successful. However, it was his seventh son, Berry Gordy Jr., who seemed to follow most closely in his father's footsteps when it came to business. A fascinating picture of a gentle, and remarkably humble, overachiever emerges from this extraordinary autobiography that reads like an oral history.

GREENFIELD, ELOISE, AND LESSIE JONES LITTLE. *Childtimes: A Three-Generation Memoir.* Harper & Row, 1979. Gr. 4–8. *

Three women—storytellers and writers, mothers and daughters—each speak in their own distinct voices to convey history in a personal way that is unique and memorable. Photographs from the family album combine with each woman's remembrances of her "childtimes" to produce an unforgettable personal glimpse into history. Pattie Frances Ridley Jones, born December 15, 1884, speaks through family stories as well as through her own writings. She was close to the slave days and remembers her mother, who worked as an unpaid maid for the family that had owned Pattie's grandmother before emancipation. Lessie Blanche Jones Little, born October 1, 1906, writes of her girlhood days and adolescence, followed by Eloise Glynn Little Greenfield's writing of North Carolina, where she was born on May 17, 1929. Each voice speaks of home, family, chores, social events, and courtship. In a direct style, deceptively simple, each woman tells of the fears and hopes, poverty and hunger, love and pride, and laughter and music during her growing-up years. The text neither draws conclusions for readers nor forces them to study history, but this unique and vibrant compilation has an effect that is poignant and moving. The patterns of the telling link one child to the next and all three children to the reader. Few books have brought the everyday life of history to readers so vividly and effectively.

HASKINS, JAMES. *Andrew Young: Young Man with a Mission.* Illustrated with photographs. Lothrop, Lee, & Shepard, 1979. Gr. 9–12. *

The son of an affluent dentist in New Orleans, Andrew Young was a precocious child who started kindergarten at age three and graduated from Howard University when he was just nineteen. He became an activist in the civil rights movement as a young minister in Thomasville, Georgia, and his talents as a diplomat and organizer soon thrust him into a leadership role within the Southern Christian Leadership Conference (SCLC). In 1972, he became the first African American congressman elected from the South since the Reconstruction era, and in 1976 he was appointed by President Jimmy Carter as the U.S. ambassador to the United Nations. In the arena of international politics, Ambassador Young became known for his directness and for his unwavering stand for human rights, a stance that was often critical of the U.S. power structure. This straightforward biography does not shy away from the controversy that surrounded Andrew Young in his public life.

HASKINS, JAMES. *James Van DerZee: The Picture Takin' Man.* Illustrated with Van DerZee photographs. Dodd, Mead, 1979. Gr. 6–9. *

The work of James Van DerZee was unrecognized and virtually unknown in the art world until his photographs of Harlem in the 1920s and 1930s were featured in a 1968 exhibition at the Metropolitan Museum of Art entitled "Harlem on My Mind." At the time, the photographer was eighty-three years old. Because James Van DerZee's life spanned the twentieth century, because he had been able to document in photographs only a small part of what his trained eye had seen over the years, and because very little had been written about him for either adults or children, Haskins was determined to get the full story down in print by conducting interviews and corresponding with the man himself. This engaging account, based on those interviews, creates a portrait with words of the intelligent, hardworking, and dignified man who became known for his portraits of African Americans—men, women, and children of Harlem who shared the traits of the man behind the camera.

SOUTHERLAND, ELLEASE. *Let the Lion Eat Straw.* Scribner, 1979. Gr. 9–12.

Abeba Williams spent her early years in the nurturing care of Mamma Habbleshaw in rural North Carolina. Abeba's tranquil life was changed when her natural mother took her to New York. Abeba is a strong, sensitive character who grows from childhood to womanhood under a variety of circumstances. She survives her mother's sometimes volatile temper, the incestuous advances of an uncle, and a marriage to a man who she later learns has a history of insanity. After raising a very large family and using her musical talent as a sustaining force, Abeba dies in peace, a well-respected woman in the community. *Let the Lion Eat Straw* is a moving story, written in rhythmic, poetic prose. It is the story of a truly genteel woman.

1979 Winner

DAVIS, OSSIE. *Escape to Freedom: A Play about Young Frederick Douglass.* Viking, 1978. Gr. 6–8.

Ossie Davis, playwright and actor, lends his artistic talent to the writing of a play that affords young readers a chance to reenact scenes from the life of the abolitionist Frederick Douglass. The scenes are dramatic and forthright, withholding none of the vindictiveness of cruel slave masters, as if to forcefully demonstrate the reasons for Douglass's determination to escape to freedom. The play tells of Douglass's accomplishments as a lecturer, a newspaper editor, and a fighter for women's rights at a time when such things were basically unheard of. Douglass's fighting spirit is summed up in a speech made after he whipped his master in a "fair fight":

> I'm free . . . I know I'm still in bondage but I got a feeling—the most important feeling in the world—I'm free.

Freedom songs are interspersed among the scenes, and there are directions for staging. However, strict copyright limitations seem to have been placed on the use of the script for "other than personal reading." But even in that context, this powerful minidrama is well worth reading and sharing.

1979 Honors

FENNER, CAROL. *The Skates of Uncle Richard.* Illustrated by Ati Forberg. Random House, 1978. Gr. K–2.

The star skating champion who once fueled the dreams of nine-year-old Marsha disappears when the ice skates she'd hoped for at Christmas turn out to be ugly, old-fashioned hockey skates that once belonged to her uncle. But the dream skater gradually returns after Marsha gets an impromptu skating lesson and a demonstration of some fancy footwork on the ice from the former owner of the skates. This is an easy-to-read transition to books divided into chapters—and a story that shows how hard work and determination are essential to making dreams come true.

HAMILTON, VIRGINIA. *Justice and Her Brothers.* Greenwillow, 1978. Gr. 3–5.

At first eleven-year-old Justice blames the pervasive sense of eeriness enveloping her home on the fact that it's the first summer she and her older brothers have been left on their own during the day while their dad is at work and their mom is enrolled in college classes. But gradually, she, her brothers, and their young neighbor, Dorian, begin to realize that the telepathic powers they all possess are greatly heightened when they work together as a unit. To their great surprise, they also realize that Justice is genetically predestined for greatness as their leader, a fact that doesn't sit well with her older brother Thomas. The compelling, original science fiction story is rooted in the reality of small-town family life, sibling rivalry, and a young girl's transformation from a fretting, uncertain child into a confident young woman ready to face whatever challenges the future may hold.

PATTERSON, LILLIE. *Benjamin Banneker: Genius of Early America.* Illustrated by David Scott Brown. Abingdon, 1978. Gr. 3–5. *

Born on his family's tobacco farm in Maryland on November 9, 1731, Benjamin Banneker was taught to read by his grandmother, who came to the colonies as Molly Walsh, an English indentured servant. Banneker's grandfather, the son of a tribal king in Senegal, and his father, a freed slave from Guinea, taught him to observe the world of plants and animals around him. In a school opened by a Quaker neighbor, Banneker learned literature, history, and mathematics.

Lillie Patterson details the impact Banneker's lifelong fascination with numbers and technology had on his neighbors and ultimately his country. He built the first clock made entirely from parts manufactured in the colonies; he calculated accurate almanacs to guide farmers, fishermen, and sailors; and, at Thomas Jefferson's suggestion, he was appointed by George Washington to help survey the new nation's capital. When Pierre L'Enfant walked out on the project and returned to France with his plans, it was Banneker's expertise and continued involvement that made possible the realization of those plans in the beautiful design of Washington, D.C.

Patterson not only makes clear that the striking beauty of the Washington, D.C., capital district is the product of this African American genius's dedication but also emphasizes his impressive foresight. Banneker's 1793 almanac outlined a plan for a U.S. Secretary of Peace to establish free schools throughout the country to work for world peace. A later almanac warned against the dangers of smoking.

Patterson gracefully combines facts with fictionalized conversations. She carefully distinguishes between fact and myth, providing enough information to dramatize history while suggesting that young readers go on to more sophisticated accounts. Underlying both this biography and Banneker's life is the wisdom, learned from his grandmother, that "life is an adventure in learning."

PETERSON, JEANNE WHITEHOUSE. *I Have a Sister, My Sister Is Deaf.* Harper & Row, 1977. Gr. K–2.

In prose that has the rhythm of poetry, Jeanne Peterson has written a story that will speak to all who work with those who cannot hear. As a loving and patient sister, she tells the reader how a deaf person understands certain things, such as the barking of a dog contrasted with the purring of a cat sitting in the person's lap. She makes note of things that bring fright to a hearing child but that do not bother the deaf child—such as a clap of thunder on a stormy night or the banging of a shutter when the wind is high. She talks of the companionship that is shared as the sisters walk through the woods: "I am the one who listens for small sounds. She is the one who watches for quick movements in the grass." The illustrations in this gentle explanatory book show a multiethnic group of children sharing in the experience of the one who has a sister who is deaf.

1978 Winner

GREENFIELD, ELOISE. *Africa Dream.* Illustrated by Carole Byard. John Day, 1977. Gr. K–2.

At first glance, Byard's pencil sketches seem airy and dreamlike, but a closer look reveals subtle details that give a sense of reality to the far-off African homeland to which a young child's imagination takes her. There is an impressive amount of historical information provided through the words and images. The illustrations of noble rulers of long ago, classic architecture, and graceful people make *Africa Dream* a book of visible pride and dignity.

1978 Honors

FAULKNER, WILLIAM J. *The Days When the Animals Talked: Black American Folktales and How They Came to Be.* Illustrated by Troy Howell. Follett, 1977. Gr. 3–6.

Looking back on his childhood, the African American folklorist William Faulkner shares stories both real and imagined. Many of the tales derive from stories he heard from a former slave, Simon Brown, who had come as a freed man to work for the Faulkner family. In part 1, the reader encounters the hardships of slavery, the frustrating powerlessness of the men and women enslaved by masters who used them as they pleased—in terms of work, sex, and aggression. These stories are told without rancor but with a depth of feeling that stirs deep emotions in the reader.

In part 2, Faulkner turns his pen to a dignified telling of animal stories with important information given about the symbolic importance of Brer Rabbit and his companions. In an introduction to this section Faulkner states:

> Signs of unrest, dissatisfaction and even outright protest are easy to detect in some of the longer dramatic tales. As the animals behaved in the stories so the slaves were motivated to behave in their struggle to survive. Although weaponless and defenseless, the slaves, like the small animals, could at times get the better of their powerful adversaries through cunning, careful planning and occasionally social action.

Faulkner's message blended with his marvelous storytelling style made him a natural choice for a Coretta Scott King honor.

GLASS, FRANKCINA. *Marvin and Tige.* St. Martin's, 1977. Gr. 6–10.

Tige at age eleven is an illiterate African American street urchin on his own after the sudden death of his mother. He survives by his wit and his ability to steal and to find adequate shelter. Finally, this continuous fight for survival gets the best of him and he plans suicide. At that moment in steps Marvin, a down-and-out, once-upon-a-time successful businessman. This unlikely interracial combination teams up and begins to make life livable—two lonely people who have found solace in each other. In a hardly credible series of events, Marvin finds Tige's father, who had abandoned Tige's mother before the child's birth. Marvin convinces Richard Davis that he must give his son a rightful place in his family. The bittersweet ending sees Tige established in his new home but with the ties to his friend Marvin still intact. This is a warm story with touches of humor, discussions about religious beliefs, and ideas about death and the value of education. It is the story of two people who care about each other with a relationship unencumbered by racial differences.

GREENFIELD, ELOISE. *Mary McLeod Bethune.* Crowell, 1977. Gr. K–4. *

This sympathetic portrayal of one of the great heroines in American history is simply told but never simplistic. Greenfield skillfully weaves into the personal history of Mary McLeod Bethune aspects of post–Civil War life in America and the trauma of segregation. This straightforward telling of Bethune's unflagging devotion to making the lives of black people better through education includes a brief introduction to some of the noted personalities with whom she worked to attain her goal—money for her educational projects. Particularly interesting is the discussion of her working relationship and warm friendship with Eleanor Roosevelt. Bethune's endless struggles to make her dreams come true are as impressive as her ability to bring African Americans together to solve problems long neglected by the establishment.

HASKINS, JAMES. *Barbara Jordan.* Illustrated with photographs. Dial, 1977. Gr. 6–10. *

> When the Constitution of the United States was completed . . . I felt somehow that George Washington and Alexander Hamilton just left me out by mistake. But through the process of amendment, interpretation, and court decision I have finally been included in "We the people."

Former congresswoman from Texas Barbara Jordan first came to national attention as a member of the House Judiciary Committee during the Watergate hearings in 1974. Her strongly held, eloquently expressed opinions have won her friends and enemies in political circles. James Haskins captures the complexity of Barbara Jordan and her times through the eyes of her supporters and her critics. Although this biography focuses on Jordan's life as a leading political figure in Washington, D.C., Haskins provides background information that helps readers acquire a full picture of her dynamic personality.

Barbara Jordan's eloquent speaking ability and decisive critical thinking skills were nurtured from early childhood by her maternal grandfather, who encouraged her to be an independent thinker. She continued to be impressive as a speaker when she was on the debating team at Texas Southern University.

Jordan's political career was marked with defeat the first few times she sought office: in 1962, when she ran for the Texas House of Representatives, and again in 1964. Jordan won her seat in the Texas House of Representatives in 1965, the first African American in the Texas House since 1883. Haskins describes Jordan's career as a member of the U.S. House of Representatives (taking office in January 1973), her appointment to the powerful Judiciary Committee, and her influential discourse during the Watergate hearings.

Haskins has provided for young adult readers the life story of a woman whose firm belief in her country may be summed up in a statement she made at the 1976 Democratic convention:

> We cannot improve on the system of government handed down to us by the founders of the Republic, but we can find new ways to implement that system and realize our destiny.

PATTERSON, LILLIE. *Coretta Scott King.* Garrard, 1977. Gr. 3–5. *

This biography begins with the talented Coretta Scott's dilemma of choosing between a musical career and the man she loves. She assumes the role of wife and mother during the years of the organized, nonviolent civil rights protests in the South. Beginning with the Montgomery bus boycott in 1955, when the threat of violence was nearly constant, Patterson recognizes the strength and stability Coretta Scott King brought to her family and their friends and acquaintances. The emphasis is on her self-sacrifice and dedication to family. The only time she raises her voice, writes Patterson, is after a sleepless night during which she received forty hate calls. The book imparts well the nonviolent attitude the Kings had to practice in their personal and private lives to stay focused on the larger goal of civil rights.

STEWART, RUTH ANN. *Portia: The Life of Portia Washington Pittman, the Daughter of Booker T. Washington.* Doubleday, 1977. Gr. 6–9. *

Written with sensitive objectivity, this biography presents a clear picture of Portia Washington Pittman, who lived a riches-to-almost-rags life with admirable dignity. From childhood she was aware of the stature and importance of her renowned father, Booker T. Washington; details of the famous educator's life are deftly woven into the Portia story. For example, it is of great interest to note that in spite of Booker T. Washington's outspoken support of segregation, he sent his only daughter to northern schools and colleges where she was the only black allowed to enroll. As a young woman Portia traveled abroad to study piano under a German master musician. At the same time, her father was getting financial support from wealthy white philanthropists who valued the concept on which Washington was founding Tuskegee Institute:

> Cast down your bucket where you are. . . . Cast it down in agriculture, mechanics, in commerce and domestic service and in the professions. We shall prosper as we learn to dignify and glorify common labor.

The biography recalls Portia Washington's meeting with her father's adversary, W. E. B. Du Bois; her dining with presidents; her studying under George Washington Carver; her marriage to architect Sidney Pittman; and the birth and death of her three children. There is a frank discussion of the life and death of her favorite son, Booker, a talented musician who died a victim of drug addiction. And one reads of her struggle in later life to save her father's birthplace in Virginia as a historical site.

The writer evokes a sense of melancholy as she describes Portia Pittman's slow decline into poverty following her dismissal from the faculty of Tuskegee Institute, a move that was seemingly politically motivated; her living in squalor in Washington, D.C.; and finally her dying at age ninety in peace and dignity in a home provided for her by members of the Washington, D.C., Tuskegee Alumni Association. Well-selected black-and-white photographs give an added dimension to this well-written biography.

1977 Winner

HASKINS, JAMES. *The Story of Stevie Wonder.* Illustrated with photographs. Lothrop, Lee, & Shepard, 1976. Gr. 6–10. *

A powerful story of remarkable achievement emerges from this well-written biography of a popular singer, songwriter, and musician. Blind from birth, Steveland Morris was always encouraged by his family to explore and develop his other senses, especially his senses of touch and hearing. While he was still a toddler, his mother bought him a set of cardboard drums and a toy harmonica. Stevie's musical abilities became so well known around his community that friends and neighbors bought him a real drum set, a real harmonica, and, when he was seven years old, a secondhand piano. By the time he came to the attention of Motown Records a few years later, he was already an accomplished musician, and Motown called him "Little Stevie Wonder, the twelve-year-old genius." Haskins tells Stevie Wonder's story by tracing his personal as well as his musical accomplishments.

1977 Honors

BLAKE, CLARENCE N., AND DONALD F. MARTIN. *Quiz Book on Black America.* Houghton Mifflin, 1976. Gr. 6–9. *

Based on scholarly research, the *Quiz Book on Black America* contains probing questions about the achievements and contributions of black Americans in every aspect of American life. The format of the book allows the user to concentrate on an area of special interest or to browse through questions in various subject areas: education, business, sports, the arts, and social action. The book covers a broad time line, with quizzes ranging from events in the mid-nineteenth century to the time of the book's publication, fulfilling its stated purpose to "make the acquisition of knowledge a pleasurable experience."

CLIFTON, LUCILLE. *Everett Anderson's Friend.* Illustrated by Ann Grifalconi. Holt, Rinehart, & Winston, 1976. Gr. K–3.

In a series of books, the voice of Everett Anderson has spoken to young readers through the words of a poet who understands childhood concerns. In "real boy" fashion, Everett Anderson takes a dislike to his neighbor, Maria. How could he like a girl who can beat him in racing and play ball better than he can! But when Everett Anderson loses his key and goes into Maria's apartment until his mother comes home, everything changes. Everett Anderson finds friendship in Apartment 3A—and even learns something about food from the Hispanic culture. With bouncy verse and quick poetic sketches, Clifton, a gifted storyteller, provides young readers not only with a joyful verse but also, more important, with a slice-of-life experience worthy of being remembered. Ann Grifalconi's illustrations capture the warmth of the author's text.

TAYLOR, MILDRED D. *Roll of Thunder, Hear My Cry.* Dial, 1976. Gr. 6–12.

Set in rural Mississippi during the Depression, this novel chronicles the lives of a strong African American family struggling to hold on to their land as seen through the eyes of their young daughter, Cassie. In spite of hard times, economically and socially, the extended Logan family fills its household with love, security, and dignity, creating and maintaining an environment from which all family members draw the strength they need to face the rigors of everyday life in the segregated South.

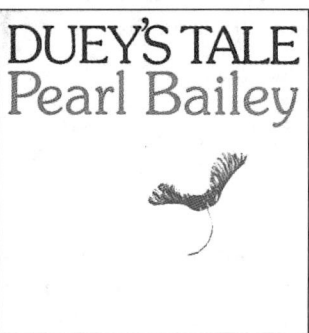

1976 Winner

BAILEY, PEARL. *Duey's Tale.* Harcourt Brace Jovanovich, 1975. Gr. 4–6.

The music that was so much a part of Pearl Bailey is reflected in the poetic prose of *Duey's Tale*. In a tale set in a philosophical mood, Duey, a seedling from a maple tree, makes observations about life and about finding out who one really is and learns a great lesson about friendship. As a seedling, Duey finds himself rudely stripped from his mother roots by a strong gust of wind. While bemoaning his loss of security, he finds adventure with a friendly log and a glass bottle. The three companions share pleasant moments together until the time comes for each to take its destined special place in the scheme of things—places that are marked by change. A saddened but wiser and mature Duey, now a sturdy maple tree, concludes that being different is not so bad, but what really matters is that everyone "needs a little attention, and that's why people have family and friends."

Duey's Tale must surely have left the Coretta Scott King awards jury with a warm feeling and a sense that this book would lead readers to reflect not only on the story but also on the author's philosophy of life.

1976 Honors

GRAHAM, SHIRLEY. *Julius K. Nyerere: Teacher of Africa.* Messner, 1975. Gr. 6–9. *

A biography that was welcomed at the time of its publication, this book supports the view of President Nyerere as a dedicated, modest leader-teacher who worked to liberate Tanganyika and then Zanzibar and to join the two as the new country of Tanzania. Written for young people, the book lucidly explains Nyerere's political philosophy, which views society as an extended family and which incorporates both tradition and tribal pride into its political system. Graham's view of Nyerere is positive. The repressive policies and interparty disputes at work in Tanzania at the time are discussed, although interpreted to fit with the generally positive view of Nyerere. The author successfully employs both fictional dialogue and excerpts from Nyerere's writings.

GREENFIELD, ELOISE. *Paul Robeson.* Illustrated by George Ford. Crowell, 1975. Gr. 3–6. *

Greenfield offers the story of Paul Robeson to young readers in easily accessible language. She smoothly compresses Robeson's personal story with his accomplishments as athlete, stage actor, and political activist. His developing political commitment and the repressive reaction against it are presented in honest, unbiased terms. The timbre, style, and impact of Robeson's musical performances are clearly conveyed. In addition, the effort and determination it took for young Robeson to succeed as an athlete are expressed in terms that children can easily understand and relate to. This impressive man's unswerving dedication to pursuing justice and opposing oppression for black and poor people is offered with obvious respect, in clear and simple terms.

MYERS, WALTER DEAN. *Fast Sam, Cool Clyde, and Stuff.* Viking, 1975. Gr. 6–12.

When Stuff was twelve and one-half years old, his family moved to 116th Street in Harlem. Six years later, he recounts his extraordinary first year with the friends he found there. Myers's first young adult novel is a tribute to the sustaining power of friendship as young people pledge to be there for one another and to understand and care for each other. "I just hope I'll always have people to care for like that and be close to," says Stuff, who seems to be speaking for the author when he adds that he would "like to be able to teach somebody else that feeling."

Myers is frank about the problems faced on 116th Street. The reader shares the pain of Clyde's father's death in an accident, of the departure of Gloria's father, of Charley's self-deceptive drug abuse, and of the school system's failure to support Clyde's academic aspirations. The group's sense of community helps them face these challenges, as does Stuff's ability to find absurdity in adversity.

Myers's wit is conveyed in his characters' language—their funny imagery and verbal sparring—and in his talent for expressing the humorous aspects of hurtful situations. When Binky's ear is bitten off during a fight, Clyde suggests a hospital visit to have it reattached. The doctor sees the frantic young people as threatening hoodlums, and the concerned friends are jailed and asked to roll up their sleeves to see if they are junkies. Readers will laugh at the almost slapstick farce, but beneath its surface they will clearly see the intolerance that confronts Stuff's crowd. When the friends retrieve a handbag stolen by two thieves, they are assumed to have stolen the bag, and again helping people is shown as futile even though the portrayal is humorous.

The closeness of the group is especially admirable when contrasted with the difficulty of open communication. Stuff's father may finally hug him when he is standing by Stuff in the face of an unjustified drug arrest, but at other times his father finds it impossible to say how much he likes his son. "I guess it's hard," Stuff observes, "for people, some people anyway, to say things like that."

By the time Stuff comes to record these memories, the neighborhood has altered, the friends have dispersed. The book, then, is about a brief moment in Stuff's life, the world in which he lived, the community that helped him confront that world, and the universal need to find such a community in our own lives.

TAYLOR, MILDRED D. *Song of the Trees.* Dial, 1975. Gr. 3–5.

Eight-year-old Cassie Logan loves the majestic old trees on her family's property almost as much as her daddy does. When two powerful white men scheme to cut down the trees for lumber, Mr. Logan comes up with a scheme of his own to foil the trespassers. Taylor's first published children's book shows the emergence of traits that would become the author's trademark in subsequent work: excellent characterizations, a strong sense of place, and the ability to weave a great story by drawing together threads of social history, the rural South, and African American family life.

1975 Winner

ROBINSON, DOROTHY. *The Legend of Africania.* Illustrated by Herbert Temple. Johnson Publishing, 1974. Gr. K–3.

The Legend of Africania is a multilevel tale. Africania is a beautiful maiden living in the harmony of her African homeland and beloved by Prince Uhuru. On a fateful day Africania is bewitched by the evil, pale-skinned Takata. She is taken to another land and imprisoned until she decides to become pale like Takata, to take on the pale-faced spirit's ways. Only when she learns that this imitation is the real prison does she become free and united with her lover, Prince Uhuru. On one level, this story is written with the flavor of the traditional folktale. The Coretta Scott King awards jury "read into it a much more significant story—almost an allegory. It is seen as a story of slavery, of resistance to a master's domination, and as a lesson in remembering to always take pride in one's blackness."

1974 Winner

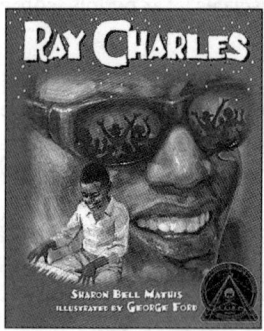

MATHIS, SHARON BELL. *Ray Charles.* Illustrated by George Ford. Crowell, 1973. Gr. K–3. *

This simplified biography gives young readers a glimpse into the life of a talented musician who, though blind, refused to see himself as disabled. The author highlights episodes from the childhood accident that caused the blindness to Ray Charles's special education and, finally, his triumph as a performer of international fame. In this inspirational portrayal, Ray Charles is seen not as handicapped but as *handicapable*.

1974 Honors

CHILDRESS, ALICE. *A Hero Ain't Nothin' but a Sandwich.* Coward, McCann, & Geoghegan, 1973. Gr. 6–12.

Benjie Johnson is thirteen and "ain't a chile no more." He is a junkie, and his habit is destroying his life and ripping apart his family. From Benjie's opening words of denial, Childress introduces the principal players in Benjie's tragic story. In alternating monologues, the reader follows Benjie's story from the perspective of his family, friends, and teachers. As the perspective shifts with each succeeding chapter, Childress weaves a tapestry of authentic voices, giving life to characters through their deeds, words, and reflection in the words of others.

Drawing upon her theater background, Childress creates a novel that moves like a play, with the spotlight shifting from character to character. Although the actors explain themselves to the reader, it is significant that they are not speaking to one another. One of the truths of this powerful work is the inability of the characters to communicate truthfully with each other or to see events from another's perspective. In one poignant moment, for instance, Benjie's mama wants to tell him that the "greatest thing in the world is to love someone and they love you too." Instead, she verbalizes this warm thought as a mundane admonition for Benjie to brush the crumbs from his jacket.

Benjie's father has left, and his mother is ready to marry Butler Craig, who lives with the mother and son. When Benjie, to support his habit, steals Butler's best clothes, Butler moves to a room downstairs. As Benjie's friend Jimmy-Lee Powell has said, "Needles divide guys," and the rift in Benjie's family seems irreparable. As Benjie flees across the roof of his building, however, Butler saves the boy from a near fall down an air shaft. Butler sees Benjie "swingin down over empty space, looking up at me, weighin' a ton and cryin' like crazy." Butler's tenuous hold on Benjie and the precipitous drop down the shaft become metaphors for their relationship.

Benjie promises to report regularly to a detoxification program, and Butler will support him by meeting him there. But as the book ends, Butler is getting cold waiting for Benjie to arrive, not sure if Benjie can see him where he is standing, not sure if Benjie is late or not coming. The reader is left to interpret Butler's closing words:

> The wind is blowing colder now, but if I go in—he might get this far, then lose courage. Come on, Benjie, I believe in you. . . . It's nation time. . . . I'm waiting for you. . . .

CLIFTON, LUCILLE. *Don't You Remember?* Illustrated by Evaline Ness. Dutton, 1973. Gr. K–2.

A familiar theme is treated with warm family love in this gentle "lap" story. Desire Mary Tate is sure that her family can never remember anything because her father postpones taking her to the plant where he works as an engineer, her mother doesn't bring home the black cake with the pink letters, and not one of her big brothers will give her the promised taste of coffee. Repeating her favorite phrase of total exasperation, "Dag, double dag," Tate retreats to her room and eventually to bed. What a surprise when the next morning—after sleeping late—Tate is awakened to find that not only will she go to the plant, but because it is her birthday she also will have the black cake with pink letters *and* coffee. In simple language that is not condescending, Clifton captures a young child's concerns. The book invites adults to read it aloud to the many little ones who feel left out and who fear that grown-ups do not remember those things that are terribly important in young lives.

CRANE, LOUISE. *Ms. Africa: Profiles of Modern African Women.* Lippincott, 1973. Gr. 6–9. *

This collection of biographies pays tribute to women from various geographical regions of Africa who have made significant achievements in widely diverse fields. Some of the women cited may seem familiar to contemporary readers, such as the talented singer Miriam Makeba or the often imprisoned fighter against apartheid Winnie Mandela. Included is the intriguing story of a woman engineer, with one of the longest names imaginable—a combination of her father's name, her husband's name, and her feminine name—who was in charge of managing the water supply for all residents in Madagascar. Her knowledge and ability finally gained the respect of the men she supervised. Efua Sutherland, a writer and a teacher from Ghana, is recognized as a catalyst for having authentic African stories published in many languages. Sutherland became interested in writing for children when she observed the dearth of Ghanian literature written for young audiences. As a part of this interest she studied folklore and involved groups in the dramatization of stories based on the trickster Ananse.

Lawyers, models, political activists, civil servants, and members of the medical profession are all a part of this book about women of color who achieved in spite of racial and political odds against them.

HUNTER, KRISTIN. *Guests in the Promised Land.* Scribner, 1973. Gr. 9–12.

Hunter speaks in the voices of young men and women in the process of defining themselves and their relationship with an often hostile society. The stories reflect the mixed hope, anger, and destructiveness of African American young people in confrontation with a racist world.

In "Hero's Return," Jody encounters his big brother Junior, home after eighteen months "in the house" for armed robbery. Where Jody expects to find a hero with improved "connections," he instead meets a brother determined to impress upon him that jail is not the romanticized retreat of street corner fantasies.

In the tragicomedy of "BeeGee's Ghost," Freddy must arrange for a proper funeral for his dog, whose ghost is haunting the family, because the pet cemetery will not accept "colored dogs." Having buried BeeGee in the backyard, Freddy wryly notes,

I'll never forget the night we spent with BeeGee's ghost in the kitchen. And I'll never stop wondering how some folks can hate other folks so much they'd take it out on a little dog. I bet if they knew it could come back and haunt them, though, they'd change.

In the title story, "Guests in the Promised Land," Hunter's naive narrator assures us that "some people," like his friend Robert, "can't stand for anybody to be too nice to them." It was not Robert's fault that the trip arranged by white businessmen to the Cedarbrook Country Club did not work out. The young people were welcomed to play on the club grounds, but a sign on the door of the elegant dining room pointedly noted "Guests not allowed without members." When Robert entered to play the piano, his hands were snatched away from the keys while the members insincerely applauded his efforts. Robert expressed his bitter frustration by slashing the piano.

> I . . . knew we'd never go back there unless we could eat in the clubhouse and listen to [Robert] play, wrong notes and all. Because it ain't no Promised Land at all if some people are always guests and others are always members.

NAGENDA, JOHN. *Mukasa.* Illustrated by Charles Lilly. Macmillan, 1973. Gr. 3–5. *

In this book, based on the author's life, Nagenda's autobiography tells of a young boy in Africa who realizes the joy and importance of an education. Mukasa was born to his parents late in their lives and became a protected "treasure" to his mother, much to his father's chagrin. When Mukasa's father would not help raise the money to send the boy to school, the boy's creative mother found a way to do it. Through Mukasa's eyes one learns something of the educational system in his village at the time of the story and of the ingenuity of the teacher who, lacking a great supply of commercial teaching materials, creatively provided students with effective homemade learning tools. In this simple setting one gains a little insight into the activities and pranks that are a part of just about every schoolchild's experience. One might accept as a high point of the book the closing incident when upon Mukasa's return home after graduation, his father asks Mukasa to teach him how to read. It is then that Mukasa decides, "Perhaps I won't be a doctor after all. Now I think I'll be a teacher."

1973 Winner

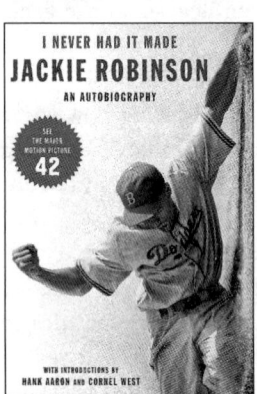

DUCKETT, ALFRED. *I Never Had It Made: The Autobiography of Jackie Robinson.* Putnam, 1972. Gr. 6–10. *

With candor, Jackie Robinson describes the difficulties of being the first black to play in major league baseball—racially motivated problems, threats of physical violence from ballplayers on his and on opposing teams, and cruel criticism from several sportswriters. Talent was not enough in a sport dominated by white players and white administrators.

Robinson does not try to gloss over personal problems that he and wife Rachel faced while trying to raise their children in the segregated South and in predominantly white areas in the North. The children seemingly suffered identity problems—and for at least one, with tragic results.

In writing of his days after baseball, Robinson discusses the trials and tribulations of working in a management position for Chock full o' Nuts. He also relates his attempts to work with the NAACP until what he calls "The Old Guard" forced his resignation. In conclusion this public hero explains the book's title, attesting that in spite of his success and triumphs, as a black man in a white world he "never had it made."

1972 Winner

FAX, ELTON. *17 Black Artists.* Dodd, Mead, 1971. Gr. 6–10. *

Using as a catalyst a slogan he read in Africa, "Sweet Are the Uses of Adversity," Elton Fax researched the lives of seventeen African American artists who succeeded against the odds. In each life was the intimation that recognition in the world of art was difficult—and for a black artist to know success was even more of a challenge. As an artist himself, Fax knew firsthand of the struggle to reach the top. Not only do the biographical sketches paint pictures of the artists as people, but also each one provides a picture of the social climate in which the individual lived and worked. At one point Fax provides an interesting historical note about the early portrayal of black figures as clowns and buffoons:

> Since it was not common prior to the 1800s for artists to portray black people with seriousness and dignity, few such portrayals exist. Race chauvinism veered white artists away from such a course, and the black artist, eager for commission, dared not risk offending his white clientele.

Fax pays tribute to an early-twentieth-century artist, James Herring, who in spite of skeptics established an art department at Howard University in 1921. The author writes candidly about the controversy surrounding the noted sculptor Edmonia Lewis, accused of murdering two fellow students on the campus of Oberlin College, and of the tragic life of Charlotte Amevor, who struggled as a single parent. Included is a chapter on Romare Bearden, who before his death in 1988 left a legacy of illustrations for young people in *A Visit to the Country* (Harper & Row, 1989). One learns of the background of nationally known Jacob Lawrence, whose plates for *Harriet and the Promised Land* were temporarily lost and then recovered, which enabled the book to be reissued (Simon & Schuster, 1968, 1993). And one is able to read of the dauntless courage of Faith Ringgold, who was the 1992 winner of the Coretta Scott King Book Award for illustrations in her first children's book, *Tar Beach*.

The book is a valuable volume in the annals of African American history and, even more important, a valuable study of the life and work of serious artists who happen to be black.

1971 Winner

ROLLINS, CHARLEMAE. *Black Troubadour: Langston Hughes.* Rand McNally, 1970. Gr. 6–12. *

Langston Hughes's poetry and prose captured the rhythms of the blues and the richness of African American speech. He created art from the full range of black experience. Charlemae Rollins met Hughes when she was children's librarian at the George C. Hall branch of the Chicago Public Library. It was during that time that Hughes was writing and discussing poetry with members of the Illinois Writers Project. A mutual interest in quality literature and in the life and concerns of African Americans led Rollins and Hughes to strike up a friendship. This friendship resulted in Rollins writing this biography for young readers.

Rollins details Hughes's childhood, spent in many far-flung places. She writes of the loving influence of Hughes's maternal grandmother, contrasting this life with the troubled visits with his father, who had settled in Mexico. The author recounts Hughes's experiences as he settled down in New York's Harlem, his disappointment in the large and impersonal classes at New York University, and the segregation at Columbia University. Eventually Hughes graduated from Lincoln University in Pennsylvania while continuing to call his beloved Harlem home.

Rollins includes details about Hughes's relationship with Mary McLeod Bethune, at whose suggestion the poet toured the South and where—through his poetry-reading concerts—he was actually able to support himself and concentrate on his writing. Rollins points out how Hughes's seemingly simple language becomes a profound comment on the America he found in his travels:

> Where is the Jim Crow section
> On this merry-go-round,
> Mister, cause I want to ride?
> Down South where I come from
> White and colored
> Can't sit side by side.
> Down South on the train
> There's a Jim Crow car.
> On the bus we're put in the back—
> But there ain't no back
> To a merry-go-round!
> Where's the horse
> For a kid that's black?

Rollins describes in some detail the breadth of Hughes's work. In the poems she cites as illustrations one is struck by the large number of now familiar images that have entered the vernacular from his creative pen. She describes the successes and discouragements of his life, his ultimate hope, and his death in 1967.

1971 Honors

ANGELOU, MAYA. *I Know Why the Caged Bird Sings.* Random House, 1969. Gr. 8–12. *

In this moving autobiography Maya Angelou takes the reader into the innermost depth of her personal self. With a masterful use of poetic prose, Angelou invokes moments of laughter, anger, tears, and shouts of victory for justice triumphant. The story begins when Angelou, who at that time was called Marguerite, is a youngster in Stamps, Arkansas. There she experiences the sting of racial prejudice and of family betrayal but also the support of her wise and compassionate brother, Bailey. With a respect for the older generation, she pays tribute to her uncle Willie, from whom she learned her multiplication tables as well as many survival lessons. Angelou's early life was full of knocks and hardships, but the reader is left with a sense of having been uplifted because the author leaves a message with young readers that with fortitude, they too can overcome. There is a significant note in the closing words. Angelou has a baby out of wedlock. A solicitous aunt insists that the frightened young mother take the child into the bed with her, despite Angelou's fear that she would roll over and smother the baby. In the morning, when she finds all is well, there is this statement of strength:

> See, you don't have to think about doing the right thing. If you're for the right thing, then you do it without thinking.

CHISHOLM, SHIRLEY. *Unbought and Unbossed.* Houghton Mifflin, 1970. Gr. 8–12. *

In 1968, Shirley Chisholm became the first African American woman to be elected to the U.S. House of Representatives. She writes:

In a just and free society, it would be foolish [to gain fame for being black and female rather than for one's accomplishments]. I hope if I am remembered it will finally be for what I have done, not for what I happen to be. And I hope that my having made it, the hard way, can be some kind of inspiration, particularly for women.

Written shortly after the 1968 election, this work is both an autobiography and a political manifesto—an exploration of Chisholm's path to Congress and her analysis of the challenges the country must meet to become just and free. She describes in some detail her early years with relatives in Barbados, away from her parents, who were struggling with the Depression in Brooklyn, where she was born. She was politicized as a student at Brooklyn College, an ostensibly progressive campus rife with racism and sexism. Entering Columbia University to earn a master's degree in early childhood education, she became active in local politics. She presents a lively portrait of clubhouse politics through the success of her Unity Democratic Club in establishing a stronghold for African American candidates and the tactics she used in the state assembly to create programs to assist disadvantaged youth in college. She also worked to establish unemployment insurance for domestic workers and to preserve tenure rights for teachers whose careers were interrupted by pregnancy. Despite her refusal to accept the "traditional politics of expediency and compromise," she was elected four years later to the Ninety-first Congress on a platform emphasizing jobs, job training, educational equity, adequate housing, enforcement of antidiscrimination laws, and support for day care—a program that would be no less relevant a quarter century later.

Having led her reader through the maze of Brooklyn politics to her landmark congressional election, Representative Chisholm proceeds to offer her analysis of the most urgent national imperatives. Though written at a very different time in our nation's history, her angry, eloquent words remain disturbingly contemporary. She traces many of the problems to the schizophrenic birth of a country that paid eloquent tribute to "liberty and justice for all" while denying full rights of citizenship to African Americans and women. To heal the breach between promises and performance, Chisholm argues that we need a Congress no longer controlled by seniority and cynicism; a society in which women's rights are a reality and women of all classes and colors have access to effective contraception and the right to choose safe, legal, affordable abortions; a united effort by blacks to assume political power; and real equality of education for all children regardless of race or income level.

We must join together to insist that this nation deliver on the promise it made nearly 200 years ago. . . . I feel an incredible urgency that we must do it now. If time has not run out, it is surely ominously short.

EVANS, MARI. *I Am a Black Woman.* Morrow, 1970. Gr. 9–12.

Mari Evans's striking collection of poems explores the personal and political dimensions of being an African American woman. The exquisitely crafted and shaped poems affirm the black woman's experiences of love, loneliness, pain, and "a black oneness, a black strength."

Using free verse and subtle rhymes, repetitive words and phrases, and evocative imagery, Evans explores the need for love and community. In tones of sadness, anger, defiance, and hope, she reaches for freedom from an oppressive society and from self-imposed constraints. She speaks of the need for reaching out for personal relationships. She applauds those who would seize collective power. And pervading all is her celebration of her African American identity.

GRAHAM, LORENZ. *Every Man Heart Lay Down.* Illustrated by Colleen Browning. Crowell, 1970. Gr. K–3.

When he served as ambassador to Liberia, Graham was most impressed by the rhythmic speech of the natives of that country. Listening to this kind of patois French that seemed to roll off the tongue, Graham was inspired to use it to write a group of biblical stories. One product of this endeavor was *Every Man Heart Lay Down*—a story that tells of God's plan to destroy his now evil-filled world. It is the story of his little "picayune" begging to be allowed to come into the world and save the people, a simple telling of the Christmas story when worshippers from afar come bringing gifts. Graham included the traditional gold and oil from the wise men, but in keeping with the story's setting, the "country people brought new rice . . . and every man heart lay down." *Every Man Heart Lay Down* is a timeless story written with a kind of poetic beauty and simplicity that begs to be read aloud.

GROSSMAN, BARNEY, WITH GLADYS GROOM AND THE PUPILS OF P.S. 150, THE BRONX, NEW YORK. *Black Means . . .* Illustrated by Charles Bible. Hill and Wang, 1970. Gr. K–3.

Gladys Groom was the teacher and Barney Grossman the principal at P.S. 150, an elementary school in a predominantly African American and Puerto Rican neighborhood. The two adults were concerned by the many negative connotations they felt were commonly associated with blackness and began seeking positive images for their students—black, Puerto Rican, and white. They first encouraged a dialogue at home and at school with the goal of developing a "thesaurus of positive images." A close look at the student-generated products spawned the idea of putting the words in a book—a format that would reach a wider audience. The final product was the award-winning *Black Means . . . .*

Charles Bible's graphic drawings—strong, positive, black-and-white images—give dramatic visual power to this beautiful and meaningful book.

JORDAN, JUNE, AND TERRI BUSH. *The Voice of the Children.* Holt, Rinehart, & Winston, 1970. Gr. 6–12.

June Jordan writes:

> [Children] are the only ones always willing to make a start; they have no choice. Children are the ways the world begins again and again. But in general, our children have no voice—that we will listen to. We force, we blank them into the bugle/bell regulated lineup of the Army/school, and we insist on silence.

To give the children a voice, the author June Jordan and then junior high school teacher Terri Bush organized a creative writing workshop in the Fort Green section of Brooklyn. The children came voluntarily on Saturdays to "rap, dance, snack, browse among the books lying around, and write their stories, poems, editorials, and jokes." Out of those sessions grew a weekly magazine, *The Voice of the Children*; poetry readings; broadcasts; wider publication—and this volume of prose and poetry by twenty-five African American and Puerto Rican young people, ages nine to fifteen, whose photographs accompany June Jordan's afterword.

Michael Goode, age twelve, writes,

> Some people talk in the hall
> Some people talk in a drawl
> Some people talk, talk, talk, talk
> And never say anything at all.

But these young people have much to say about a world gone awry. They speak of loneliness, of anger, of pain, and of the ultimate futility of hate.

Vanessa Howard, age thirteen, warns ominously of

> The last scream
> The last cry of pain
> The last tear
> Last bleeding face
> Last baby drops
> Last riot
> Last of the human race.

But we are offered alternative visions as well, as in "Drums of Freedom," by Glen Thompson, age thirteen:

> Some of us will die
> but the drums will beat.
> We may even lose but,
> but the drums will beat.
> They will beat loud and strong,
> and
> on
> and
> on
> For we shall get what we want
> and the drums will beat.

Jerome Holland, age fifteen, tries to answer his own inner question in "Will I Make It?"

> I clear my throat with a slight cough,
> clear my eyes to see the way,
> hold my shoulders up high trying to
> forget the danger that might exist,
> because I'm black and wanna make it.

PETERS, MARGARET. *The Ebony Book of Black Achievement.* Johnson Publishing, 1970. Gr. 6–9. *

As a high school teacher of English and American history, Peters was concerned about the dearth of information about African American history available to her students. She devoted her life to bringing information to the schools and to correcting distorted information. In this volume, she briefly sketches the lives of more than twenty black men and women from the fourteenth through the twentieth centuries who distinguished themselves as inventors, explorers, revolutionaries, educators, abolitionists, and businesspeople, among other fields. Included are familiar names as well as others less frequently included in collective biographies, such as Granville Woods, whose air brake, induction telegraph, and third-rail system had a profound impact on American rail transportation. In brief sketches, Peters clearly presents her subjects' accomplishments, commitment, determination, and dedication to civilization.

UDRY, JANICE MAY. *Mary Jo's Grandmother.* Illustrated by Eleanor Mill. Whitman, 1970. Gr. K–3.

An early example of the cross-generation theme, Mary Jo visits her grandmother, who lives in the country. The activities in which Mary Jo and her family participate are the gentle things that speak of unhurried and stress-free time—learning how to sew, playing with the animals on the farm, making goodies in the kitchen under Grandmother's careful guidance, and acting very maturely when Grandmother has an accident.

This book is one in a series of Mary Jo stories. It might be reasonable to surmise that the Coretta Scott King awards jury selected it as an honor book to recognize a nonblack author for her sensitive treatment of a character from a minority culture.

1970 Winner

PATTERSON, LILLIE. *Dr. Martin Luther King, Jr.: Man of Peace.* Illustrated with photographs. Garrard, 1969. Gr. K–3. *

This book, written for young readers, is an introduction to the life of Martin Luther King Jr. and his nonviolent approach to achieving racial equality. The simply stated information and the timeliness of the book, published just after King's assassination, were among the factors that made this book the first title to receive the Coretta Scott King Book Award. ∎

Q & A

A Conversation with Gabrielle Douglas

Gabrielle Douglas is a U.S. Women's artistic gymnast. At the 2012 London Summer Olympics, she won gold medals in both the team and individual all-around competitions. Gabrielle is the first woman of color of any nationality and the first African American gymnast in Olympic history to become the Individual All-Around Champion. She is also the first American gymnast to win gold in both the gymnastic individual all-around and team competitions at the same Olympic games.

What did you read when you were growing up? How did it impact you?

I really enjoyed reading the *Diary of Anne Frank*. I was so moved by how the human spirit can soar in spite of having basic freedom and rights taken away. It continues to remind me that I have a responsibility to celebrate and honor my freedom by pursuing my dreams and using my gifts and talents to positively impact my generation!

Why do you think it is important for multicultural children's books to be available?

Being able to read about another culture is such a treasure. Knowledge invites understanding, which I believe helps create unity. It is so important that children be exposed to other cultures so that they learn differences are to be honored not despised.

Why do you think books about one's own ethnicity would add value to a child's experience?

Every race has great heroes, and it's so encouraging to be taught about those pioneers within your own ethnicity. I believe that one of life's greatest gifts is being able to see yourself in them and then striving to achieve your own level of greatness!

How do you think books about other ethnicities enrich a child's social awareness?

I think exposing a child to books about other ethnicities is very important. When children learn about another culture's successes and struggles, it enables them to appreciate what someone else has been through and conquered. I also believe that this exposure allows them to be more engaged and compassionate. ■

Illustrator Awards
1974–2014

An * indicates nonfiction

2014 Winner

BEATY, DANIEL. *Knock Knock: My Dad's Dream for Me.* **Illustrated by Bryan Collier.** Little, Brown, 2013. Gr. Pre-K–2.

Beginning with the title page, paper collage scraps of different hues and newspaper print create a compact urban landscape of brownstones, skyscrapers, water towers, and vacant fire escapes. The earth tones of the city contrast vividly with a bright blue sky of pieces of paper expertly woven together, suggesting that anything is possible on such a beautiful day. The story begins with a young boy pretending to sleep and waiting for his father to wake him in the morning. The young boy and his father play a game called Knock Knock and the father knocks on his son's bedroom door every morning to wake him and tell him that he loves him. One day the knock doesn't come anymore and the son is left to wonder where his father is. "Does he come when I'm not home?" wonders the young boy as he waits for his father day after day. The father doesn't return and the young son soon becomes a young man.

Beaty and Collier are true partners in this timely work. Beaty's sparse, but somber, text meshes beautifully with Collier's abundant landscape of texture and color. The pairing in the message of the longing for a parent with the strength and resiliency of a child is handled with extraordinary care by Collier and Beaty. There is a richness of spirit and hope in this work that captures the imagination of young children and the universal love of parents for their children, no matter the circumstance. —*Lana Adlawan*

2014 Honor

NELSON, KADIR. *Nelson Mandela.* HarperCollins, 2013. Gr. K–3. *

Mandela was singled out of his thirteen siblings to attend school miles away from his family when he was only nine years old. It was there that he received the name Nelson. Nelson grew and learned as he listened to the elders' tales of how the people in old Africa were overwhelmed by the Europeans, losing their land and freedoms to the foreign invaders. Nelson continued his education, eventually becoming an attorney taking on the plight of his less fortunate countrymen. Nelson enthusiastically joined in the protests of the early dissenters of apartheid. The success of the resistance campaign and Nelson's leadership made him a target for the authorities, eventually forcing him to go underground. His success landed him in jail several times before he finally received a life sentence as a political prisoner.

Nelson's influence and power among South Africans was not diminished by his incarceration. His supporters were emboldened to fight the apartheid system, bringing international visibility to their plight. Nelson was released after serving twenty-seven years as a political prisoner. His popularity and influence led to his election as the first black president of South Africa four years later. —*Carole J. McCollough*

2014 John Steptoe Award for New Talent

HILL, LABAN CARRICK. *When the Beat Was Born: DJ Kool Herc and the Creation of Hip Hop.* **Illustrated by Theodore Taylor III.** Roaring Brook Press, 2013. Gr. 2–4. *

As a child growing up in Jamaica, young Clive loved to watch DJ King George set up for his Saturday night dance parties. When his family later moved to New York City, Clive felt displaced until he discovered the power he had in music. Developing his own DJ style of hip hop as DJ Kool Herc, Clive was the first to combine two turntables to extend the music breaks, shouting out to recognize audience members by name, and encouraging dancers to do their own break dance moves.

From the opening page that shows him fingering an imaginary trumpet, through Clive's evolution into DJ Kool Herc, the architect of hip hop, Laban Carrick Hill and Theodore Taylor III have created an exciting biography (with a timeline and bibliography), which also serves as an excellent example of a picture book where picture and text work together wonderfully. Taylor uses color choices of muted greens, grays, blacks, and oranges accented with a standout splash of red and exaggerated size to highlight how important the music is in this John Steptoe award-winning biography. Especially powerful are the illustrations of a visually small Clive sitting on a stack of records watching equally small couples dance on the top of speakers and the picture of his hands manipulating the two turntables. —*Therese Bigelow*

2013 Winner

HUGHES, LANGSTON. *I, Too, Am America.* **Illustrated by Bryan Collier.** Simon & Schuster, 2012. Gr. K–4.

A young African American boy peeks through the stripes on an iconic American flag for the cover of "I, Too, Am America." Before one has even cracked the spine of this powerful work, the beauty of the boy and his steadfast look of determination over the word "America" makes a powerful statement spanning hundreds of years in a single image. Collier's collage rendering of Langston Hughes's 1925 poem, "I, Too" is set on fast-moving trains traversing the United States with the Pullman Porters, a group of African American men who worked the railways in the late nineteenth to mid-twentieth centuries. Known for their level of service and dedication—even while enduring questionable working conditions—the Porters helped educate others along their railway lines by taking discarded passenger items such as newspapers or records and distributing them to those without access.

In this sparsely worded text, Collier's interpretation of the words of Langston Hughes through the life of a Pullman Porter promotes hope, community, and advancement of African Americans in stark contrast to the lines of Hughes's poem that damn inequality and promote justice. Collier uses his gift of collage to carry the metaphor of the discarded Pullman newspapers from the past to the present—also included on the end papers—to arrive in present-day New York City by subway. Pieces of the American Flag float through time and place to land on characters' faces and landscapes—a subtle reminder that we are all America. —*Lana Adlawan*

2013 Honors

LYONS, KELLY STARLING. *Ellen's Broom.* **Illustrated by Daniel Minter.** G.P. Putnam's Sons, 2012. Gr. K–3.

Daniel Minter captures the sweetness of romantic love, family, and community in his hand-painted linoleum blocks. Bright pinks, blues, and purples, and warm golden yellows bring movement to a technique that is often thought of as stiff and emotionless. In Kelly Lyons's tale of a family during Reconstruction, Minter's characters leap off the page as they worship in church and celebrate the fact that all marriages can now be legally registered. Just as powerful are the pages that illustrate the family discussions of slavery. Minter uses sepia tones to denote the past. The facial expressions clearly demonstrate loss as family, friends, and lovers are ripped apart. However, the sepia tones also express joy as Papa and Mama jump the broom. Minter's linoleum block technique suggests forward movement into a hopeful future. His illustrations truly extend the text, reflecting the warmth of family and community and the hopefulness of the future that will always be grounded in tradition. —*Debra Gold*

MYERS, CHRISTOPHER. *H.O.R.S.E.: A Game of Basketball and Imagination.* Egmont, 2013. Gr. K–5.

In *H.O.R.S.E.*, Christopher Myers mixes photo collage and two painted figures, elongated TALL guys who aren't just using their height to take their shots with a bright orange basketball. As the two friends prepare their shots with long, long arms ready to compete, their words take over the game, and it morphs into a boast-fest of one fantastic shot after another. As their game goes stratospheric, and possibly even intergalactic, the text leaps from its confines and curves overhead and around planets.

Myers's page-spanning paintings even feature a guest appearance by Hayden Planetarium Director Neil deGrasse Tyson, who points to the path of the "new basketball-shaped comet." Young readers may or may not get this visual joke or Myers's note, which is a tribute to an artist friend who is bonded to Myers by history, imagination, and athleticism. However, Myers is exactly on young readers' wavelength in the two players' one-upmanship and boys of all ages will undoubtedly relish the fantastical tongue dunk. His players inhabit free and expansive blank spaces until their ball takes off for outer space. The sparse use of photos of formal earthbound city buildings provides contrast to the free-flowing paintings and text. —*Sue Sherif*

KING, MARTIN LUTHER, JR. Illustrated by Kadir Nelson.
I Have a Dream: Martin Luther King, Jr. Schwartz and Wade Books/Random House Children's Books, 2012. Gr. K–5.

Kadir Nelson's homage to Dr. King truly captures the "artistic expression of the African American experience" as described in the purpose of the Coretta Scott King Award. The artist's signature oil paintings bring the moment of the speech to life as well as a variety of less specific (but not less powerful) moments. It is important to note the "I Have A Dream" speech has been abbreviated within the scope of the picture book itself. However, readers can listen to the entire speech that is available on an enclosed CD contained in the back matter. The way the speech is excerpted enabled Nelson to pair images with particular sentiments from the speech. In this way, Nelson has created a unique version of the speech with emphasis carefully placed on Dr. King's stature, spirituality, and sustaining memory. The pictures vary in terms of focus and layout. Double-page spreads are used to create a sense of place (long view from the reflecting pool), for dramatic emphasis (white and black hands clasped), and to add a personal face to the struggle, a family portrait. As is expected from this artist, the striking realism and rich colors will draw readers in and keep their attention. —*Lesley Colabucci*

2012 Winner

EVANS, SHANE W. *Underground: Finding the Light to Freedom.* Roaring Brook Press, 2011. Gr. 2–6.

While it can be a fairly exhausting task to consider the intricacies and hardships of the Underground Railroad, it takes a fair amount of genius to explain it to young children. Shane Evans has created a wonderful introduction to this complex system in his book *Underground*. With sparse text and evocative striking images, Evans describes the dangerous and desperate journey of a group of slaves as they travel through the endless nights, looking up to the stars and moon to guide the way to freedom. Skillful use of perspective helps convey the movement of the Underground Railroad, through a muted palette of dark blues that gives way to progressively brighter tones on double-spread pages. Taking the most harrowing of conditions and condensing them into succinct yet powerful statements, Evans tells a story understood by audiences of all ages. —*Eboni Curry*

2012 Honor

NELSON, KADIR. *Heart and Soul: The Story of America and African Americans.* Balzer & Bray, 2011. Gr. 3–7. *

Heart and Soul is like a treasured family photograph album that captures the highlights and heartaches of African American history. An elder African American "Everywoman" tells the story of her life and America's history. The reader will linger over the full-page illustrations and double-page spreads in this oversized book. Kadir Nelson's stunning oil paintings portray bold images of known and unknown historical personalities. The portrait of a nameless African American Revolutionary War soldier is just as powerful as the one of abolitionist Frederick Douglass. The sepia-toned picture of a young girl in a vintage oval picture frame and one of a well-dressed 1920s Harlem couple are striking enlarged reproductions of the studio photographs of that era. Nelson has selectively chosen to illustrate pivotal events in African American history. The determination on the faces of the men depicted in the labor strike picture captures the spirit of activism in the African American community. The dramatic use of color in the scene of a blazing burning cross is a contrast to the close-up of the hands of a senior citizen holding an "I voted" button. As the narrator says, "You have to know where you come from so you can move forward." Children and teens will be attracted to this book's vivid illustrations that show them the past and promise a bright future. —*Martha Ruff*

2011 Winner

HILL, LABAN CARRICK. *Dave the Potter.* **Illustrated by Bryan Collier.** Little, Brown, 2010. Gr. K–3. *

A picture book homage to a strong, brilliant artist, Collier uses his own prodigious talent to bring the life of Dave the Potter to young readers. Using collage and earth-toned paints, Collier both reveres and respects the artist whose works still amaze potters today. In the foreground of many spreads we see Dave working in "mud pie heaven," while the background honestly shows the life of a slave. He is an artist who refuses to allow his lack of freedom to stop him from being an artist. The image of Dave standing in front of the tree, with it seemingly growing out of his head, includes family images in the branches that expand on the embrace of the large jar described in the text on the facing page. The play of light and shadow, particularly on Dave's hands, arms, and clothing, gives the illustrations depth and power. Emotional without being didactic, Collier gets the details of the craft right—the caked palms, the dry, chapped skin, tongue-thrusted concentration, the magical moment when a round of wedged clay becomes a perfectly centered pot. This is a book that is like one of Dave's pots—at first glance, simple to look at, but, upon inspection, centered and filled with power. —*Robin Smith*

2011 Honor

GOLIO, GARY. *Jimi: Sounds Like a Rainbow: A Story of the Young Jimi Hendrix.* **Illustrated by Javaka Steptoe.** Clarion Books, 2010. Gr. 3–5. *

The very beginning of the story introduces the reader to artistically talented young Jimmy Hendrix.

> Electricity ripped through the air . . . Jimmy's hand jumped, and a rainbow of color pencils went tumbling to the floor . . . Jimmy grabbed his one-string ukuele. He could play only simple tunes, but now he had a new idea . . ." The new idea was to create and play notes that sound like raindrops and ultimately "paint pictures with sound."

Living with his father in a boarding house in Seattle, Jimmy creatively used objects and instruments given to him. He also used his imagination and told stories. When Jimmy received a second-hand guitar, it broadened his musical ingenuity. Later, Jimmy acquired an electric guitar and amplifiers. "He learned to use it as an artist uses paint, creating new worlds with the colors of sound."

Gary Golio's lyrical text sets the tone of the story at the very beginning. Using words that have musical connotations like "electricity," "pound," and "rock" immediately thrusts young readers into Jimmy's musical world. When readers see the text in circular and wavy lines, it may remind them of notes and scales on a music sheet. Golio focuses on Jimmy's music and artistic talents rather than his impoverished life. A list of resources is provided in the author's note. Javaka Steptoe's illustrations match perfectly with Golio's text and Jimmy's story. The rainbow of colors depicts Jimmy's colorful personality, his artistic style, and finally the colors of the sound Jimmy makes with his guitar. The mixed media makes the point of Jimmy's many talents in art, music, drama, and storytelling. On each page, Jimmy is in the forefront, listening, drawing, dreaming, and playing until the very end of the story. —*Karen Lemmons*

2011 John Steptoe Award for New Talent

JOHNSON, JEN CULLERTON. *Seeds of Change.* **Illustrated by Sonia Lynn Sadler.** Lee & Low, 2010. Gr. 2–4. *

Seeds of Change is a well-written picture book biography of Wangari Maathai, Kenyan women's activist, environmentalist, scientist, and Nobel Laureate. Wangari's love of learning and nature was instilled in her as a young girl by her mother. She was taught to treasure trees for food, wildlife, and clean water, and promised never to cut down the trees. Although it was not customary for Kenyan girls to be educated, her parents decided to send her to school. Wangari went to America to study science and learned that even as a woman she could accomplish whatever she set her mind to. Learning took her to America where she studied science and discovered that a woman could accomplish whatever she wanted to do. Returning home to Kenya she founded the Green Belt Movement, changing the country's landscape and ultimately spreading the message of planting trees and caring for the environment around the world.

Wangari's life of devotion to protecting the natural world she loved serves as an example to young readers of how one person can inspire others to appreciate and care for the environment. The rhythmic, poetic text is complemented by artful illustrations. Illustrator Sonia Lynn Sadler's vivid, bright colors and textures infuse vibrancy into this biography with every turn of the page. —*Eunice Anderson*

2010 Winner

HUGHES, LANGSTON. *My People.* **Illustrated by Charles R. Smith Jr.** Atheneum Books for Young Readers, 2009. Gr. Pre-K–3.

Bold, antiqued, sepia-toned photographs that accompany and complement one of Langston Hughes's most memorable poems define this stunning book. Each page is a celebration of African American people of all ages, colors, and hues. Whether the subject is laughing, thinking, dancing, or crying, each page pops with emotion and celebration of the beauty and variety of African American people. The sophisticated design employs typefaces of varying sizes, emphasizing each word of this thirty-three-word masterpiece. Adding to the rhythm and pacing, Smith includes lightly shaded filmstrip-like photos along the edges of most spreads. Smith's eye for detail and his extraordinary photographs eloquently express the pride and love the poet felt for his people, capturing equally the curiosity and excitement of youth and the experience and wisdom of elders. This is the first time photography has been honored by the Committee. —*Robin Smith*

2010 Honor

HUGHES, LANGSTON. *The Negro Speaks of Rivers.* **Illustrated by E. B. Lewis.** Disney/Jump at the Sun, 2009. Gr. K–8.

In Hughes's classic poem brief language is deceptively simple; a deep current of emotion rises to the surface through Lewis's beautifully painted images of people and waters in pastoral shades of blue, green, and gold. Each stanza, written in the first person, is presented on one double-page spread, ensuring a suitably dramatic visual interpretation of such powerful statements as "I've known rivers ancient as the world / and older than the flow of human blood in human veins." The former is illustrated by a wide, gray-blue river sparkling with sunshine and the silhouette of a thin, lone figure poling a small boat; the latter by a close-up image of strong brown hands holding an earthenware or copper pot by the side of a greenish-brown stream. The juxtaposition of the majestic, wide waterway with the earthy, quotidian portrait of hands and pot set the theme for this volume: rivers represent a continuum of life, and in particular here, African American life throughout history. Some rivers significant to this history are named: "I bathed in the Euphrates when dawns were young. / I built my hut near the Congo and it lulled me to sleep." Some of the paintings are realistic, including a charming image of a man and a boy fishing on the banks of the Mississippi; others are more spiritual, such as a self-portrait of Lewis himself (identified as such in an illustrator's note), shown praying against a backdrop of dark green, presumably deep water with rippling lines flowing across a stylized depiction of his upper body. Written in 1920, this poem remains relevant and eloquent, especially as interpreted through Lewis's affecting watercolors. —*Diane Foote*

2009 Winner

THOMAS, JOYCE CAROL. *The Blacker the Berry: Poems.* **Illustrated by Floyd Cooper.** HarperCollins, 2008. Gr. 3–6.

Songwriters, poets, and authors often refer to the color black as if it were one dark density: "Black is the color of my true love's hair"; "Out of the night that covers me, / Black as the Pit from pole to pole"; "I am a Negro, black as the night is black." Artist Floyd Cooper captures all the nuances of the color in perfect response to Thomas's words. There's Grandma drinking coffee so thick and black "a spoon could stand in it"; the "biscuit brown" face of a young boy; a girl, dark skin contrasting with her bright yellow dress, who realizes that it's the dark of night that makes a bright dawn possible; and the smiling, red-haired child, whose face looks almost white, who is proud of the single drop of blood that makes her black. Cooper's closing painting, a multicultural gathering of children of all shades of black, extends Thomas's message that every shade of black is beautiful.

2009 Honors

NELSON, KADIR. *We Are the Ship: The Story of Negro League Baseball.* Jump at the Sun/Hyperion Books for Children, 2008. Gr. 3–8. *

Kadir Nelson captures the spirit of Negro League Baseball in *We Are the Ship*. With artistic realism, he takes us back and makes time stand still. His elegant, up-close renderings of players, such as Raleigh "Biz" Mackey and Wilber "Bullet" Rogan, or of players standing in dappled sunlight (Leroy "Satchel" Paige in Yankee Stadium), bring to life the human drama of these often forgotten athletes and their contributions to our great national pastime. Nelson captures the seduction of the night game with halos of light against a great dark sky, miniaturizing the players as if to signify the monumental obstacles encountered by these determined African Americans. The gatefold showcasing the players of the first Colored World Series in 1924, at Muehlebach Field in Kansas City, Missouri, is a stunning example of the scope of the artist's talent. Each of the forty-one players is different. Deep, rich color fills the other single and double-page spreads as well. All are enhanced by a brilliant use of light, accented by an occasional pale blue sky. Nelson brings the players and the game to life with sensitivity and reverence.

ASTON, DIANNA HUTTS. *The Moon Over Star.* **Illustrated by Jerry Pinkney.** Dial, 2008. Gr. Pre K–3.

As Mae's Grandpa leads the singing in church, Mae is thinking of the *Apollo 11* astronauts who are about to land on the moon. Jerry Pinkney's pencil, ink, and watercolor illustrations allow readers to experience the enormity of the historic event while identifying with Mae's dream of joining the space program. Pinkney has a distinguished history of depicting space travel; in 1982, he was hired by NASA to commemorate the launch of the shuttle *Columbia*. His experience is evident throughout this book as he moves readers back and forth between the historical images and scenes from Mae's warm world—her father giving her a reassuring embrace, her friends building a makeshift rocket from wheels, ladders, and barrels found in the barn. The double-page, wordless spread of the fiery *Apollo* takeoff, vivid and dramatic, is balanced by the wonder in a beautiful scene of Mae's family staring up at the sky while enjoying an evening picnic. In a black-and-white spread suggestive of the television broadcast watched by 600 million people around the world, Pinkney depicts the astronauts cavorting on the surface of the moon. The closing image of the astronauts' footsteps on the lunar surface invites Mae (and readers) to fill those shoes.

WEATHERFORD, CAROLE BOSTON. *Before John Was a Jazz Giant: A Song of John Coltrane.* **Illustrated by Sean Qualls.** Henry Holt, 2008. Gr. K–3.

Carole Boston Weatherford's brief text describes the musical influences that shaped the life of the renowned jazz saxophonist John Coltrane. Coltrane grew up in High Point, North Carolina, where "he heard hambones knocking in Grandma's pots, / Daddy strumming the ukulele / . . . Mama playing hymns for the senior choir / . . . and a saxophone's soulful solo, / blue notes crooning his name." Painting in acrylics and using collage and pencil accents, Sean Qualls illustrates the picture-book tribute with a muted, harmonious palette of blue, brown, terra-cotta, and black. Floating notes, bubbles, and ribbons of sound evoke the rhythmic world that shaped this musical great. The paint-saturated pages combine representational images with abstract shapes, beautifully reflecting Coltrane's music, which surrounded listeners with riffs on familiar melodies.

2009 John Steptoe Award for New Talent

ELLIOTT, ZETTA. *Bird.* **Illustrated by Shadra Strickland.** Lee & Low, 2008. Gr. 2–5.

Although he's still struggling with his grandfather's death, Mehkai (nicknamed Bird by Granddad) realizes that he and his family suffer even more from the death of drug-addicted Marcus, Bird's older brother. The illustrations, a combination of gouache, watercolor, pencil, and charcoal, carry a heavy emotional load, but Strickland's palette, mostly muted grays, blues, and browns, conveys the reflective mood with a lightness of touch. Uncle Son, Granddad's friend, is mentoring Bird, providing him with words of comfort and encouraging him to practice his drawing, revel in his love of birds, and develop his "own special something" that will help him soar. Lines drawn in soft gray pencil accompany the more realistic depictions of characters and events, balancing the hard facts of life with an imagined world. Grief haunts each picture, but there's a surprising uplifting quality in the close relationship between the boy and the adult who serves as his support. Strickland's careful use of light and dark (hope and despair) turns the sensitive poetry into a visual jazz riff that honors both the reality of Bird's life and his feelings and thoughts.

2008 Winner

BRYAN, ASHLEY. *Let It Shine: Three Favorite Spirituals.* Atheneum, 2007. Gr. K–3.

When does a stack of brightly colored papers become a wondrous work of art? It happens when the skilled fingers and creative imagination of Ashley Bryan converge. The result is an image-filled collage giving brilliant visual interpretation to the artist's best-loved spirituals. The ingenious use of the media of collage invites the reader to scrutinize each illustration for those details that add dimension to the seemingly simple words. In the first selection, each "little light" is different, from the candle to the lantern to a flashlight and others. The smoothly turned curves in the double-page spread of the mother cuddling her child convey the sense of comfort and security that says He truly holds "the little bitty baby in His hands." Tambourines, drums, maracas, a myriad of musical instruments provide a visual rhythmic beat as "the Saints go marching in." The universal appeal of this musical form is captured in the clearly definable multicultural personalities pictured on the pages. Figures for each carefully thought-out scene are cut with the memory-filled sewing shears and embroidery scissors inherited from the artist's mother. In tribute, facsimiles of both pairs are woven into the endpaper designs.

Let It Shine is an informative, handsomely illustrated gem, meant to be savored by all ages. Recognizing that these reverential and historically important spirituals are meant to be sung, Bryan includes notations, done with crafted block prints of musical scores for each of the three selections: "This Little Light of Mine"; "When the Saints Go Marching In"; and "He's Got the Whole World in His Hands." Ashley Bryan's 2008 Coretta Scott King Book Award winner for illustrations is a color-filled invitation to open the pages and sing.

2008 Honors

JOY, N. *The Secret Olivia Told Me.* **Illustrated by Nancy Devard.** Just Us Books, 2007. Gr. K–3.

With a limited color palette of black, white, gray, bright red, and brick tones, Devard's illustrations of shape, line, and color illustrate a story that opens with a heart-to-heart conversation and ends with a dramatic explosion. Devard depicts the story using silhouettes, which appear at once shadowy and rock solid. This technique recalls the creation of that art form in the work of the African American artist Kara Walker. Children in action, passing along stories not meant for other ears, and a bright red balloon hovering with its string trailing through the air symbolize a tale told from mouth to ear, from cell phone to cell phone, even on the playground. These are among the striking images of friendship almost broken—even as the red balloon explodes. Clever use of the scissors lets the reader see characters with innovative hairdos, a wide variety of clothing, and individualized physical features. The large heads balanced upon slender necks give the figures of the girls and boys a kind of fragility in a world that can be easily destabilized.

DILLON, LEO, AND DIANE DILLON. *Jazz on a Saturday Night.* Blue Sky Press/Scholastic, 2007. Gr. K–3. *

Subdued shades and tints of brown, blue, and green with touches of yellow set the scene for an evening of jazz—all fine and mellow. Each page is a spirited invitation to enjoy the music of the historically great jazz personalities of another era. Dapper musicians dressed in cuff-linked shirts, with jacket and tie—and a few hats—join the fashionably dressed vocalist who will entertain an across-the-generations audience. The lights go up and Charlie Be-Bop Parker's golden saxophone responds to the notes from Miles Davis's trumpet. Skull-capped Thelonious Monk challenges the audience to respond to his unusual piano innovations. The audience seems enraptured as Ella Fitzgerald trickles her tongue around the rhythms of "scat" in a manner unequaled by any other.

The abundant use of circular lines in body positions, in facial expressions, and even in the patterns designed in the audience's clothing convey a sense of joyous rhythmic motion as listeners seem to sway with the changing tempos of the music. With a subtle touch, this most creative art team obliterates shades of yellow in the spotlights, letting the audience in attendance, and the reader, know that the evening is over. The stage is empty. The musicians have gone. *Jazz on a Saturday Night* is a memory until the next time. But the musical feast is extended with original and informative poetic couplets on each page and biographical sketches of the musicians in the endnotes.

2007 Winner

WEATHERFORD, CAROLE BOSTON. *Moses: When Harriet Tubman Led Her People to Freedom.* **Illustrated by Kadir Nelson.** Jump at the Sun/Hyperion Books for Children, 2006. Gr. K–3. *

The account of the heroic slave who escaped and led three hundred of her people to freedom is well known. With an aura of deep spirituality, Nelson tells the story of Harriet Tubman's personal trials during her own escape. Dramatic paintings capture the pathos of the moment in dark shades of brown, blue, and deep green and then, with a masterstroke, keep an ever-present sign of hope and faith in the glow of yellow. In one scene Tubman is wielding a huge ax, cutting into a huge tree stump. With the escapee on the move, we see in the dark of night the huge ax stuck, as if forever immobile, in that same tree stump—Tubman's determined end to servitude. We feel the pain, weariness, and loneliness as Harriet slumps against a darkened tree and bathes her feet in the cool creek water. Through it all, Nelson increases the symbolic color yellow, and at the end of her journey this light becomes like a radiant beam of praise as gnarled hands are raised in prayer and thanksgiving.

2007 Honors

RAMPERSAD, ARNOLD, AND DAVID ROESSEL, EDS. *Langston Hughes. Poetry for Young People series.* **Illustrated by Benny Andrews.** Sterling, 2006. Gr. 7–10.

Andrews's spirited paintings illustrate twenty-six poems selected from the works of Langston Hughes. The combination of word and art portrays the African American experience with themes of hope, dreams of the future, the influence of music and dance, recollections of slavery and discrimination, and the resilience of the human spirit. Andrews's art, distinguished by elongated figures and minimal but effective use of detail, is painted mostly in varying shades of red, green, and blue. Providing an emotional as well as an aesthetic experience, this Coretta Scott King honor book will find a place in homes, schools, libraries, and the hearts of its readers.

MYERS, WALTER DEAN. *Jazz.* **Illustrated by Christopher Myers.** Holiday House, 2006. Gr. K–6.

It starts with the title page. With a flair of the dramatic, Christopher Myers immediately invites one to "hear" the music of the jazz era with, seemingly, a sound from the slender figures of a drummer. Pages filled with images then introduce the piano player, then the trumpet player whose full-blown cheeks blow out the notes. The rhythm of an unseen band has the Lindy Hoppers swinging across the double-page spread. The bass player, silhouetted against a blue background, captures the nostalgic sadness of Walter Dean Myers's blues poetry, "Waiting for me to come out to swing onto the empty avenue." *Jazz* has a harmonious blend of colors, skillfully constructed physical features, and a balanced representation of a variety of musicians. Through the effective combination of words and visuals, it can be shared as an important contribution to the history of music.

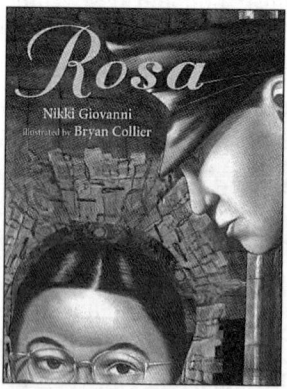

2006 Winner

GIOVANNI, NIKKI. *Rosa.* **Illustrated by Bryan Collier.** Henry Holt, 2005. Gr. 3–5. *

Noted for images featuring texture, pattern, and color that echo the complexities of the patchwork quilts created by African American artisans, Bryan Collier joins artists such as Romaire Bearden and Jacob Lawrence who have made the art of collage their very own.

In one of the opening portraits of Collier's Coretta Scott King Book Award book, the artist depicts Rosa Parks as a serene young seamstress in her work environment. Large eyes shine out from behind glasses, welcoming the reader to join her on the journey to equality. Contrasting that image with the menacing hulk of the police hovering over her on the book's cover, the reader will feel the drama that's soon to come.

Collier understands Mrs. Parks's role as an exalted member of the human rights movement and has subtly included two images of her with her head surrounded with a golden halo. A variety of facial expressions and imploring hands that seem almost to be speaking are among the trouble-filled images symbolic of the racism of the American South. Collier creates a world that is timeless, yet anchored in 1955. Each visual, standing alone, has its own power. Collectively, the illustrations tell a story of black resistance and determination and victory, through the life of one singular woman.

2006 Honor

WILLIAMS, MARY. *Brothers in Hope: The Story of the Lost Boys of Sudan.* **Illustrated by R. Gregory Christie.** Lee & Low, 2005. Gr. 3–6.

Using acrylic paints, Christie captures the drama and trauma of thousands of young boys torn from their families in the horrific raids on the villages of Sudan. With an economy of deft touches, the scenes come to life, showing a multitude of scantily clothed, cocoa-colored young boys making a fear-filled trek into unknown territory. The repetition of the earth tones of the African tundra dramatically reflects the seemingly endless journey. A swirling swatch of green depicts the wide river that the boys must cross if they are to reach safety. Touches of paint become bobbing heads as one by one the band of "brothers" emerge on the shore, with no loss of life. Christie's understated simplicity helps emphasize the importance of education as the key to survival, first through the picture of young boys struggling to replace play with attention to school books, and later through the image of a lone young man reading a book, preparing for the future. An interesting note—the main character in *Brothers in Hope* is in reality Valentino Deng, now studying international law. As in previous books, Christie's characters have oversized heads. When asked why he depicts them that way, Christie responded quietly and philosophically: "That is where the mind is."

2005 Winner

SHANGE, NTOZAKE. *Ellington Was Not a Street.* **Illustrated by Kadir Nelson.** Simon & Schuster Books for Young Readers, 2004. Gr. 3–5.

Today Ellington is a tiny street in lower Manhattan. But the street Nelson shows us is one where the movers and shakers of the mid-1920s and '30s met to discuss important social matters of the time. A precocious young lady with an impish face welcomes the towering Paul Robeson into the parlor. While the "hostess" sleeps, Robeson joins in serious conversation with graying, but ever alert, W. E. B. Du Bois. Many musicians are among those who cross the threshold. With a skill that comes from careful study, Nelson gives each character a distinctive identity. In a place that is truly home, neatly dressed gentlemen discuss the affairs of the day while enjoying a game of cards, spied on by the tiny Miss of the house. With all the comings and goings, there is still a constant sense of family.

Along with the realistic personal portrayals, Nelson's background scenes give evidence of careful study of the period. We note the flowered wallpaper in the parlor, the huge grandfather clock in the spacious hallway, the oversized furniture, and then the tiny lace doily on the coffee table. For a look back in time and an introduction to influential personalities of an earlier generation, *Ellington Was Not a Street*—a visual treat—extends the author's recollections in lyrical verse.

2005 Honors

HAMILTON, VIRGINIA. *The People Could Fly: The Picture Book.* **Illustrated by Leo Dillon and Diane Dillon.** Knopf, 2004. Gr. K–5.

Somber black endpapers with a feeling of embossed feathers are an intimation of the sorrow-filled legend told in the Dillons' dramatic illustrations for *The People Could Fly*. The picture book is a new interpretation of Hamilton's masterful storytelling in which some who are dragged into captivity happen to have wings. With creative use of muted earth colors in one scene, the symbiotic Dillon palette captures the agony and fear and helplessness of those chained in a ship's hold. Working seamlessly together, the artistic pair continue the story—a mother's sorrow, a baby's pain and discomfort, and a whip-swinging overseer's cruelty. The placement of hands speaks volumes as an ancient bearded "spirit of freedom" appears, knowing the time has come to set wings in motion. Like a graceful dancer, the first flier leaps toward the heavens. Others, suddenly adorned in clothing of geometric splendor—at first unsteadily, then with growing confidence—begin the flight to freedom.

On the closing page, the Dillons pay a final tribute to their dear friend Virginia Hamilton, who, with a gentle smile and almost imperceptible wave to all those left behind, joins the assembly of the people who, with wings unfurled, could fly. One look is not enough to absorb all the stories, all the emotions, all the mystic history that the Dillons have embodied in this picture-book version.

HOLIDAY, BILLIE, AND ARTHUR HERZOG JR. *God Bless the Child.* **Illustrated by Jerry Pinkney.** Amistad/HarperCollins, 2004. Gr. 2–6.

Illustrator Pinkney remarks that his art has to begin with research. This relationship between art and history is evident when we look closely at the illustrations in *God Bless the Child*—Pinkney's visual interpretation of Billie Holiday's vocal commemoration of the Great Migration of the 1930s. Look closely at the toil-worn faces of Negroes of all ages, toiling endlessly in southern cotton fields. The use of drab colors for a family's shapeless clothing speaks of poverty. Deft use of line and color captures the range of moods of family members as one group heads north. There is joy, sadness, anticipation, as scant belongings are piled atop an ancient automobile. How creatively the artist captures the total poignancy of the moment through the setting of a single chair sitting abandoned in front of a now empty home. A turn of the page and we find a startling contrast with scenes of hustle and bustle in the city—El trains, automobiles, tall buildings, and busy factories.

Contrasting shades and tints of the same color in the clothing, and posturing in body positions, bespeak a subtle snobbery between the ones who have "made it" in the city and the new arrivals. It's a full story told with a few strokes of a brush! And Pinkney extends the story in the endpapers: the walls of a wooden shack are replaced with flowery wallpaper that was all the vogue in this era. The meaningful closing scene shows a well-dressed youngster in school—a wordless message that education is the key for each one who would "have his own." From a study of history to his own creative artistry, a master storyteller with brush and paint has given visual life to the meaning of *God Bless the Child*. (The accompanying CD is a reproduction of Billie Holiday singing this plaintive song.)

2005 John Steptoe Award for New Talent

ROBERTS, BRENDA C. *Jazzy Miz Mozetta.* **Illustrated by Frank Morrison.** Farrar, Straus, & Giroux, 2004. Gr. Pre-K–3.

In a neomannerist style, Morrison portrays an African American ethnic community full of life and joyous energy. His story of an evening of dance and friendship employs color and movement to create a warm, close relationship between readers and characters in the book, who come alive through the artist's use of physical and emotional expression, body posture, and color. The movement of the dance can be experienced by all.

As Miz Mozetta, in her fancy dress and special blue dancing shoes, ventures out into the evening, vibrant colors heighten the excitement, and almost exaggerated shapes express life in action among intergenerational members of the community. We can feel the tension when Miz Mozetta turns her back, if only momentarily, on those who rejected her and the understanding when Miz Mozetta and the others realize that their community isn't complete without the youth. It's a joyous closing when young and old join in a breathless jitterbug fling. Morrison's perceptive interpretation of Robert's story of what it means to be a community deservedly earned him a Coretta Scott King Book Award for new talent.

2004 Winner

BRYAN, ASHLEY. *Beautiful Blackbird.* Atheneum, 2003. Gr. K–2.

Ashley Bryan reclaims yet another African tale for the twenty-first-century reader. From the Ila-speaking people of Zambia, *Beautiful Blackbird* achieves excellence in the canons of children's literature through both the illustrative and the textual artistry of its creator. Bryan's ability to capture the rhythm and cadence of the African folk tradition is unparalleled. From endpaper to endpaper Bryan's cut-paper figures fill the pages with strong imagery. The collage technique, combining the powerful blackness of the central character with the brilliant contrasting colors of the birds, all set against stark white pages, makes this memorable story a visual treat.

Bryan has perfected the language of movement in this retelling of how each in a merry throng of birds comes to sport a bit of black in his plumage. Dancing words frolic across the pages, exciting the reader's verbal and visual imagination. *Beautiful Blackbird* carries a strong message of pride and self-confidence, attesting to the fact that black is beautiful. There is a final underlying message in this cautionary tale, with its superb marriage of word and picture. When Ringdove begs for a bit of color, Blackbird admonishes, "Color on the outside is not what's on the inside. . . . I'll be me and you'll be you." A delightful selection for reading aloud or for looking at over and over.

2004 Honors

NELSON, VAUNDA MICHEAUX. *Almost to Freedom.* **Illustrated by Colin Bootman.** Carolrhoda, 2003. Gr. 1–3.

Painted against a stark background, each scene in this poignant story interprets a part of the author's historically based telling of the African American slave's constant quest for freedom. The narrator is a tiny homemade doll who, although her face remains expressionless, through Bootman's use of brush and palette, emanates an aura of response and interaction. As the drama unfolds, the visuals capture the many moods surrounding the events in the escape attempt: the catalyst, the merciless beating of an innocent child; the compassion shown by a comforting parent; the daub of yellow paint representing a light in a distant window, the sign of a place of safety; and the pathos and determination of those huddled together in the last steps of their perilous journey. The use of muted colors in the clothing of each character, coupled with the carefully designed body positions of each, sustain the tension of the story from its very beginning. Then, in keeping with the comforting surprise ending of the story and in contrast to the muted tones that prevail in the solemn early parts of the narration, the artist clothes the newest owner of the homemade doll in a dress of brilliant sunshine yellow.

This award-winning book is a most satisfying and seamless blend of word and illustration.

NOLEN, JERDINE. *Thunder Rose.* **Illustrated by Kadir Nelson.** Whistle/Harcourt, 2003. Gr. K–3.

Jerdine Nolen wrote this original tall tale to celebrate African Americans who settled the American West. Kadir Nelson's illustrations capture the joy and the power of its young heroine. Using oil, watercolor, and pencil, Nelson depicts the storm that greets Rose's birth, the literally electrifying moment when the newborn girl grabs hold of a lightning bolt, and the family's love and wonder in the presence of their extraordinary child. Shades of brown and blue convey the closeness of Thunder Rose's family and the endless western skies under which they live. Nelson is especially successful in creating expressive characters. Readers will laugh at a startled cow being suckled by the infant girl and sense Rose's strength as she wrestles steer to the ground. Whether Rose is surveying the parched land or taming a tornado, Nelson's illustrations depict a spunky, endearing child with larger-than-life powers.

2004 John Steptoe Award for New Talent

COX, JUDY. *My Family Plays Music.* **Illustrated by Elbrite Brown.** Holiday House, 2003. Gr. Pre-K–3.

Clang the cymbals, tap the triangle, ring the handbell, shake the tambourine, dance in the street! Executed with brilliantly colored cut-paper figures, the artwork of this book invites one and all to celebrate the joys of music that ranges from classical string quartets to bluegrass to modern jazz and much more.

Brown's illustrations capture the exuberance of a multiethnic group of people sharing the joy and universality of harmonious sound. The creatively prolific use of rounded lines depicting characters and instruments, set against an uncluttered background, extends this merry tale. The simplicity of the instruments played by the always identifiable protagonist with her well-tended cornrow braids is an invitation for readers to make their own music. Colorful mini-reproductions of the music scenes add visual interest to the book's informative glossary. This book is a visual treat that sings and dances from cover to cover.

2003 Winner

GRIMES, NIKKI. *Talkin' About Bessie: The Story of Aviator Elizabeth Coleman.* **Illustrated by E. B. Lewis.** Orchard, 2002. Gr. 2–5. *

E. B. Lewis's watercolors illustrate Nikki Grimes's poetic prose and free verse to portray the life of the first female pilot of African American descent and one of America's most daring barnstormers. The format chosen has Coleman's friends and relatives gathered at Bessie's death to reminisce about her life. For each speaker, Lewis has painted a small sepia portrait and a full-page representation of the speaker's recollections. His water-saturated colors and limited palette—predominantly browns, blues, and greens—hint at the photographs of an earlier time. As the mourners gather, Bessie watches, smiling from a photograph on the mantel. By placing a mirror behind the photograph, Lewis makes room for the reader to join the gathering. Expressive compositions and careful choice of details contribute to the narrative power of the illustrations. In one scene, Bessie hangs laundry on the line, but large and in the foreground are jars in which she is saving precious coins for her education. In another scene, a bigoted white woman recalls Bessie's assertiveness. Lewis shows Bessie and the woman holding tight to a laundry basket. The tension in their grip is a mark of Bessie's strength and determination. From the close-up portrait of Bessie on the cover to the soaring plane in the book's final scene, Lewis's illustrations convey the struggles and triumphs of Bessie Coleman's life. The authenticity of clothing, artifacts, and settings are based on Lewis's careful research of the period in which Coleman lived (1896–1926).

2003 Honors

PERDOMO, WILLIE. *Visiting Langston.* **Illustrated by Bryan Collier.** Henry Holt, 2002. Gr. 2–4 *

Visiting Langston takes Collier to the streets of his Harlem neighborhood to celebrate the centennial of Renaissance poet Langston Hughes's birth. A smiling young girl, her writing journal held close to her heart, goes with her father to visit the house where Hughes wrote "poems like jazz," "sang like love," and "cried like blues." The artist's signature watercolors and cut-paper collage provide texture and detail for Perdomo's poetic text. As the words sing of "what Africa means to me," our young girl gazes out her window at a sky that takes on the shape of that continent. The creative inclusion of an old-fashioned typewriter, the use of a technique that gives texture to the brownstone stoop, the painting of airy green leaves, and the use of fabric patterns blend seamlessly to give visibility to a now gone time. The positioning of father and daughter in each scene, like an ode to love, speaks convincingly of the warm relationship they share as together they experience the pride and joy of a young African American girl's visit to the home of her literary hero.

DILLON, LEO, AND DIANE DILLON. *Rap a Tap Tap: Here's Bojangles—Think of That!* Blue Sky Press/Scholastic, 2002. Gr. Pre-K—2.

Rap a Tap Tap is the delicious sound tapped out by Mr. Bill "Bojangles" Robinson for city children, park-sitting parents, folk making a living through small businesses, poor people waiting at soup kitchens, and dressed-up ladies and gentlemen.

As Bill "Bojangles" dances through the pages, readers get a view of city life—the overhead trains, street vendors' vegetable carts, high rises, and even rainy-day parades.

Each new page shows the dancer in a different position so that the viewer gets a sense of the almost perpetual motion that was one of the hallmarks of this talented performer. Robinson's figure, painted in tones of brown and gray, moves gracefully against a sparkling white background. But Robinson is not dancing alone. In the background of each scene, like ones following a pied piper, a colorfully dressed ethnic mix of joyous people of all ages is seen swinging to the moves of this high-stepping dancer. With their impeccable skill, Leo and Diane Dillon have seamlessly woven into this story biographical matter and social commentary.

While enjoying the rap-a-tap rhyme or studying each distinctive illustration, one can hardly refrain from humming, "Think of that!"

Set in Robinson's hometown, Harlem, *Rap a Tap Tap* is a creative introduction to the art of a talented performer and a handsome book for readers of all ages.

2003 John Steptoe Award for New Talent

DuBURKE, RANDY. *The Moon Ring.* Chronicle, 2002. Gr. K–2.

With full-page illustrations in exuberant color, Randy DuBurke, author and illustrator, tells the story of Maxine, a young girl who feels the magic in the air as she sits on the porch with her grandmother on a hot summer night. It is the night of the blue moon, the second full moon in that month. The fun begins when Maxine finds a silver ring the size of a stove burner ring. She wishes the weather was cooler, and suddenly she's transported to the Antarctic. There the penguins teach her how to catch fish and show her the "right way to walk." Still holding the ring, she has a great ride on the back of a seal, but when she feels a little frightened she wishes she was "outa here." Just that quickly she finds herself riding a giraffe across the African savanna, accompanied by the seal and the penguin. Suddenly the group is attacked by a troop of lions and Maxine wishes she was far away in New York City—and there she is—atop the Empire State Building. The romp continues until Maxine finds herself back home and, in the morning at breakfast, trying to tell her family about her adventures. Of course the family decides it was either a dream or the product of a great imagination—that is, all except Grandma. Along with Maxine, Grandma saw the seal, the penguin, and the giraffe outside the kitchen window.

From the blue backgrounds to Grandma's blue shoes, Maxine's blue and white tennies, the silver ring, and Maxine's great goggle-eyed glasses, DuBurke's cartoonlike illustrations are filled with exaggerated shapes, sizes, and expressions. The approach is a perfect complement to this fancy-filled, magical tale. That Maxine is a lively, happy child is reflected in both the athleticism with which she moves and the joy-filled expressions on her face as she experiences her once-in-a-blue-moon adventure.

2002 Winner

McKISSACK, PATRICIA C. *Goin' Someplace Special.* **Illustrated by Jerry Pinkney.** Atheneum, 2001. Gr. K–5.

With watercolor over pencil illustrations, Jerry Pinkney brings warmth, movement, and vivid color to this story of a young girl on her first trip alone in the segregated southern town of Nashville. The accuracy of the clothing, hairstyles, and details on automobiles makes the 1950s setting come alive. It is the use of rich colors for 'Tricia Ann and those she loves, contrasting with the paler, more neutral shades used for people and the places around her, that help keep the reader focused. Full-page spreads are ingeniously designed to work well with text and provide a sense of movement on the journey. Advice and support from her friends help 'Tricia Ann to deal with the injustices imposed on her, with each advisor looking directly at her. The expressive faces of the characters during their conversations break the isolation that the Jim Crow laws attempt to impose. Pinkney uses composition and art to accentuate the strength, courage, and perseverance described in the text. The overlaid pencil strokes provide a remarkable floating quality to selected scenes, just as the lightness of the watercolors helps to keep the scenes unintimidating and reassures readers that arrival at "Someplace Special" will be safely accomplished. The yellow light glowing in the culminating scene highlighting the Nashville Public Library emphasizes the warmth of success and freedom achieved.

2002 Honor

RAPPAPORT, DOREEN. *Martin's Big Words: The Life of Dr. Martin Luther King, Jr.* **Illustrated by Bryan Collier.** Jump at the Sun/Hyperion Books for Children, 2001. Gr. K–2. *

The smiling, beckoning face of the Nobel Prize winner that dominates the book's cover seems to call to readers to open the pages. No identifying title is needed to proclaim the subject. Designed for young readers, Rappaport's brief, skillfully woven, carefully selected quotations present defining moments in Dr. King's life. Collier's watercolors and collage enhance the drama, devotion, and dedication of the man and his mission. Collier includes details from history in each piece of art. A Civil War flag hangs high as a young Martin points to the "white only" drinking fountain. A United Nations flag is held aloft during a civil rights march, symbolic of the worldwide struggle for equal rights. The American flag is front and center as two freedom marchers hold hands and Dr. King speaks during the March on Washington. A technique that produces images of light is another powerful element. Light shining through a stained-glass panel illuminates Dr. King's face as he preaches. The endpapers reflect stained-glass windows in vibrant shades that might seem to symbolize a world made up of the many colors of people. A small touch of white paint and one sees a votive candle being lit by a mother and daughter. The bright reds and oranges of fearful fire light the nights during the years of protest. Four white candles burn in memory of the little girls who perished in Alabama and the man who was killed in Memphis. Collier's work reflects his attention to all details of design and his strong feeling for his subject. His use of color and imagery have the power to linger in the mind's eye longer than the thousands of photographs that illustrate so many other titles.

2002 John Steptoe Award for New Talent

WILES, DEBORAH. *Freedom Summer.* **Illustrated by Jerome Lagarrigue.** Simon & Schuster, 2001. Gr. K–3.

An innovative use of color marks Jerome Lagarrigue's illustrations in this story based on the author's experience. The heat of the underlying golds, greens, and browns is reminiscent of a hot summer day. The cool shades of purple, pink, and blue add depth that matches the strong feeling evoked by the story of an integrated friendship in a segregated community. Joe and John Henry have shared summers together their whole lives but have had to adapt to stringent rules that govern the options for John Henry—just because of his color. At last, the courts have ruled that everything must be integrated. Emotional ups and downs are mirrored in the paintings' colors as well as in the expressions on the two boys' faces. Adults are mostly background figures, vague and somewhat blurry. The focus is on the boys. The illustrator captures with dramatic accuracy the way these young people cope with injustice. The resolution is as discomforting as it is realistic, but Lagarrigue's vibrant illustrations bring warmth and tenderness to the main characters without falsifying history.

2001 Winner

COLLIER, BRYAN. *Uptown.* Henry Holt, 2000. Gr. K–3.

On the title page, a confident young man stands poised to give readers a personal tour of the streets of Harlem. Collier, who lives and works in that community, uses watercolors and cut-page collage in vibrant colors and intriguing patterns to illustrate his own brief but lively text. In changing scenes, historic brownstone houses are fashioned from chocolate bars, shoppers wear richly textured African fabrics, Van DerZee photographs are displayed on building walls, and young girls in Sunday finery walk to church. The sounds of jazz and the Boys Choir of Harlem fill "Harlem . . . Harlem is my World." The reds, yellows, greens, and blues used to letter the title and text cheerfully complement the multileveled but very accessible design.

Young readers will respond to this proud and loving tribute that portrays a community alive with music, food, faith, and art.

2001 Honors

ROCKWELL, ANNE. *Only Passing Through: The Story of Sojourner Truth.* **Illustrated by R. Gregory Christie.** Random House, 2000. Gr. 3–5. *

Distinctively Negroid features, rendered with respect and sensitivity, distinguish the African American characters in this young readers' edition of the life of Sojourner Truth. When viewing Christie's illustrations, the first thing one notices is the emphasis on the characters' heads, heads that are large, atop elongated bodies. When asked about this particular trait, the illustrator's quiet reply was, "I focus on the head because that is where the mind is." Close study of the facial expressions of the slave owners and those they would keep in bondage reveals a solid contrast of evil versus good. Somber tones of brown, black, and terra-cotta dominate the pages as one traces Sojourner Truth's heroic journey from slavery to freedom.

RAPPAPORT, DOREEN. *Freedom River.* **Illustrated by Bryan Collier.** Jump at the Sun/Hyperion Books for Children, 2000. Gr. 3–5. *

Based on a true event, *Freedom River* is the inspiring story of John Parker, one of the conductors on the Underground Railroad. He leads a family to freedom across the Ohio River from Kentucky to Ohio. Parker, born a slave, after buying his freedom, repeatedly risks his life to help others. For one journey, he must sneak into the slaveholder's bedroom, where Isaac and Sarah's baby slept at night. This arrangement was planned to thwart the parents' desire to flee. The escape, though filled with danger, is successful. Rappaport's text conveys a sense of intense anxiety. Collier uses cut-paper collage and watercolors as perfect accompaniments to the mood. Intense shades of purple and blue are used in the nighttime scenes. The endpapers show a map of the route along the Ohio River. A special feature of the book's design can be seen in the portraits of the ancestors who provided spiritual guidance to African Americans. Collier used the leaders of his church as models and adorned their photographs with wavy lines representing the undulating motion of the river to freedom.

HOWARD, ELIZABETH. *Virgie Goes to School with Us Boys.* **Illustrated by E. B. Lewis.** Simon & Schuster, 2000. Gr. K–2.

Lewis's expressive full-page watercolors capture the greens and browns of the rural setting for this true story of a family's quest for education and its availability at the Quaker-run Warner Institute in Jonesborough, Tennessee.

The illustrator masterfully contrasts the starkness of the family's living conditions in their drab brown cabin with the brightening hues on the clothing of both the boys and Virgie as they take the long walk to school. One cannot miss the slight touch of humor as a mud-splattered Virgie smiles after falling into a creek that lies along the way. The seemingly limitless length of dark trees and the road that has neither beginning nor end evoke the distance the young people must travel in their quest for an education. To suggest the time period, Lewis uses special touches of paint to illustrate the quill pen, the slate, and the rough-hewn desk and benches. In the final picture, Virgie's sparkling eyes and infectious smile perfectly capture the book's theme, the joy of "learning—to be free."

2000 Winner

SIEGELSON, KIM. *In the Time of the Drums.* **Illustrated by Brian Pinkney.** Jump at the Sun/Hyperion Books for Children, 1999. Gr. 3–5.

"In the long ago time before now on an island fringed by marsh meadows and washed by ocean tides, men and women and their children lived enslaved." Thus begins Kim Siegelson's story inspired by Gullah oral traditions. It is the story of Twi, her grandson Mentu, and her magical escape from bondage. No more apt artist than Brian Pinkney could have illustrated the people who made goatskin drums to remind them of Mother Africa. Pinkney is an accomplished drummer, and the African drums he depicts are modeled on drums in his own collection. The swinging shapes of Pinkney's scratchboard illustrations capture Mentu's mischievousness, the ancient rhythms Twi taught him, and the churning waters into which Twi leads newly arrived Ibo slaves as they seek to return to their homeland. The harmonious colors of the illustrations, mainly greens, blues, browns, and yellows, depict the heat of the sun, the cool of the water, and the brown earth that the slaves "worked from dark of morning to dark of night, harvesting what they could not keep." As Mentu drummed with Twi until the rhythms felt as natural to him as his own heart beating, "the bronze color of the drums complement the beautiful bronze shades of their bodies." Near the book's end, Pinkney illustrates a calm sunset scene with Mentu watching a flock of birds rising from the water. The rising birds suggest the spirits of the slaves now free from bondage. The scene is an evocative prelude to the lively closing illustration in which a contemporary boy and girl play skin drums as Mentu taught his children "and they taught their own children . . . through slave time and freedom time and on up until now time."

2000 Honors

MOLLEL, TOLOLWA. *My Rows and Piles of Coins.* **Illustrated by E. B. Lewis.** Clarion, 1999. Gr. K–2.

Set in Tanzania in the 1960s, this story is based on events in the author's childhood. Young Saruni always helps his mother at the market, and on this particular day she gives him ten-cent coins to buy something for himself. While tempted by things like cake or a toy, he decides to use the money to buy a bicycle so that he can help his mother carry her products to market. As time passes, and with many mishaps, Saruni learns to ride a bicycle but finds out that the bicycle merchant has sold the bike he wanted. Finally, with help and understanding, he gets the transportation he needs to help his mother. As a fine end to the story, Saruni next dreams of saving enough money to buy a cart to pull behind the bicycle to further lighten his mother's load.

E. B. Lewis's expressive, full-color watercolor illustrations re-create the bustling activity of the Tanzanian marketplace and the village Saruni calls home. The pictures capture the hopes and feelings of the young boy as he works with his mother and as he practices riding a bike. One sees the pride with which Saruni walks through the marketplace, wearing the coat given him by his father, and the fright with which he struggles as he rides the bicycle with a pumpkin on his back to help him keep his balance. There is no guessing at the protective concern of both the mother and the father watching their son and at the final triumph as Saruni purchases his bicycle with his "rows and piles of coins." With deft touches of color, Lewis provides readers with a view not only of another culture but also of the universality of family love and appreciation.

MYERS, CHRISTOPHER. *Black Cat.* Scholastic, 1999. Gr. 3–6.

There is an unmistakable sense of independence in the way the sleek Black Cat walks the streets of Harlem, balancing faultlessly past empty bottles on an old brick wall or in quest of a mouse meal, challenging a subway as it races through its dark tunnel. Myers's innovative use of acrylics, collage, and photography invites readers to view Harlem from Black Cat's perspective, moving gracefully through the blur of rushing traffic or defying gravity while walking along the roof edges of dimly lit tenement houses. Myers captures the changing shapes of the cat as it squeezes through the crisscrosses of a fence to leap effortlessly through the bright orange basketball rim on a deserted court. At the close of the day, signaled by the changing blues of the evening sky, Black Cat, with defiant, fiery yellow eyes, seems to respond to the reader's question, "We want to know where's your home?" Black Cat answers, "Anywhere I roam."

The stalwart Black Cat's city journey is a masterful blend of poetry and picture.

1999 Winner

IGUS, TOYOMI. *I See the Rhythm.* **Illustrated by Michele Wood.** Children's Book Press, 1998. Gr. 3–5.

I See the Rhythm is a multilayered history of African American music that celebrates the far-reaching impact of this art form. The rich text includes words from songs of various eras, definitions of musical styles, and valuable chronological time lines. Vibrant, energetic, expressionistic paintings, blended with innovative fonts and creative page design, enrich this visual chronicle of African American music from the drumbeats of Africa to stirring gospel to the contemporary rhythms of funk, rap, and hip hop.

Wood's paintings mix a variety of styles and vivid colors to suggest musical style and tone. The illustrator has also incorporated much historical detail in her paintings, making them rich explorations of the text. The choice of colors and the variety in layout make this volume a feast for the eyes and drive home in a most dramatic fashion the importance, the depth, and the vitality of the musical forms that the work encompasses.

1999 Honors

THOMAS, JOYCE CAROL. *I Have Heard of a Land.* **Illustrated by Floyd Cooper.** HarperCollins, 1998. Gr. 3–6. *

Lush paintings on double-page spreads heighten the sense of place in this depiction of the historic land runs of the late 1800s. It was a time when black pioneer settlers were offered the freedom of land ownership in the Oklahoma Territory. The book especially honors the female participants who "dared to act on their dreams." This artistic rendering presents the vastness of the Oklahoma Territory and reflects the strength and determination of the African American pioneers.

The skillful use of light and color evokes a vivid picture of the character of the land. The rich earth tones perfectly fit the descriptions in the text. Artist Cooper is most successful in depicting the contrast between the great expanse of land and the individuals who sought to tame it as well as the connectedness between the land and those same individuals. With studied but not overworked detail, Cooper captures the challenge and spirit in the faces of the settlers he portrays. This illustrated history will bring to life for young readers a little-known aspect of African American history.

CURTIS, GAVIN. *The Bat Boy and His Violin.* **Illustrated by E. B. Lewis.** Simon & Schuster, 1998. Gr. 3–5.

Evocative watercolor paintings illuminate this warm family story set in the late 1940s. Music lover Reginald wants to practice his violin, but his dad, the manager of the Dukes of the Negro National League, needs a batboy. Despite the fact that Reginald is preparing for an upcoming concert, his dad insists that he accompany the team. However, Reginald finds a way while traveling with the team to pursue his first love—music—and at the same time lift the morale of the players.

E. B. Lewis's graceful watercolor paintings bring a special dimension to this unique story of intergenerational male bonding. The artist skillfully uses this technique to portray the time, the place, and the mood of the story. His careful attention to detail provides an authenticity that makes this book worthy of special attention. The almost delicate watercolor paintings provide an interesting backdrop to the masculinity of the baseball scenes and imply the gentle and sensitive nature of the men despite the physical nature of their game.

PINKNEY, ANDREA DAVIS. *Duke Ellington: The Piano Prince and His Orchestra.* Illustrated by Brian Pinkney. Hyperion Books for Children, 1998. Gr. 3–5. *

Andrea Davis Pinkney's rhythmic text and artist Brian Pinkney's vibrant illustrations trace Duke Ellington's career from his childhood as a reluctant piano student to his triumphant success as a composer and orchestra leader. The swirling patterns and pulsing colors of Brian Pinkney's illustrations capture the dynamism of Duke Ellington's music. The artist uses scratchboard renderings with dyes, gouache, and paint to make the text come alive. At times, the visuals are larger than life. The creative placement of figures on each page informs the reader of the important role that music played in Ellington's life. With the passage of time, Ellington's musical influence grew and expanded, and the artist shows this to the reader while the author explains it in the text.

Pinkney's use of line and color brings a vibrancy to the text that reflects the many moods of Ellington's music. His use of visuals and space, from the music exploding from the instruments right up to the A train seemingly riding off the page, will engage not only young readers but also music lovers of all ages.

1999 John Steptoe Award for New Talent

CHOCOLATE, DEBBI. *The Piano Man.* **Illustrated by Eric Velasquez.** Walker, 1998. Gr. K–2.

In this intergenerational story, a young girl tells, with great affection, the story of her grandfather, a musician who played the piano for many years. His love for music carried him from silent movies to vaudeville and finally to legitimate theater. When opportunities for performing were no longer available, he tuned pianos for a living, always passing on his love for music from era to era to his daughter and granddaughter.

Eric Velasquez's spirited paintings engage the reader and add life to the story. His clever illustrations begin with the closed curtain on the endpaper of the front cover and move to an open curtain on the title page. The animation in the faces transmits the exuberance the characters feel. Color choice is strong, and the effective use of light balances the many warm shades of brown.

1998 Winner

JAVAKA STEPTOE. *In Daddy's Arms I Am Tall: African Americans Celebrating Fathers.* Lee & Low, 1997. Gr. K–2.

With imagination and creativity Javaka Steptoe designed the illustrations in this eye-intriguing volume to complement poems by several poets writing in praise of fathers and fatherhood. The designs are developed from such three-dimensional objects as buttons, chalk, pieces of window screen, paper collages, and other materials, thus giving exciting life and color to the selected poems. Steptoe discusses the variety of images:

> Each of the poems was so different, and I wanted each to have its own individuality. And so each illustration invites you to take a second look, less some innovative detail be missed.

When speaking of the art in *In Daddy's Arms I Am Tall*, Steptoe says:

> I've thought about illustrating children's books all my life . . . [then] I was thinking a lot about my relationships with my father and ideas of manhood. I thought this would be the perfect book.

The four years that it took to complete this book attest to the seriousness with which Javaka Steptoe reflected on his relationship with his father, the late, great illustrator John Steptoe.

1998 Honors

BRYAN, ASHLEY. *Ashley Bryan's ABC of African American Poetry.* Atheneum, 1997. Gr. K–5.

Vivid tempera paintings, replete with significant symbolic information, grace the pages of this oversized volume. With care and focus, Bryan has selected the works of twenty-five African and African American poets and one ever popular spiritual to introduce the youth of all cultures to the strength and beauty of these writers' words. The moods vary from poignant to humorous to unforgettably thought provoking. In a masterful blend of sound and symbols, one sees and hears the breaking of the chains as Robert Hayden tells of Sojourner Truth walking barefoot out of slavery or God's laughter in Samuel Hayden's tribute in "Satch." Blazing firmaments, strength-filled dark eyes, love-filled brown faces of family, and the eloquent portrayal of the sturdy though time-worn face in Margaret Walker's tribute to grandmothers are just a few of the elements that showed the Coretta Scott King awards jury that this was an unforgettable collection worthy to be honored.

DIAKITÉ, BABA WAGUÉ. *The Hunterman and the Crocodile: A West African Folktale.* Scholastic, 1997. Gr. 3–5.

Bamba the crocodile and his family are on a pilgrimage to Mecca when they run out of food and water and plead with Donso the Hunterman to help them return home. After reluctantly agreeing, Donso is betrayed by Bamba, who threatens to eat him. From this beginning the reader is led into a tale of treachery—a reminder of humankind's selfish use of plants and animals. The tale underscores the importance of learning to live together in harmony.

Wagué Diakité has illustrated the storytelling with stylized, hand-painted tiles whose folkloric quality complement the text. Black figures cavort on a background of muted earth tones with subtle touches of color. The striking design of the book is evident in its interplay of decorative and representational elements, its rhythmic patterns, and its dynamic use of line. All of these features do much to extend this telling of a traditional tale. Although Wagué Diakité's work reflects his West African background, his playful illustrations are an expression of a unique artistic talent that reaches beyond all geographic boundaries.

MYERS, WALTER DEAN. *Harlem.* **Illustrated by Christopher Myers.** Scholastic, 1997. Gr. 6–8.

The community of Harlem has for decades served as a touchstone for numerous writers and visual artists. This father-and-son collaboration adds to that rich body of work. Christopher Myers portrays street scenes, rooftops, a church interior, the A train subway, fire escapes, nightclubs, a basketball court, living rooms, and individual people in single- and double-page spreads. His collages incorporate singular moments—hair braiding, hoop shooting, funerals, and neighbors chatting—vignettes of life in this vitality-filled community. Myers's mixed-media works illuminate the poetic history of the past and the present glories of Harlem's people, their music, and their art and literature, and provide a visual counterpoint to the lyrical poetry of his father. The original artwork from this oversized dynamic picture book of cultural history has been exhibited at the Studio Museum of Harlem on 125th Street.

1997 Winner

SCHROEDER, ALAN. *Minty: A Story of Young Harriet Tubman.* **Illustrated by Jerry Pinkney.** Dial, 1996. Gr. K–2.

Alan Schroeder's fictionalized account of young Harriet Tubman, who refused to be the "docile slave," provides the setting for Jerry Pinkney's dramatic visual interpretation of the vitality, determination, and ingenuity that marked this remarkable heroine's life. Careful research enabled this serious illustrator to depict authentic details about the dress, food, and living conditions of the plantation slaves. His own sensitivity, historical background, and passionate concern allowed Pinkney to portray in moving scenes the strength, courage, fears, and dangers young Harriet faced with unmitigated courage. Detailed watercolor spreads coupled with a master illustrator's use of space, color, and perspective provide scenes of cabin life, threatening forests, and the wild-eyed fear of the would-be runaway. The artistic attention given to all aspects of the story enrich this narration that introduces young readers to an unforgettable personality later known as the Moses of her people.

1997 Honors

ADEDJOUMA, DAVIDA, ED. *The Palm of My Heart: Poetry by African American Children.* **Illustrated by R. Gregory Christie.** Lee & Low, 1996. Gr. K–3.

African American young people who are a part of the Inner City Youth League wrote the stirring, pride-filled words that inspired Gregory Christie's illustrations in this very special collaboration. The artist's paintings capture the joy and exultation with which the young writers see their future. His depiction of a young lady on stilts raises a proud black girl to unknown heights even as she proclaims that "Black is me—Tall, dark and wonderful." In some scenes there is a sense of spirituality, such as in the image of a church that looks down protectively on a close-knit gathering. The writers honor the elders, and Christie's art gives visual reality to the honor in a simple cross-generational painting that says, indeed, that "Black power is . . . long life."

Christie's muted paintings, like a musical accompaniment, support and interpret but never overpower the lyrical writings of the young poets.

LAUTURE, DENIZÉ. *Running the Road to ABC.* **Illustrated by Reynold Ruffins.** Simon & Schuster, 1996. Gr. K–3.

Sparkling with life in both its text and its illustration, Running the Road to ABC imbues the reader with the joy of the desire for learning. The story, set in Haiti, tells of six children who rise before dawn and run through the beautiful countryside on their way to school. Ruffins's magnificent, brightly colored gouache illustrations complement Lauture's poetic text. His images capture many stories of the culture—a breakfast of cornmeal, yams, and perhaps some Congo beans; book bags made from palm leaves; and the simple, open-windowed schoolroom.

The pictures give one a sense of place as the illustrator uses the bright colors of the Caribbean to great effect. There is visual poetry as the paintings show first dawn in the village, stars still twinkling in the sky, the rooster sleeping while a mother bids her son good-bye on his way to ABC. From this beginning to the double-page illustration of the eager children watching attentively, paper and pencil in hand, this book sings with joy in words and pictures. Ruffins's paintings, filled with flora and fauna, frogs, snails, lizards, butterflies, donkeys, and gorgeously plumed birds, transport the reader to this tropic land. Through his use of varying perspectives and page design, shadow and light, and line and shape, the artist creates endlessly fascinating illustrations.

ENGLISH, KAREN. *Neeny Coming, Neeny Going.* **Illustrated by Synthia Saint James.** BridgeWater, 1996. Gr. K–3.

Karen English takes readers back to the 1950s, a time of change when residents of the Daufuskie Island left their homes to seek another way of life on the mainland. Young Essie awaits the return of her cousin Neeny, who was one who had left the island. Synthia Saint James has captured the bittersweet mood of Essie's excitement at the thought of Neeny's return, and the emptiness she feels because she realizes that Neeny, although physically there, has not really come back.

Flat collagelike illustrations portray life on the island: bogging for crabs, weaving baskets from sweetgrass, and picking blackberries. Simple features and bright shapes show Essie running excitedly through the island to tell of Neeny's return. With this same simplicity, Saint James illustrates the fading joy and the indignation and sadness as Neeny says good-bye. Readers will find particular significance in the memory quilt Essie gives Neeny on Neeny's departure. Words and pictures in Neeny Coming, Neeny Going convey to the reader a culturally specific place and a part of the African American experience that has a sense of universality.

1996 Winner

FEELINGS, TOM. *The Middle Passage: White Ships/Black Cargo.* Dial, 1995. Gr. 9–12. *

More than thirty years ago a Ghanaian friend of Tom Feelings asked him what had happened to blacks when they were taken away from Africa to American slavery. The way to express the horror of that experience came to the artist some years later while he was living in Guyana. However, he felt he could not realize his vision without returning to the United States, where he would have to confront the pain that is so much a part of the African American experience. As Feelings read about the slave trade, he saw that "callous indifference or outright brutal characterizations of Africans are embedded in the language of the Western World." He was determined to tell the story with as few words as possible. Feelings moved back to New York City, where he completed the preliminary drawings in two and a half years. It took almost twenty years more to revise the images so they would speak with the honesty and passion he had intended.

Feelings created a series of illustrations that eloquently describe the capture of slaves in Africa and their horrendous trip across the Atlantic to America. *The Middle Passage* opens with a sun-filled African landscape. In successive images Feelings depicts the forced march of captured slaves, the violence and claustrophobia of slave ships, and the desperate and futile attempts to escape the ships by diving into the shark-infested waters. Powerful bodies of black slaves stand out against the ghostly forms of their white tormentors. Swirling shapes echo howls of despair and yearnings for freedom.

In the introduction Feelings writes that it was while he was living in Ghana that his "drawings became more fluid and flowing. Rhythmic lines of motion, like a drumbeat, started to appear in my work, and a style that incorporated a dance consciousness surfaced." This style makes more palpable, perhaps, the horror of *The Middle Passage*. The images, executed in pen and ink and tempera on rice paper, are meticulously reproduced in tritone, using two black inks and one gray, plus a neutral press varnish. The care with which this oversized volume was published does honor to Feelings's work.

In completing *The Middle Passage*, Feelings expressed the hope that "those chains of the past, those shackles that physically bound us together against our wills could, in the telling, become spiritual links that willingly bind us together now and into the future."

1996 Honors

HAMILTON, VIRGINIA. *Her Stories: African American Folktales, Fairy Tales, and True Tales.* **Illustrated by Leo Dillon and Diane Dillon.** Scholastic, 1995. Gr. 5–8.

The paintings that illustrate *Her Stories* capture the mood of each female-oriented tale, with meticulous attention shown to the details needed to give visual vitality to this superb collection. One cannot miss the crafty eyes in the diminutive rabbit in "Little Girl and Buh Rabby." The mermaid with stringy, vinelike hair does indeed float in a jar of green water. Note how menacing the eerie, cold-green, chiseled-tooth, wart-faced hag is that rides Marie's back in "Marie and the Boo Hag." By contrast, there is the quiet dignity of reality in the portraits of the women in the biographical section. The reader's eye will respond to the art of the award-winning Dillons, even as the ear responds to the words of *Her Stories*.

SAN SOUCI, ROBERT. *The Faithful Friend.* **Illustrated by Brian Pinkney.** Simon & Schuster, 1995. Gr. K–4.

Set on the island of Martinique, Robert San Souci's story of two faithful friends, one white and one black, is replete with elements of the area's culture: magic, zombies, dark forces, and romance. Brian Pinkney's specialized scratchboard technique, enriched with touches of oil-paint colors, captures the changing moods of the story. Dramatic moments from the narrative come to life when the artist shows the faithful Hippolyte slowly turned to stone through the magic of the zombies. The zombies are formidable figures in their dark clothing, weaving their spells in the gloom of the tropical landscape. In contrast, the illustrator shows the delicate texture of the young bride's dress at her marriage to Clement. One can almost feel the material of the clothing of other characters. Through the drawings of the furnishings in the home, scenery in the lush tropical landscape, and small details of facial expressions and body language, the illustrator displays his skill in putting into visual perspective the words of the story.

1995 Winner

JOHNSON, JAMES WELDON. *The Creation.* **Illustrated by James E. Ransome.** Holiday House, 1994. Gr. K–3.

A tribute to the ageless quality of James Weldon Johnson's poetic narration of the creation of the world is captured in a dramatic contemporary setting especially appropriate for today's youth. James Ransome, reflecting the power of oral tradition, portrays a wise and warm storyteller sharing the events with a rapt audience of young people. The illustrator gives life to the stirring words with tones of color and a use of perspective that interprets the vastness of God's world and the move from emptiness to inhabitation. The lyrical beauty of the words is enhanced by the surrounding borders that depict the step-by-step development of the sermon until the dramatic moment when "man became a living soul" whose very physique exudes strength and purpose.

1994 Winner

FEELINGS, TOM. *Soul Looks Back in Wonder.* Dial, 1993. Gr. 3–5.

To convey the joy, beauty, and challenge of being African American, Tom Feelings invited African American poets to contribute original poems to accompany his paintings. A never-before-published poem by Langston Hughes is also included. Using a variety of techniques and mixed media, such as collage, color crayon, and wallpaper, Feelings has created a book that is captivating to the eye and musical to those who listen. The artist offers striking images of copper-colored boys and girls, children with beautiful dark faces—the youth this book was designed to inspire. In this, the artist's first book done in color throughout, the predominant colors are the blended and textured blues, greens, and browns of Feelings's beloved Mother Africa. Brief biographical sketches of each of the contributing poets are included.

1994 Honors

THOMAS, JOYCE CAROL. *Brown Honey in Broomwheat Tea.* **Illustrated by Floyd Cooper.** HarperCollins, 1993. Gr. 3–5.

The striking paintings of African Americans in *Brown Honey in Broomwheat Tea* give dramatic visualization to Joyce Carol Thomas's provocative poetry. Stirring examples of this visual feast can be seen in the strength and dignity of the white-haired elder's face when sipping broomwheat tea, in the artist's interpretation of the African American lineage as generations rise from the interwoven roots of a sturdy tree, and in the trusting face of the child who asks that "as you would cherish a thing of beauty, cherish me."

A touch of sunshine yellow illuminates some part of each page—symbolic of the light of hope that is the strength of the African American race. Cooper's art reveals a sensitivity to Thomas's words, resulting in a book that in word and picture is a celebration of African American life.

1995 Honors

GRIMES, NIKKI. *Meet Danitra Brown.* **Illustrated by Floyd Cooper.** Lothrop, Lee, & Shepard, 1994. Gr. 3–5.

Danitra Brown is an exuberant, spunky, self-assured young person. Through Nikki Grimes's poetry Danitra expresses her "philosophy" on the importance of exposure to things of culture, how to react to those who try to "put you down," the beauty of blackness, and other important facts of life. Floyd Cooper's illustrations capture Danitra's energy in images of her often leaping into the air, engaging in spirited dancing, and, in pensive moments, with a sense of life and well-being in her sparkling eyes shining through black-rimmed glasses. Cooper consistently dresses Danitra in tones of her favorite color—purple—sometimes stripes, sometimes plaids, sometimes plain, but always purple. The illustrator symbolically uses muted tones of brown for the background as well as for the skin tones of the characters in the poetry. The words and pictures reveal Danitra Brown through wise and joyful animation—"the greatest and most splendiferous girl in town."

MEDEARIS, ANGELA SHELF. *The Singing Man.* **Illustrated by Terea Shaffer.** Holiday House, 1994. Gr. 3–5.

The Singing Man is a folktale that lauds the importance of the griot, or praise singer, whose responsibility it is to preserve and pass on the stories of Africa's glorious history—the achievements of its rulers, artisans, and scholars. Terea Shaffer's rich oil paintings not only add drama to the story but also give visualization to the diversity of the people in Nigerian regions as readers travel with the praise singer, Banzar, and his teacher Sholo. The sun-baked lands over which they travel, the variations in clothing design, the facial features that distinguish one group of people from another, and the musical instruments that were used to tell the griot's stories are caught in the expressive, informative illustrations that give life to an age-old tale.

MITCHELL, MARGAREE KING. *Uncle Jed's Barbershop.* **Illustrated by James E. Ransome.** Simon & Schuster, 1993. Gr. 3–5.

Set in the rural South, *Uncle Jed's Barbershop* is a story about holding fast to a dream in spite of seemingly overwhelming obstacles. Uncle Jed's goal in life was to own his own barbershop with four chairs, mirrors, sinks with running water, and a red and white barber pole on the outside. Beset by the Depression, bank failures, and prejudice, Uncle Jed is forced to defer his dream. Finally, at age seventy-nine, he opens his barbershop to the delight of all who were his "customers" over the years.

James Ransome's paintings, full of vibrant colors, capture the moods and extend the text of Mitchell's story. Uncle Jed is a sturdy man, cheerful and undefeated. He is surrounded by a warm and smiling family. The homestead is a picture of care and neatness. One can observe the artist's attention to historical accuracy in the paintings of the potbellied stove, the crystal-set radio, the oval rag rug—all typical of the era in which the story is set. Ransome's use of circular lines in the rotund bodies of many of the characters, the furniture, the oval mirrors in the barbershop, and even the round aftershave tonic bottles on the shelf impart emotions of joy.

Ransome pays a tribute to his mentor, the artist Jerry Pinkney, by including a character that resembles Pinkney in the picture of the people who cared about and supported Uncle Jed in his quest.

1993 Winner

ANDERSON, DAVID A. *The Origin of Life on Earth: An African Creation Myth.* **Illustrated by Kathleen Atkins Wilson.** Sights, 1991. Gr. K–5.

The Origin of Life on Earth is a Yoruba legend of how the world began. Kathleen Atkins Wilson saw in the story a moving part of her own heritage. With breathtaking skill she used her distinctive style of portraying "silhouette expressions of portraits in black" to translate the story into a visual "telling." As the Coretta Scott King awards jury looked at this book, they felt wonderment at how many details of the text were expanded in the illustrations. There was the care of detailing the stages in the molding of each figure and the quiet respect for the shapes of the disabled—representing the orisha Obatala's moment of drunken weakness. And what a contrast between the distinctive and expressive features of the silhouetted story characters and the luminous clothing in which they are garbed! Wilson's unique artistic style gives unforgettable life to a well-told story that shouts her joy and pride in her African heritage.

1993 Honors

WILLIAMS, SHERLEY ANNE. *Working Cotton.* **Illustrated by Carole Byard.** Harcourt Brace Jovanovich, 1992. Gr. Pre-K–3.

Double-page spreads illustrated in acrylics with mottled hues set the mood in this powerful visual rendition of a day in the life of a black migrant family. As the day unfolds through the voice and eyes of young Shelan, Byard depicts the strength of this family through large close-up images and lush colors. The beauty of the illustrations never softens the powerful images of work and struggle that are conveyed in the text. We see the immensity of the cotton fields and the strain of hard work, yet the tenderness of the expressions reminds us of the power of love and family as the summer heat heightens weariness. It is a celebration of strength in an unjust world that makes such strength necessary to survive.

WAHL, JAN. *Little Eight John.* **Illustrated by Wil Clay.** Lodestar, 1992. Gr. K–2.

Little Eight John, a familiar character in African American folklore, is an extremely handsome young fellow but just as naughty as he is good looking. Wil Clay has captured every nuance of this mischievous child's behavior in what seem like double-vision settings. When the text speaks of one of Eight John's tricks, which causes his mother to have the hiccups, the illustration creates an illusion of movement similar to seasickness. When Eight John is admonished not to sit backward in a chair, the chair suddenly becomes a horse being whipped into frenzied action by the overactive boy. Wahl's adaptation of this popular story has a happy ending, which Clay captures in the affectionate scene between a relieved mother and a repentant Little Eight John. For a visual treat, readers will enjoy examining each picture for the details that tell so much more of the story.

SAN SOUCI, ROBERT. *Sukey and the Mermaid.* **Illustrated by Brian Pinkney.** Four Winds, 1992. Gr. 3–5

With his scratchboard technique, Brian Pinkney has captured many subtle nuances that give an added dimension to San Souci's interpretation of this tale from the folklore of South Carolina. Using gentle touches of color, Pinkney brings the figures to life in true character—the darkness of the evil father, the emerald sea colors of the mermaid, and the childlike pink in the clothing of the beleaguered young Sukey, who is abused by her greedy father. A closer look shows that the artist is also attentive to such tiny details as the part in Sukey's hair or the wisps of smoke from the father's pipe. The skillful blend of words and pictures assures the reader that *Sukey and the Mermaid* is a story to be read, to be told, and to be looked at over and over.

1992 Winner

RINGGOLD, FAITH. *Tar Beach.* Crown, 1991. Gr. K–3.

Faith Ringgold is an artist. Faith Ringgold is a quilter. With her creative ingenuity, Ringgold weaves a wonderful story of hope, dreams, and dauntless courage stitched with the innocence of childhood. The reader meets Cassie Louise Lightfoot as she spends a hot summer evening on the roof of the apartment house—the city child's "tar beach." Looking at the sky, Cassie flies over a world in which her talented father will be able to work on tall buildings because, even though he is black, he will be able to join the union. She sees her family with enough income so that her hardworking mother will be able to sleep late some mornings. Then, with a mood swing that is a natural part of childhood, Cassie dreams of having ice cream for dessert every night because she will own the Ice Cream Factory. On all her imaginary travels she takes her little brother BeBe and all who read this thoughtful picture book. The choice of colors and patterns for the material in the *Tar Beach* quilt and the arrangement of figures in the various scenes offer both a feast for the eye and food for thought.

In addition to winning the Coretta Scott King Book Award, Faith Ringgold received Caldecott honors for this, her first picture book.

1992 Honors

BRYAN, ASHLEY. *All Night, All Day: A Child's First Book of African-American Spirituals.* Atheneum, 1991. Gr. Pre-K–5.

More than once Ashley Bryan has voiced his concern that young African Americans and other youth are not being exposed to the melodic beauty and the historical significance of Negro spirituals. *All Night, All Day* is one of several books that this artist and scholar has designed to make the words and the music of the spirituals accessible and aesthetically pleasing to young audiences.

Bryan uses tints and shades of tempera colors to illustrate the changing moods of the twenty titles included in this collection. Bright yellow glimmers in the abstract candles in "This Little Light of Mine," and swirling blues and sea greens wash around brown-hued feet in "Wade in the Water." And one cannot miss the joyous, repetitious, double-page spread of the huge bells accompanying the spiritual "Peter, Go Ring the Bells."

At the 1992 Coretta Scott King Book Awards breakfast there was an unforgettable moment of silence when, as his acceptance "speech" for this honor book, Ashley Bryan played the title piece, "All Night, All Day," on his recorder. Bryan has given us a book and an experience to be remembered for many nights and many days.

GREENFIELD, ELOISE. *Night on Neighborhood Street.* **Illustrated by Jan Spivey Gilchrist.** Dial, 1991. Gr. K–3.

Jan Spivey Gilchrist's use of warm shading together with blue, gold, and green clearly illustrates the characters portrayed in Eloise Greenfield's warm and delightful poetry. The expressions on the faces of the children and adults and the subtle use of body language complement and enhance the author's beautiful and expressive poetry. The visual impact is intensified by the artist's use of silhouette and shadings of black and white. Given that the passage of time plays a strong role in the book, Gilchrist's use of light and shadow to denote the time of day is impressive, and such details as curtains blowing as night approaches set a mood and enhance the overall effect.

Evidence of complete communication between writer and artist can be seen in how the words and the pictures evoke visual images that change with each poem. The children's faces show adoration, mischievousness, apprehension, fear, sadness, or grief as called for by the corresponding poems. The adults, even when captured only in shadow or silhouette, convey movement and emotion. A fine example of this is the piece "In the Church." The interaction between children and adults is well presented in such pieces as "Goodnight Juma," "Fambly Time," and "The Seller." Night on Neighborhood Street is a magnificent creation of mystical appearances through the use of color, light, and shading.

1991 Winner

PRICE, LEONTYNE, ADAPT. *Aïda.* **Illustrated by Leo Dillon and Diane Dillon.** Harcourt Brace Jovanovich, 1990. Gr. 3–8.

Upon opening the pages of *Aïda*, one stands in the entrance of a mighty palace whose marble halls invite the viewer to participate in a breathtaking artistic experience. Leo and Diane Dillon, inspired by the voice of Leontyne Price singing the title role of *Aïda*, knew that the diva's adaptation of this tragic opera was a book they were meant to illustrate. Each bordered, full-page illustration reveals some aspect of a palace of ancient Egypt, the powerful Egypt that existed as a seat of learning and a source of inspiration to the Greeks who followed in the Egyptians' wake. Although the layperson may not understand the artists' technical approach, the dedication to honesty in the portrayal of the characters, their clothing, the setting in which they functioned, and the grandeur of the period is clearly visible. One feels the texture of the robes. One senses the gigantic size of the temple gods and the strength of the supporting palace columns. The Dillons have taken care to give individuality to the face of each character in the huge and diverse cast of this tragic drama. As if this were not enough, the Dillons' creativity extends to the friezes across the top of the page—a pageant of Egyptian personages adds to the visualization of the text. The depth of the Dillons' research reflects their commitment to providing an accurate picture of the dignity of an ancient and learned people. *Aïda* is a story of warring factions, unrequited love, and, finally, the fatal price of loyalty. *Aïda* is a book that will be opened over and over, and each time the viewer will enjoy a new artistic experience.

1990 Winner

GREENFIELD, ELOISE. *Nathaniel Talking.* **Illustrated by Jan Spivey Gilchrist.** Black Butterfly Children's Books, 1988. Gr. K–5.

Jan Spivey Gilchrist uses only black-and-white pencil sketches to portray a wide range of emotions—sadness, grief, joy, pensiveness—that are the themes of some of Eloise Greenfield's poems. In "My Daddy," Nathaniel's face shows us he is completely at one with his father's music and secure in his father's love for him. Nathaniel says, "He ain't never been on TV, but to me he's a big star." There is sadness in Nathaniel's face as he sits in his room, thinking about his mama, who died last year. But one perceives a source of comfort in the shadowed figure of the father entering his son's room. Pictures in close harmony with the words demonstrate the artist's sensitivity as she depicts events in the life of the spunky Nathaniel and his friends. Gilchrist clearly understands all the nuances in Greenfield's poetry and interprets the poems with clarity and a warmness of spirit.

1990 Honor

SAN SOUCI, ROBERT D., RETELLER. *The Talking Eggs.* **Illustrated by Jerry Pinkney.** Dial, 1989. Gr. K–5.

A Creole folktale from the southern U.S. oral tradition, *The Talking Eggs* features two sisters: a favored, spoiled, and lazy girl named Rose and a generous, kind, and a hard-working girl named Blanche. The girls are given identical tasks by a mysterious woman in the woods, and Blanche is rewarded for her trust and obedience. This beautifully designed and printed version of a folktale previously known to many in its Anglo-European variant features African American characters wonderfully realized by Jerry Pinkney. His drawing and painting show fresh observations of people and of the animal world. They embody a richness of detail and motion that is harmonious with the tale's idiom, time, and place. In addition to being a Coretta Scott King honor book, *The Talking Eggs* was a Caldecott honor book.

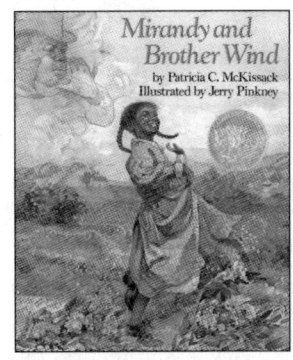

1989 Winner

McKISSACK, PATRICIA C. *Mirandy and Brother Wind.* **Illustrated by Jerry Pinkney.** Knopf, 1988. Gr. K–5.

Mirandy overlooks her obvious partner for her first cakewalk after she brags that she will be accompanied by the wind himself and sets out to catch her partner. The engaging full-color paintings are filled with historical details of African American life in the rural South at the turn of the century. They perfectly interpret and enhance the lighthearted exuberance inherent in the story and memorably characterize the pride, self-confidence, and determination of Mirandy.

1989 Honors

STOLZ, MARY. *Storm in the Night.* **Illustrated by Pat Cummings.** Harper & Row, 1988. Gr. Pre-K–3.

Grandfather's lively recollection about his own childhood fear of a thunderstorm occupies young Thomas's attention during an electrical power failure and helps the boy overcome his worries. A visual story-within-a-story assists readers with the flashbacks. Cummings's ability to challenge the eye with color and perspective is as effective as her poignant portrayal of the African American grandfather and grandson inside their cozy single-family home on a rainy summer night.

GREENFIELD, ELOISE. *Under the Sunday Tree.* **Illustrated by Mr. Amos Ferguson.** Harper & Row, 1988. Gr. K–6.

Twenty exquisite paintings introduce children to the artwork of the Bahamian artist Mr. Amos Ferguson. The playfully vivid paintings, which boldly depict aspects of life in the Bahamas, have great child appeal. Poet Eloise Greenfield has written poems to accompany every painting, further extending each painting's mood and meaning.

1988 Winner

STEPTOE, JOHN. *Mufaro's Beautiful Daughters: An African Tale.* Lothrop, Lee, & Shepard, 1987. Gr. K–5.

Two beautiful sisters—one vain, the other kind—compete for the king's attention when he announces he is looking for a wife. Brilliant full-color paintings illustrate the classic tale of just rewards. The artist skillfully uses light and color to give emotional power to illustrations that richly detail the natural beauty of a specific region in Zimbabwe.

1988 Honors

LANGSTAFF, JOHN, COMPOSER. *What a Morning! The Christmas Story in Black Spirituals.* **Illustrated by Ashley Bryan.** Margaret K. McElderry, 1987. Gr. K–6.

The Christmas story is told through a chronological arrangement of five African American spirituals, lavishly illustrated by brilliant tempera paintings. Brief biblical quotes accompanying each of the spirituals provide a religious context, while Bryan's shining iconographic portraits of a black Nativity provide a historical, geographical, and emotional context.

ROHMER, HARRIET, OCTAVIO CHOW, AND MORRIS VIDAURE. *The Invisible Hunters: A Legend from the Miskito Indians of Nicaragua / Los Cazadores Invisibles: Una Leyenda de los Indios Miskitos de Nicaragua.* **Illustrated by JoeSam.** Children's Book Press, 1987.

An early Central American legend tells of the ultimate price of greed as well as the tragedy of deceiving one's own people. Themes concerning colonialism are developed in colorful, unique paper constructions and collages.

1987 Winner

DRAGONWAGON, CRESCENT. *Half a Moon and One Whole Star.* **Illustrated by Jerry Pinkney.** Macmillan, 1986. Gr. Pre-K–3.

Half a Moon and One Whole Star is a lullaby that invites the reader to share in the safety of untroubled sleep. It is the song of man and of creature and their different activities as the sun goes down. It is as if Pinkney were an unseen observer in the actions of each character in this gentle story. One sees the brightly colored parrots "rest in jungles deep." And at the same time Pinkney takes the reader with him to see "Johnny with his saxophone" standing against an early night sky, Johnny who will play at the club at night. And while the activities are either stopping or starting, with mood-setting colors the illustrator introduces the reader to the child who at the end of the day is lulled to untroubled sleep. In a blend of words and pictures the reader, too, can sing of the night that is marked with *Half a Moon and One Whole Star.*

1987 Honors

BRYAN, ASHLEY. *Lion and the Ostrich Chicks: And Other African Folk Tales.* Atheneum, 1986. Gr. K–6.

Using his special talent for blending rhythmic word patterns with all the details of a well-told story, Bryan has adapted a diverse collection of African tales that beg to be read aloud. Through his research into the history and culture of several tribes, this author-illustrator found the roots of the stories in many geographical regions and, in his inimitable writing style, retold the tales for young readers. Complete scholar that he is, Bryan has included a bibliography listing his sources for all the stories in the book.

One cannot miss the folktale concept of the triumph of good over evil, whether it is in the title story, in which the lion tries to claim the ostrich chicks as his own, or in a telling of how the born-foolish boy outwits the trickster Ananse.

Bryan extends the text with his own art prints in sharp black-and-white figures or in illustrations using the earth colors of the land in which the tales are set. The Coretta Scott King awards jury enjoyed both the humor and the lessons in *Lion and the Ostrich Chicks.*

CUMMINGS, PAT. *C.L.O.U.D.S.* Lothrop, Lee, & Shepard, 1986. Gr. 3–5.

In a flight of fancy Cummings lets readers share in an imaginary trip to an artist's studio where the painter hopes to see exciting new colors spring from his palette. Chuku is a painter for Creative Lights Opticals and Unusual Designs in the Sky. His excitement about a new assignment fades when he is sent to paint the sky over New York City and to produce rigid and realistic interpretations. But his creativity is not to be thwarted. Each day he draws sky pictures in unusual colors and intriguing cloud shapes. There are Lovely Light Lavender sunsets, Cloud-Lining Silver, and Unbelievingly Brilliant Gold. The clouds take the shapes of tigers, giraffes, and birds, all of which are done especially for a little girl, Chrissy, the only one in New York who ever seems to look up.

But all readers who see Chuku's figures in *C.L.O.U.D.S.* will find themselves looking for colorful skies in New York and elsewhere. They may even look for a real Chuku, who is a very purple young man.

1986 Winner

FLOURNOY, VALERIE. *The Patchwork Quilt.* **Illustrated by Jerry Pinkney.** Dial, 1985. Gr. Pre-K–3.

The Patchwork Quilt is a story of family unity. In this story parents care, children are loved, and a grandmother is a loving and integral part of the household. Each member of the family contributes a memorable piece of clothing to the patchwork quilt, which symbolically bonds the family. Jerry Pinkney saw all these elements in the text and gave his personal artistic interpretation to the story and its characters. In the colorful quilt one sees a variety of textures, shapes, and forms. This same concept extends itself to the characterization of the family members. Pinkney captures the nuances of skin color, the individual hairstyles, and the personal choices of dress. This care for making each character an individual speaks to the artist's philosophy of making sure those who see his art realize that the beauty of the African American is as varied as the people who make up this culture. The artwork in *The Patchwork Quilt* invites readers to visit a cross-generational African American family living in harmony in a home that celebrates togetherness.

1986 Honor

HAMILTON, VIRGINIA. *The People Could Fly: American Black Folktales.* **Illustrated by Leo Dillon and Diane Dillon.** Knopf, 1985. Gr. 3–6.

Forty stunning, stylized, black-and-white illustrations accompany Virginia Hamilton's retellings of African American folktales, echoing the dignity of the text by extending each tale's distinctive mood. The harmony of all book-design elements provides a handsome presentation of stories for families to share, scholars to study, and individuals of all ages and backgrounds to enjoy.

1984 Winner

WALTER, MILDRED PITTS. *My Mama Needs Me.* **Illustrated by Pat Cummings.** Lothrop, Lee, & Shepard, 1983. Gr. K–2.

Walter's simple text describes a universal dilemma—the concern and discomfort of the older child when a new baby comes home—and Cummings gives visual interpretation to the concept. She chooses mainly mocha brown for the family figures and uses other colors to give the story a multicultural setting, thus extending the universality of the concept. An outstanding feature of the illustrations can be seen in the expressive eyes of the troubled Jason—eyes that show the perplexity of wanting to be needed yet seeming to be rejected. There is a visual sense of family, of love and tenderness, when Jason shares the mother's nursing moments and learns to rub the baby's ear to make it want to suckle more, and when he is asked to help bathe the baby. From Jason's feelings of being an outsider to the assurance that his mama needs him, Cummings's bright colors and decorative designs capture the joy of this family story.

1983 Winner

MAGUBANE, PETER. *Black Child.* Knopf, 1982. Gr. 6–12. *

A stream of emotions ran through the jury—surprise, horror, excitement, distress, anger, and occasionally a sense of hope. It was the Coretta Scott King awards jury together examining Peter Magubane's *Black Child*.

Taking advantage of the sharp contrasts that are best captured in black-and-white photography, photojournalist Magubane has shown the disparate worlds of South Africa through the eyes of its black children. The pictures tell stories of the deplorable working conditions of teenagers who should be enjoying life but are instead sweating in the maize fields of Delmas and who return at day's end to windowless dormitories for restless sleep. One wonders about the future of the skinny-legged, barefoot boy begging a few coins from a well-dressed white woman on a street in Johannesburg. As a tribute to the human spirit, Magubane photographed a youth making joyful music on a homemade guitar. The book closes with a dramatic picture of the grave of Hector Peterson—the thirteen-year-old who was the first to die in the Soweto riots.

There seems to be a special message in the selection of the solid black endpapers with which this powerful photo documentary opens and closes. For the many messages in the book, Magubane received the Coretta Scott King Book Award for illustrations. His "acceptance speech" was a series of slides sent from South Africa and presented in his absence at the awards breakfast.

1983 Honors

BRYAN, ASHLEY, SELECTOR AND ILLUSTRATOR. *I'm Going to Sing: Black American Spirituals. v. 2.* Atheneum, 1982. Gr. K–12.

Bryan has spent many hours in the research of African American history in subject areas from folklore and legend to poetry and music. With a concern for making spirituals accessible and meaningful to young people, he designed and illustrated his second volume of those songs using woodblock images reflecting the "spirit of the early religious woodblock books." With special skill, Bryan depicts facial expressions and body movements that reflect the moods of the songs—which range from hopeful, to longing, to joyful and triumphant. In what the artist describes as a desire for visual unity, with a technique that must have required unbelievable patience, he carved the notes using the same woodblock style as the illustrations. The Coretta Scott King awards jury was impressed not only with the words and music but also with the fact that the notes all had to be cut in reverse so that they would print out correctly. In selecting this title for illustration honors the committee agreed that now more young people were surely going to sing.

CAINES, JEANNETTE. *Just Us Women.* Illustrated by Pat Cummings. Harper & Row, 1982. Gr. K–3.

The text is simple and very positively feminine. Aunt Martha is taking her young niece to North Carolina in her new convertible. The trip is to be made with "No boys and no men, just us women." Cummings captures the joy of the trip in two-tone color illustrations that extend the text. One sees a small picture of shoe boxes overflowing with lunch goodies; a double spread shows the fun of roadside shopping; a background of moon and stars completes the picture when the travelers decide to have breakfast at night. The warmth of companionship is undeniable when at the end of the trip the two "women," with arms around each other, approach the relatives' home at the end of a joyous journey. *Just Us Women* is a rich and positive concept interpreted with artistic skill.

ADOFF, ARNOLD. *All the Colors of the Race.* **Illustrated by John Steptoe.** Lothrop, Lee, & Shepard, 1982. Gr. 5–12.

Distinguished brown-tone paintings provide the perfect accompaniment to Adoff's free-form poems written from the point of view of a girl born to parents of different ethnic backgrounds—one white, one African American. Steptoe's expressionistic portraits capture the many moods of a young girl searching for identity, respect, and security as she struggles to assert herself in a sometimes hostile world.

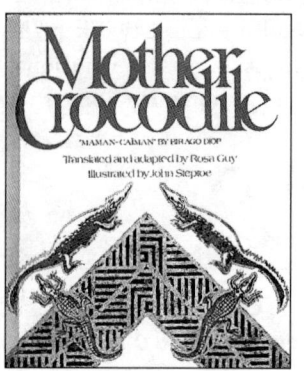

1982 Winner

DIOP, BIRAGO. Trans. and adapted by Rosa Guy. *Mother Crocodile / Maman-Caiman.* **Illustrated by John Steptoe.** Delacorte, 1981. (New edition: *Mother Crocodile: An Uncle Amadou Tale from Senegal.* Delacorte, 1982.) Gr. K–3.

When Mother Crocodile warns her children to swim away, they close their ears. Only later, when it's almost too late, do they realize the truth in her words. Steptoe's breathtaking abstract illustrations are appropriately presented in a spectrum of underwater colors to create a strong sense of place while at the same time allowing for interpretation of symbolic history in this cautionary Ovolof tale from West Africa.

1982 Honor

GREENFIELD, ELOISE. *Daydreamers.* **Illustrated by Tom Feelings.** Dial, 1981. Gr. K–5.

To read *Daydreamers*, one must first closely study the faces of the children brought sensitively to life by the artist Feelings. The figures of children outlined in chocolate brown, charcoal gray, and sepia convey determination, self-confidence, and a strong feeling that they are a part of the future. There is a message in the set of the jaw of some of the young men remembering their history and "drawing strength from the spirit of their ancestors."

Is it the placement of hand on hip that shouts, "I am somebody"? One wonders what thoughts are going through the mind of the toddler pensively sucking on a tiny finger. The eyes of some of the children—eyes looking into the future—seem to reflect Greenfield's words, "daydreamers letting the world dizzy itself without them." From toddler to young adult, the characters in Feelings's illustrations proclaim that "dreaming has made them new."

Feelings's illustrations have more than an aesthetic impact. There is a message of ethnic pride and cultural strength that is totally integrated with Greenfield's poetic text.

1981 Winner

BRYAN, ASHLEY. *Beat the Story-Drum, Pum-Pum.* Atheneum, 1980. Gr. 3–5.

The striking force of Bryan's lusty woodcut technique had instant appeal to the Coretta Scott King awards jury that selected this collection of tales based on Nigerian folklore. There is a rhythm in the curve of the animals' bodies that captures the rollicking beat and humor of Bryan's storytelling. Subtle use of lines gives expressions to the faces of the characters in the stories—stories that explain why the elephant and the bush cow do not get along or that take a jab at human foibles as in the tale of the man who could not keep a wife because he insisted on counting each spoonful of food placed on his plate.

Reflecting Bryan's strong concern for truth, there is a consistency between the setting—the plains of Africa—and the choice of colors. This is particularly discernible in the full-page illustrations that show blends of earth tones—reds, browns, oranges—as one would see in the homeland of these stories.

1981 Honors

GREENFIELD, ELOISE. *Grandma's Joy.* Illustrated by Carole Byard. Philomel, 1980. Gr. Pre-K–3.

Charcoal drawings on cream paper tenderly express Greenfield's story of Rhondy's attempts to cheer her grandmother, who is sadly packing their belongings into boxes as they prepare to move away. Remembering the special closeness they have shared since Rhondy was a little baby finally cheers and comforts Grandmama. The expressiveness of the illustrations brings an immediacy and a loving respect for people struggling against difficult times, pulling the reader into the story and championing the strength of family ties that carry us through. The illustrations honestly portray both the sadness of the story and the glow of joy and love that comforts child and adult.

ZASLAVSKY, CLAUDIA. *Count on Your Fingers African Style.* **Illustrated by Jerry Pinkney.** Crowell, 1980. Gr. K–3.

In an African marketplace, young readers are introduced to a way of counting based on the system used in some areas of that vast continent. Pinkney gives graphic life to the concept through clear, black-and-white illustrations. Even without color one can clearly visualize the marketplace and sense its busyness. And indeed the absence of color makes very clear the position of the fingers and the movements of the hands that distinguish one number from another. The uncluttered illustrations in this book serve as a fun-filled, participatory introduction to an element of mathematics in another language.

1980 Winner

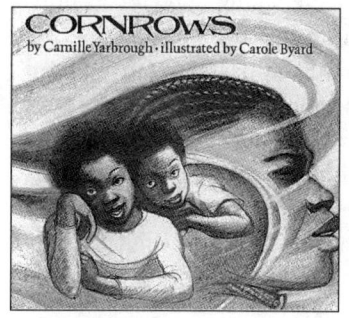

YARBROUGH, CAMILLE. *Cornrows.* **Illustrated by Carole Byard.** Coward, McCann, & Geoghegan, 1979. Gr. 3–6.

As a modern-day grandmother and mama braid their children's hair in cornrows, the three generations share the stories of the braid patterns that are a part of their African heritage. The charcoal drawings with swirling shapes and dramatic close-ups present a series of visions, first taking the reader to Africa and then offering a series of distinct portraits of famous black Americans. Shifting from masks and drums to Malcolm X and Rosa Parks, the drawings soften or become crisp as appropriate. The illustrations of African carvings impart solidity, while the drawings depicting the joy of dancing flutter with movement. In the series of portraits of leaders and heroes of black America, each person is easily recognizable and aptly presented. Included are Langston Hughes, Malcolm X, and Marian Anderson. There are no stilted copies of studio portraits here but instead vivid people joyously and proudly leading their kin—people like the three generations of family glorying in their heritage, in the ordinary world of home, storytelling, and braiding cornrows.

1979 Winner

GRIMES, NIKKI. *Something on My Mind.* **Illustrated by Tom Feelings.** Dial, 1978. Gr. 4–8.

Tom Feelings captures the essence of Nikki Grimes's words in the faces and body language of the inner-city children of whom she writes. The words are often poignant, speaking of the need to belong, the wish to understand "the secrets grown-ups share," or just to understand grown-ups. Feelings's charcoal and sepia drawings leave no doubt about the message of each piece. There is quiet puzzlement on the face of the young lady, for example, who tries to understand the dichotomy of the mother who urges her to hurry into her Sunday best to go to the Lord's house and then emits some telling curses when she bangs her toe. "Why," asks the child, "instead of going to the Lord's house, don't we invite him to visit ours?" Feelings's line drawings are deceptively simple. The beauty of African American features shows in the face of each child portrayed in this thought-provoking collection.

1978 Winner

GREENFIELD, ELOISE. *Africa Dream.* **Illustrated by Carole Byard.** John Day, 1977. Gr. K–2.

In a dream sequence, a huge, crashing wave transports a sleeping child from her home in one land to her homeland in Africa. Together the girl and the reader celebrate the wonders of her heritage—magnificent examples of majestic buildings, the sounds of drums and song, a glimpse of everyday activities, and the powerful strength of noble ancestors welcoming her home. The varying shades of charcoal used throughout seem to symbolize a time past. The creative use of dimension conveys the dramatic contrast between the leaders of old and the little figure to whom welcoming arms are extended. *Africa Dream,* and the story it tells, is deceptively simple in word and picture.

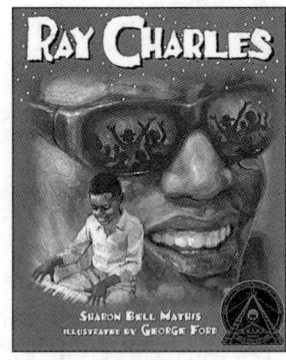

1974 Winner

MATHIS, SHARON BELL. *Ray Charles.* **Illustrated by George Ford.** Crowell, 1973. Gr 3–6. *

When Ford did the illustrations for Mathis's *Ray Charles*, little did he know that he would become a part of history! Indeed, the drawings in this young readers' biography made Ford the very first illustrator to receive the coveted Coretta Scott King Book Award plaque and an honorarium.

Ford expresses the joy of Ray Charles's music beginning with the very cover picture—a smiling musician with swaying dancers reflected in his dark glasses. Looking at black-and-white sketches interspersed with yellow-toned figures, one can follow the talented pianist from his early days, when he lost his sight, through the school where he learned to write down his own musical notations and on to scenes of large audiences enjoying the sounds of spirituals, blues, and jazz. ■

Selected Biographies

Jaime Adoff 1967-

The son of acclaimed poet Arnold Adoff and the late Virginia Hamilton Adoff, Coretta Scott King and Newbery award winner Jaime Adoff was born in New York City but grew up in Yellow Springs, Ohio, where his mother's family has lived for generations. He has described his family as one that "buzzed twenty-four hours a day with imagination." Adoff earned a bachelor of music degree from Central State University in Ohio, studying drums and percussion. He later studied drums and voice at New York's Manhattan School of Music. Pursuing a career in songwriting, he led his own rock band and released two CDs of his own music under his middle name, Jaime Levi. Tired of playing clubs on the music circuit, Adoff thought about a creative outlet that would have a positive impact on young people and decided to pursue the "family business." Accustomed to hearing his parents read their works-in-progress to one another when he was a child, Adoff experimented with language as a way to express his love of music. His first book for young people, *The Song Shoots Out of My Mouth* (2002), an illustrated collection of free-verse poems that express teenagers' experiences with music, was named a Lee Bennett Hopkins Poetry Award honor book. His first young adult novel, *Names Will Never Hurt Me* (2004), was followed in 2005 by *Jimi & Me,* which was honored with the 2006 Coretta Scott King/John Steptoe New Talent Award. Adoff now lives with his wife and children in the one-hundred-year-old house in which his mother was born.

Benny Andrews 1930-2006

Benny Andrews was born in 1930 in the small farming town of Plain View, near Madison in northern Georgia. He was one of ten children in a sharecropping family. His father, George, was a self-taught artist. His mother emphasized the importance of religion, education, and freedom of expression. Andrews was the first member of his family to graduate from high school. For his fine grades he received a scholarship that enabled him to attend Fort Valley State College in Fort Valley, Georgia. There he studied art, and after four years of military service he enrolled at the Art Institute of Chicago, where he earned a bachelor of fine arts degree. Andrews's work had been rejected by every art show at the Institute, but six years later, in New York City, he had become an established artist. Over many years his work has been featured at exhibits around the country and internationally.

Andrews taught at Queens College of the City University of New York for twenty-nine years and was a visiting lecturer at many other colleges and universities. His creation of a prison arts program became of model for other artists to follow. Not only were his humanitarian interests instrumental in helping form the National Endowment for the Arts, but he was also a prominent spokesperson for artists whose works were not considered for exhibition in the large public institutions in New York. Among Andrews's many awards is the renowned Abby Award for lifetime achievement in the arts. He was elected to the National Academy in 1997. His work is owned by more than thirty major art museums, including New York's Metropolitan Museum of Art and Museum of Modern Art, the Art Institute of Chicago, and the Art Institute in Detroit, Michigan. With what has been described as an expressionistic style, Andrews often takes as his themes such difficult concepts as the African American experience, with a focus on daily life, suffering, and injustice; Native American forced migrations; the Holocaust; and most recently Hurricane Katrina. At the same time, his illustrations often celebrate life and the strength of the human spirit. Before his passing, Andrews lived in New York City with his artist wife Nene and their three children. Posthumously, Benny Andrews received the Coretta Scott King 2007 honor for the creative art work in *Langston Hughes, Poetry for Young People* series.

Andrew Aydin   1983–

Andrew Aydin currently serves in Rep. John Lewis's Washington, D.C., office where he handles telecommunications and technology policy as well as new media, having previously served as communications director and press secretary during Rep. Lewis's 2008 and 2010 re-election campaigns. A native of Atlanta, Aydin holds a B.A. degree from Trinity College in Hartford and an M.A. from Georgetown University. With John Lewis, Aydin coauthored *March: Book One*, the first in a planned trilogy of graphic novels telling the story of Rep. Lewis's life.

Pearl Bailey   1918–1990

Pearl Bailey was born in Newport News, Virginia. At the age of four, she moved with her family to Washington, D.C. Her interest in performing onstage began when her brother Bill, a tap dancer, encouraged her to appear in an amateur-hour contest at the Palace Theater in Philadelphia at the age of fifteen. A few years later, after winning the amateur contest at the famous New York Apollo Theater, Bailey knew what her life work would be. Her career in show business included a Broadway debut in *St. Louis Woman*, regular appearances at the Village Vanguard, and singing with bands conducted by Cootie Williams and Cab Calloway.

Retiring from show business in 1975, Bailey made several television appearances before her appointment as special advisor to the United States mission of the United Nations. In 1976, her book *Duey's Tale* received the Coretta Scott King Book Award.

In 1980, Bailey returned to school, attending Georgetown University, where she earned a B.A. degree in theology in 1985. Among the many honors Bailey received was the Presidential Medal of Freedom awarded to her by President Ronald Reagan in 1988.

James Berry   1924–

James Berry is known as a distinguished writer of both prose and poetry. Born and raised in a coastal village in Jamaica, West Indies, this award-winning writer now calls England home. He has been honored internationally for writing that is described as "making a great contribution to people of all ages." His interest in multicultural education manifests itself both in his writing and in his personal involvement in programs that focus on that matter. Among his recognitions are the Order of the British Empire, from the United Kingdom, and the 1993 *Boston Globe–Horn Book* Award for the poignant story of *Ajeemah and His Son* (HarperCollins).

Clarence N. Blake   1926–

Born in Cottonplant, Arkansas, Clarence N. Blake grew up in Detroit but spent many years in such far-flung places as Fairbanks, Alaska; Klamath, California; and Ubon, Thailand. His education includes a B.S. from Wayne State University, an M.A. in counseling and guidance from Gonzaga University in Spokane, Washington, and an Ed.D. in adult education from George Washington University. Blake traveled extensively as an Air Force officer, and once noted that he had traveled to every state in the United States except Oklahoma and every continent except Africa. When not traveling and teaching, Blake relaxes by playing the mandolin and the piano, fishing, and taking photographs.

His impetus for the *Quiz Book on Black America*, which he developed with Dr. Donald F. Martin, came from observing the lack of knowledge of black history "on the part of blacks and whites in the United States."

Tonya Bolden   1959–

New Yorker Tonya Bolden is the author of more than twenty books, including novels, self-help books, reference books, and poetry. Many of her best-received titles are works of nonfiction for young people. Her *Tell All the Children Our Story: Memories and Mementos of Being Young* and *Black in America* (2001) was named a Best Book of the Year by *School Library Journal*.

In an interview with Deborah Hopkinson in *BookPage*, Bolden describes how incidents remembered from childhood inform her work. Her experiences in a strong family, grounded in church, gave her the strength to strive to be her best. "I love Black history. History makes me whole," Bolden explained to an interviewer for *The Crisis* magazine. "With every book I do on a Black person or a Black experience, I'm getting stronger. And, I'm getting clearer from whence I come."

Bolden graduated magna cum laude from Princeton University with a baccalaureate in Slavic languages and literature, concentrating on Russian. She earned a master's degree in the same fields from Columbia University and a Certificate for the Advanced Study of the Soviet Union from Columbia's Harriman Institute of Russian, Eurasian, and Eastern European Studies. Bolden, recognized for her fine writing style and readable narratives, has also received many honors for her meticulous research. Included among them is the James Madison Award for *Maritcha*. The Madison Award is given each year to the book that "best represents excellence in bringing knowledge of American history to children in elementary and middle school." It honors James Madison, fourth president of the United States. For relaxation, Tonya Bolden lists as her hobbies collecting antique inks, doing jigsaw puzzles, and—influenced by research for her latest title, *George Washington Carver*—gardening. She lives in the Bronx, New York.

Victoria Bond 1979–

Victoria Bond is lecturer in English at the John Jay College of Criminal Justice and a contributor to *The Huffington Post*. She received her B.A. from Vassar College and her M.F.A. from Brooklyn College. Her debut novel, *Zora and Me*, coauthored with T. R. Simon, is a fictional account of Zora Neale Hurston's childhood, a canonical Harlem Renaissance writer, imagining her as a girl detective. The book has received several honors, including the Coretta Scott King/John Steptoe Award for New Talent for Bond and Simon. Bond lives in New York.

Colin Bootman 1963–

Colin Bootman was born on the Caribbean island of Trinidad, where he lived for the first seven years of his life. He attended the LaGuardia High School of the Arts in the Bronx, New York, and, after graduation, went on to receive a bachelor of fine arts from the School of Visual Arts, New York.

Bootman's talents as an illustrator can be seen in several children's books, including in the 2004 Coretta Scott King honor book *Almost to Freedom*. Away from his studio, Bootman draws constant inspiration from visiting museums and galleries and "is highly inspired by the grit of New York City."

Colin Bootman makes his home in Brooklyn, New York.

Candy Dawson Boyd 1946–

Candy Dawson Boyd was born and raised in Chicago, Illinois. She earned her bachelor's degree at Northeastern Illinois and Illinois State universities and a master's degree and a Ph.D. from the University of California, Berkeley. She teaches at Saint Mary's College in Moraga, California—the first African American to hold a tenured position at that institution. Boyd was named 1992–93 Professor of the Year at the college; the citation described Boyd as a "gifted and passionate teacher, writer, and colleague."

The themes that one can find in many of Dawson's books reflect her activities with the civil rights movement of the 1960s, her association with Martin Luther King Jr., and her experiences as a field worker in the Southern Christian Leadership Conference.

Boyd's first novel, *Circle of Gold*, was a 1985 Coretta Scott King honor book. It was followed by several other novels that speak directly to African American experience for young readers.

Boyd lives with her husband, Robert, in San Pablo, California.

Elbrite Brown 1970–

Elbrite Brown was born and raised in Philadelphia, Pennsylvania. His interest in art evinced itself at an early age and was encouraged by his whole family, but particularly by his mother. She helped him to learn his alphabet by drawing pictures for each letter—and the budding artist found himself creating his own letter-related pictures.

Brown was a shy youth who learned to communicate through his art. He integrated his art into a small business venture by illustrating covers for his peers' school reports and also earned money from a decorative button-making business. After graduation from Murrell Dobbins Vocational and Technical High School, the artist continued his education, earning a bachelor's and a master's degree in art from the University of the Arts, Philadelphia. Presently Brown's talents are being shared with students in Camden Middle School in Camden, New Jersey, where he teaches young people in kindergarten and in grades 5 through 8. Aware of the power of sports in today's society, as a caring teacher, he shares with his students the philosophy that art can play an important role in the world of sports—even if a person is unable to dunk a basketball or make a touchdown. He encourages students to think of the art that goes into designing uniforms, media ads, and realia, all of which are connected to sports.

Brown's hobbies include visiting antique stores that specialize in period furniture, collecting and mounting theater lobby posters, and relaxing with handsome books that focus on various forms of art, from quilt making to the elegant design of early American homes. *My Family Makes Music,* for which Brown received the 2004 Coretta Scott King/John Steptoe New Talent Award, is his first children's book to be published

Elbrite Brown makes his home in Philadelphia.

Ashley Bryan   1923–

Ashley Bryan was born in Antigua but raised in New York City in what he describes as a "household crowded with parents, five brothers and sisters, three cousins, one hundred birds, and lots of music." In his neighborhood, people shared stories and family experiences, and it is to this that he attributes his unending passion for the written word and for music. Those interests continue to come together in the body of work Bryan has produced: volumes of poetry and collections of African American folktales based on research and embellished for telling laughter. Bryan states that the goal in his books of spirituals and folktales is to bring to young and old a picturesque yet accurate interpretation of the rich store of African and African American history.

Bryan's interests extend beyond music and the written word into the world of art. After graduation from Columbia University with a degree in philosophy, he studied art at Cooper Union School of Art in New York City. His works reflect his ability to suit the medium to the mood and setting of a story—from woodcuts used in his early books of spirituals, to the fine fluid line drawings that capture the fun and mischief in *The Dancing Granny and The Cat's Purr,* to the tempera paints that enrich the illustrations in later books of spirituals and his 1998 Coretta Scott King honor book *Ashley Bryan's ABC of African American Poetry.* In 2004, Bryan received the Coretta Scott King Book Award for his illustrations in *Beautiful Blackbird,* a story told with paper-cut figures, a medium entirely new to him. In recognition of his contributions to diverse aspects of the humanities, Bryan was awarded honorary doctorates from Framingham College in Massachusetts (1995), the University of Wisconsin at Madison (1998), the University of Oakland in Detroit, Michigan (2003), and the Bank Street College of Education, New York City (2008). Each year, more and more honors are bestowed in recognition of his high standards for producing meaningful books for readers of all ages. In addition to winning the 2008 Coretta Scott King Book Award for *Let It Shine,* he was also nominated for the 2007 Hans Christian Andersen Award, sponsored by the International Board on Books for Young People. His work has been exhibited in the Eric Carle Museum of Picture Book Art in Amherst, Massachusetts. When not traveling, lecturing, or sharing poetry with avid listeners, Ashley Bryan makes his home in Islesford, Maine.

Carole Byard   1942–

Carole Byard was born in Atlantic City, New Jersey, on July 22, 1942. Her mother died when Byard was very young, and she was raised by her father with the help of a grandmother. Every time art was offered in school Byard would try to take advantage of the opportunity, but she always felt secretive about her efforts, as though her work were something private. During high school a teacher recognized her talent and helped Byard obtain a full-tuition scholarship to an art school in Ohio. Unable to raise the necessary money, she wrote to the school asking if her place could be held until she could earn enough to attend. Although that dream was never realized, she found a civil service job that enabled her to attend Fleischer Art Memorial in Philadelphia from 1961 to 1963 and then Phoenix School of Design in New York, where she became an instructor. She has also taught for the Studio Museum in Harlem, Metropolitan Museum of Art, New York Foundation for the Arts, Baltimore School of Arts, Maryland Institute College of Art, and Parsons School of Design.

Byard has had many exhibitions in major and alternative galleries across the country, as well as special commissions. In 1971, Byard was a founding member of the Black Artists Guild. She received a grant from the Ford Motor Company to go to Africa in 1972. The trip to Senegal, Ghana, Ethiopia, and Egypt was a moving experience and a strong influence on her work.

Carole Byard has received many awards since the 1978 Coretta Scott King awards jury recognized her along with Eloise Greenfield for her illustrations in *Africa Dream.* In

1980, she received the Coretta Scott King Book Award for her history-filled illustrations in Camille Yarbrough's *Cornrows*, and she received Coretta Scott King honors in 1981 for *Grandma's Joy* and in 1993 for *Working Cotton*.

Alice Childress 1916–1994

Alice Childress—playwright, actress, and essayist—was born in Charleston, South Carolina. At the age of five she was sent to live with her grandmother in Harlem, New York. Childress recalled that her life was poor in terms of money but enriched by love, patience, and her grandmother's appreciation of the arts—a love that she passed on to her young granddaughter. After dropping out of school at an early age, Childress discovered the public library and began to read at least two books each day.

Childress's writing career began in 1940. By 1943, she moved into acting when she became a part of the American Negro Theater. In 1955, she was the first African American woman to receive an Obie Award for her off-Broadway play *Trouble in Mind*, which spoke out against the stereotyping of blacks.

As Childress wrote, she focused on reaching African American youth and offered them hope in the "struggle to survive in capitalist America." She earned Coretta Scott King honors in 1974 for *A Hero Ain't Nothin' but a Sandwich* and in 1982 for *Rainbow Jordan*. Critics acclaim Childress as a master at her craft—known for deft handling of language.

Shirley Chisholm 1924–2005

Shirley Chisholm, the first African American woman to serve in the U.S. House of Representatives, was born in Brooklyn but spent her early years in Barbados living with her grandparents. She returned to the United States to attend high school, graduated from Brooklyn College in 1946, and earned a master's degree from Columbia University in 1952. Intending to devote her life to early childhood education, she taught nursery school, directed two child-care centers, and served as a consultant to the day-care division of the New York City Bureau of Child Welfare.

Chisholm's encounters with racism and sexism in college and her interest in community organization inspired her involvement in electoral politics. She served in the New York State Assembly from 1964 to 1968 and was elected to Congress in 1968 from the newly created Twelfth Congressional District in Brooklyn's Bedford Stuyvesant section. Although she was fiercely independent and an outspoken critic of the congressional seniority system, she served on such influential committees as Education and Labor and the Rules Committee. As she had in the state assembly, she pioneered progressive programs to support women and the poor. She championed support for education and urban needs while attempting to limit expenditures for armaments. In 1971, Chisholm earned a Coretta Scott King honor for *Unbought and Unbossed*, an autobiography and political manifesto combined.

In 1972, Chisholm traveled the country campaigning for the Democratic presidential nomination. She appeared on the ballot in twelve state primaries and received 151 delegate votes at the Democratic convention. Retiring from Congress after serving for fourteen years, she remained active on the boards of groups that support education, health care, urban concerns, and minority and women's rights.

R. Gregory Christie 1971–

Even at the age of five, Gregory Christie was tagged an artist, an appellation that remained throughout his school years. Born in Plainfield, New Jersey, Christie traveled from there to the prestigious School of Visual Arts in New York, where he graduated with a degree in fine arts. Working as a security guard at the Guggenheim Museum strengthened his appreciation for artists who were not always recognized for their work during their lifetimes. In view of the recognition he has already received, he is happily aware that this did not happen to him. Christie has received many accolades for his work, but he values most the response from his parents. "I can tell they're proud. My family has always supported my art. My father exposed me to jazz, classical music, cooking, and reading. My mother put me through school. I can never forget the sacrifices she's made for me. It honestly pushes me to success."

Comparing his own artistic process to learning a second language, Christie explains, "Realism is the base language, the one we use as a tool to comprehend the new language—abstraction, or rather, the way I visualize people and objects." Magnificent examples of Christie's visualization can be found in *The Palm of My Heart*, a Coretta Scott King honor book for illustration in 1997, and in Anne Rockwell's *Only Passing Through: The Story of Sojourner Truth*, a Coretta Scott King honor book for illustration in 2001. When working on a book, Christie finds that an initial piece will act as a "messenger" for the rest of the book, setting the tone and acting as the foundation on which to build.

Christie now lives and paints in the historic Fort Greene section of Brooklyn, a city he cites as a constant influence.

Wil Clay **1938–2011**

Wil Clay was born in Bessemer, Alabama, where, at Macomber Vocational High School, he began his career in the field of commercial art. Over the years he studied at the George Vesper School of Art in Boston and at the University of Toledo, where he concentrated on art history and sculpture. During a three-month journey to Cameroon, Africa, he studied the beadwork, painting, and woodworking of the Bamileke and Fulani people and how those art forms related to their tribal festivals and lifestyles. Exhibits of Clay's paintings and sculpture can be found in private collections around the United States, Canada, Cameroon, and Sierra Leone. His six-foot, bronze-and-steel sculpture of Martin Luther King Jr. entitled "Radiance," located in downtown Toledo, was selected the winner of an international contest sponsored by the Arts Commission of Toledo, Ohio.

Clay received a Coretta Scott King honor in 1993 for his illustrations in *Little John Eight*. His illustrations for children's books reveal the joy and humor he feels when painting and sculpting and sharing stories with youthful audiences.

Lucille Clifton **1936–2010**

Lucille Clifton, a native of Depew, New York, carved a distinguished career in the field of literature by writing for both children and adults. The high quality of her poetry was recognized more than once by the Pulitzer Award committee, and in 1987 she was one of three finalists. She won the Woman of Words Award, was honored by the New York Public Library as Literary Lion 1989, and in 1993 was inducted into the Maryland Women's Hall of Fame. From 1974 to 1985, this talented writer achieved the distinction of Poet Laureate of Maryland.

With a major focus in the field of humanities, Clifton served on Pulitzer Prize juries and was a jurist for the National Endowment for the Arts and for the Poetry Society of America. Clifton also wrote several children's books and had stories accepted for publication in *Atlantic*, *Redbook*, and *House and Garden*.

As an educator, Clifton was recognized as the Distinguished Professor of Humanities at St. Mary's College of Maryland. She also taught at George Washington University and at the University of California, Santa Cruz. She received the Coretta Scott King Book Award in 1984 for *Everett Anderson's Goodbye* and Coretta Scott King honors in 1974 for *Don't You Remember?* and in 1977 for *Everett Anderson's Friend*.

Widowed in 1984, Clifton had six adult children and four grandchildren.

Bryan Collier **1967–**

Bryan Collier was born in the small town of Pocomoke City, Maryland. He grew up close to his grandmother, from whom he learned about the African American tradition of quilting. He began painting in high school and was always encouraged to pursue a career in art. In 1985, Collier won first place for a submission in a congressional competition, and his art was exhibited in the Capitol building in Washington, D.C. In 1989, this talented artist received his bachelor of fine arts degree from Pratt Institute, New York, graduating with honors. After moving to Harlem, Collier became the director of Harlem Horizon Art School, a Harlem Hospital program for children and teenagers.

Titles illustrated by Bryan Collier include *These Hands*, by Hope Lynne (Hyperion, 1999), and *Uptown*, which received both the 2001 Coretta Scott King Book Award for illustrations and the Ezra Jack Keats New Illustrator Award. *Uptown* was also recognized by the National Council of Social Studies as a Notable Children's Trade Book in the field of social studies. He has received Coretta Scott King honor recognition for *Visiting Langston*, by Willie Perdomo (2003), and *Freedom River*, by Doreen Rappaport (2001). In addition to a 2002 Coretta Scott King honor, Collier received a Caldecott honor for the illustrations in *Martin's Big Words*, by Doreen Rappaport.

Collier loves to cook and has compared his collage techniques to preparing a good soup. "Collage is more than just an art style. Collage is all about bringing different elements together. Once you form a sensibility about connection, how different elements relate to each other, you deepen your understanding of yourself and others." Collier photographs members of his family and church and uses them as models. The little boy depicted in *Uptown* is a nephew.

This outgoing artist enjoys talking to children and encouraging them to explore art. Bryan Collier lives in Harlem with his wife and one daughter.

Floyd Cooper **1956–**

Floyd Cooper is a native of Tulsa, Oklahoma, where he attended Tulsa Central High School, and he continued his education by earning a bachelor of fine arts degree from the University of Oklahoma at Norman. Early in his art career Cooper worked for an advertising firm and spent time creating illustrations for Hallmark cards in Missouri. Having found that such art stifled his creative senses, Cooper moved to the East Coast, where he was introduced to the idea of illustrating children's books. His first illustrations, for Eloise Greenfields's *Grandpa's Face* (1988), earned high praise from reviewers, and *Grandpa's Face* was listed as an ALA Notable Book in 1989. Cooper has received Coretta Scott King honors for his illustrations in *Brown Honey in Broomwheat Tea* (1994), *Meet Danitra Brown* (1995), and *I Have Heard of a Land* (1999). He received the Coretta Scott King Book Award for *The Blacker the Berry* in 2009.

In reflecting on his feelings about illustrating books for children, Cooper says, "I feel children are in the front line of improving society. I feel children's picture books play a role in counteracting all the violence and other negative images conveyed in the media." About the goals he has set for himself as an illustrator, Cooper states, "I want to take the reader on a journey into the story, to get a sense of the smells, the atmosphere, and the emotions conveyed by the characters."

In addition to illustrating the work of others, Cooper has written and illustrated his own book, *Coming Home: From the Life of Langston Hughes* (Philomel, 1994). Cooper, his wife, Velma, and their two sons make their home in New Jersey.

Pat Cummings 1950-

Pat Cummings was born in Chicago, but as a child in a military family, she traveled so extensively that she might well call the world her home. When frequent moves from school to school precluded her from making lasting friendships, this talented artist found that her skill with pen, crayons, and imagination could win her acceptance from her peers, even if only temporarily. Those who have met Cummings would be inclined to add "and also her sense of humor." In spite of many moves, Cummings did stay in one area long enough to earn a bachelor's degree from Pratt Institute in 1974.

When Cummings speaks of her art, in the same breath she speaks of the need for freedom of imagination, listing as one of her concerns the rigid rules of art she witnesses as she makes school visitations. One can see her putting her philosophy in action in her choice of colors, angles of perspective, and unusual design details. Perhaps this philosophy is most clearly observed in her 1987 Coretta Scott King honor book *C.L.O.U.D.S.* with its action in the sky, decidedly different color names, and a protagonist who is believably purple. Cummings also earned the 1984 Coretta Scott King Book Award for her illustrations in *My Mama Needs Me* and Coretta Scott King honors for *Just Us Women* (1983) and *Storm in the Night* (1989).

Cummings and her husband, Chuku Lee, live in Brooklyn.

Christopher Paul Curtis 1953-

Christopher Paul Curtis was born in Flint, Michigan, where he completed his high school education. His first work experience was as an employee of Flint's historic Fisher Body Plant #1. He subsequently held a variety of jobs, and in this atmosphere of change he began an early draft of *The Watsons Go to Birmingham—1963*. While attending the University of Michigan, Curtis won the Avery Hopwood Prize for some essays he wrote and the Jules Hopwood Prize for the early draft of the Watson family story—his first novel.

Curtis credits his family, particularly his wife, Kaysandra, for the inspiration to make writing his career. He also finds inspiration in the honesty of young people and their ability to detect "what rings true or what feels right in a particular piece of writing." In addition to receiving a Coretta Scott King honor, *The Watsons Go to Birmingham—1963* was a 1996 Newbery honor book and a Young Adult Choice from the International Reading Association. It was listed in selections from the National Council for Social Studies, noted as a *New York Times* Book Review Best Book, and included in *Booklist*'s Top 25 Black History Picks for Youth.

In 2000, Curtis received not only the Coretta Scott King Book Award but also the Newbery Award for *Bud, Not Buddy*. In addition to winning the Coretta Scott King Book Award for *Elijah of Buxton*, this title was also chosen as a Jane Addams honor book. This award focuses on themes of peace and social justice. Curtis and his wife and children now live in Canada.

Ossie Davis 1917-2005

Ossie Davis was born in Waycross, Georgia. After spending his early years in the South, Davis journeyed north and attended Howard University, where he earned a B.A. degree in 1939. An early project in the field of performing arts was his direction of the show *Cotton Comes to Harlem*. In 1978, he completed the authorship of *Purlie Victorious*, which enjoyed a long run on Broadway before touring the United States. For *Purlie Victorious* and other works, Davis was inducted into the NAACP Images Awards Hall of Fame in 1978. By 1970, Davis and his actress wife, Ruby Dee, were deeply involved in the civil rights movement, working hard to continue the campaign of Dr. Martin Luther King Jr. Awards for his civil rights activities include the 1975 Actors Equity Paul Robeson Citation "for outstanding contributions in both the performing arts and society at large."

In 1998, the two co-wrote a book entitled *With Ossie and Ruby: In This Life Together* (Morrow).

Tanita S. Davis — N/A

Tanita Davis is originally from the San Francisco area and currently lives in Northern California. She earned her MFA at Mills College in 2004. She published her first novel for young adults, *A La Carte*, in 2008, and she has since published two additional novels: *Mare's War* (2009) and *Happy Families* (2012). *Mare's War* received numerous awards, including a 2010 Coretta Scott King author honor. Davis is also an active blogger, contributing to *Finding Wonderland: The WritingYA Weblog, Brandy Trekkers, Guys Lit Wire*, and running her own blog *fiction, instead of lies*.

Alexis De Veaux — 1948–

Alexis De Veaux, a native of New York City, is an internationally known poet, playwright, essayist, and short story writer who has published in five languages: English, Spanish, Dutch, Japanese, and Serbo-Croatian. One of her earliest children's books was *Na-ni*, published in 1973. For older readers she wrote *Don't Explain*, a poetic biography of Billie Holiday that was a Coretta Scott King honor book in 1981. A second children's book, *An Enchanted Hair Tale* (1987)—a fantasy written in poetry—was among the Coretta Scott King honor books in 1988 and was selected to receive the Lorraine Hansberry Award for Excellence in African American Children's Literature in 1991. Among the plays produced by this talented writer are *Circles* (1972), *The Tapestry* (1976), *No* (1981), and *Elbow Room* (1987). Many of these works were seen at off-Broadway theaters, in regional theaters around the United States, and on television. Among the television productions was a documentary, *Motherlands: From Manhattan to Managua to Africa Hand to Hand* (1986). De Veaux's work can also be found in poetry anthologies, short story collections, and such diverse publications as *Essence, Village Voice, Black Feminist Anthology*, and *Buffalo Women's Journal of Law and Social Policy*.

Having earned her doctorate in American studies from the State University of New York at Buffalo, De Veaux now serves on the faculty at that university while continuing to juggle a demanding schedule of travel, personal appearances, and, of course, writing.

Nancy Devard — 1963–

Nancy Devard is a former engineer turned professional artist. After earning a bachelor of science from Temple University and working as a development engineer, Devard finally decided to pursue her passion—fine art and illustration. She began her career as staff artist for Hallmark Cards, crafting best-selling original designs primarily for the Mahogany and Kids divisions. Today, as a freelance illustrator, she uses gesture and expression to tell stories, real or imaginary. "My thrill comes when I look at work I've completed, feel a sense of satisfaction, and receive feedback from my clients that they are delighted with the results." *The Secret Olivia Told Me*, her very first illustrated trade book, won a 2008 Coretta Scott King honor for illustration.

Baba Wagué Diakité — 1961–

Baba Wagué Diakité was born in Bamako, Mali, on the west coast of Africa. There he grew up drawing and enjoying the traditional stories told by his mother and grandparents. He has said that as he heard the stories he could "see trees speak, shrubs move, and logs talk, and all things—dogs, elephants, moon, and stars—move and talk like human beings." It is the heritage of those traditional tales that infuses Diakité's approach to his art and painting.

After coming to the United States in 1985, Diakité's art took a new direction as he began working with clay and painted pottery. He divides his time between his home in Mali and his home in Oregon. When in Mali, he works with members of the community to restore and decorate their mud homes and continues to study the art of mud cloth design under his mother's guidance. When in Oregon, he visits schools as an itinerant storyteller (using the name Wagué) and organizes his many art exhibits. With his artist wife, Roma, he has also produced a prize-winning video, *Don't Paint Lizards on My House*, a celebration of cultural diversity.

Diakité received a Coretta Scott King honor in 1998 for his first picture book—*The Hunterman and the Crocodile*. He and his wife and two daughters live in Portland, Oregon.

Diane Dillon   1933–
Leo Dillon   1933–2012

Diane Dillon was born in Glendale, California, the daughter of a classroom teacher father and a pianist mother. She recalls that her mother encouraged her interest in art over her interest in music because "she could not stand to hear me practice!" After high school Diane Dillon studied at Los Angeles City College and then at Skidmore. Her critical study of art forms and techniques was expanded when she attended the Parsons School of Design and the School of Visual Arts in New York from 1954 to 1958. It is virtually impossible to discuss Diane Dillon the artist without discussing her husband, Leo Dillon the artist, whom she met and married in 1957.

Leo Dillon was born in Brooklyn, New York, the son of parents who migrated to the United States from Trinidad in the West Indies. Leo Dillon credited his earliest interest in art and his inspiration to become an artist to a friend and mentor, Ralph Volman, a native of Trinidad. Volman supplied him not only with materials but with constant encouragement.

After a two-year tour of duty with the United States Navy, Leo Dillon attended the Parsons School of Design from 1953 to 1956 and the School of Visual Arts in 1958. He worked as an instructor at the School of Visual Arts from 1969 to 1977. It was during his years of study at the Parsons School of Design that he first saw the work of an artist whose skill he admired and determined to surpass: his soon-to-be wife, Diane Dillon.

Leo and Diane Dillon were, indeed, inseparable in the artwork they produced. They balanced their techniques, creative ideas, and perspective so that the finished product was truly the result of two minds working as one. For their award-winning illustrations they used techniques that ranged from woodcuts, to waxed pencil on toned paper, to acetate painting on polished wood, to, most recently, cut paper.

Together the Dillons won awards in the United States and abroad, including two successive Caldecott Medals for *Why Mosquitoes Buzz in People's Ears* in 1976 and the African alphabet/information book *Ashanti to Zulu* in 1977. They received the 1991 Coretta Scott King Book Award for their illustrations in *Aïda* and illustrated three Coretta Scott King honor books: *The People Could Fly: American Black Folktales* (1986); *Her Stories: African American Folktales, Fairy Tales, and True Tales* (1996); and *Rap a Tap Tap: Here's Bojangles— Think of That!* (2003). In their concern to express the truth of a culture in their illustrations, the couple traveled widely to capture the flavor and authenticity of their subject matter.

The Dillons' art has been exhibited in the United States at the Brooklyn Museum of Art, the Pentagon, the American Institute of Graphic Arts, and the Museum of Modern Art in New York and abroad at the Bratislava Book Fair. Some of their artwork is a permanent part of the Kerlan Collection at the University of Minnesota.

Sharon Draper   1952–

Sharon Draper was the recipient in 1995 of the first New Talent Award for her first book, *Tears of a Tiger*. Draper, a native of Cleveland, Ohio, attended Pepperdine University as a National Merit Scholar. After graduating, she moved to Cincinnati and began teaching in the public schools. Her writing career was launched in 1991, when one of her students challenged her to enter an *Ebony* magazine short story contest. She later developed her winning entry, "One Small Torch," into the full-length novel *Forged by Fire*, for which she earned the 1998 Coretta Scott King Book Award. Another of her novels, *The Battle of Jericho*, was a Coretta Scott King honor book in 2004.

Draper's goal has been to "write meaningful literature, readable yet with depth, to speak to today's young people—particularly those labeled as reluctant readers." Her hard-hitting, realistic writing is informed by the lives of the young people she observed as a teacher. One of the country's most distinguished educators, Draper was named 1997 National Teacher of the Year. She taught junior and senior high school English for more than thirty years, and her website describes the "I Survived the Draper Paper" T-shirt that her students received when they completed her legendary senior research assignment. She has served on the board of the Carnegie Foundation for the Advancement of Teaching and is currently on the board of the National Commission on Teaching and America's Future. She has been a consultant to educators and students in Russia, Ghana, Togo, Kenya, and Ethiopia. No longer teaching in a classroom, she continues to write and to speak widely on literary and educational issues.

A mother of four, Draper lives with her husband, Larry, in Cincinnati, Ohio, along with their golden retriever, Honey.

Randy DuBurke   1962–

Randy DuBurke was born in Washington, Georgia, but at an early age moved with his parents to New York City. From his early youth he showed outstanding artistic talent, first drawing cartoon characters with great accuracy and then, with maturing interest, studying the works of the great masters, particularly Michelangelo and Degas. Although at first a self-taught painter, DuBurke did formal study at New York Technical College. Following graduation, his artistic talents opened the door to a wide range of working experiences, including ad and lighting design for major fashion leaders, production of storyboards for army recruiting films, animation work for MTV, and illustrations for *Mad* magazine.

Moon Ring, for which DuBurke received the 2003 Coretta Scott King/John Steptoe New Talent Award, is his first children's book. It was inspired by his reflections on the storytelling tradition that filled his childhood and the natural beauty surrounding his home in the rural South.

Randy DuBurke and his wife, Olivia, spend their time between homes in Basel, Switzerland, and New York City.

Alfred Duckett 1917–1984

Alfred Duckett was born and raised in New York City. His mother was a housekeeper and his father a Pullman porter. Following high school, Duckett began work as a newspaper boy for the *New York Age*, a Harlem weekly. This job marked the beginning of a career in journalism and reporting that included writing for the *Pittsburgh Courier*, Harlem's *Amsterdam News*, and Johnson Publishing in Chicago. Following service in the U.S. Army during World War II, Duckett returned to school and formally studied journalism at Columbia University. His last job was that of operating his own press agency, handling press releases for such noted clients as Mahalia Jackson, Duke Ellington, and Harry Belafonte.

When asked about his collaboration with Jackie Robinson on the book *I Never Had It Made*, for which he won the 1973 Coretta Scott King Book Award, Duckett said that he looked upon Robinson as a role model whose story, which extended far beyond his heroics on the baseball diamond, needed to be told.

Duckett, described as a pioneer press agent, was the father of one daughter.

Karen English 1947–

Karen English was born in California, where she received most of her education, including a B.A. in psychology from California State University in Los Angeles. She currently teaches elementary school in California's Bay Area.

When she speaks of her 2000 Coretta Scott King honor book, *Francie*, she reflects that it was partially inspired by her mother's stories of life in the "racist, segregated climate" of the South, where she was born and raised.

When asked about her hobbies, this award-winning author's response was, "Reading, reading, reading!"

Karen English and her husband, Isaac, are the parents of four children and live in Richmond, California.

Mari Evans 1923–

Mari Evans was born in Toledo, Ohio. After graduate studies at Toledo University, Evans accepted a position as an instructor in black literature and writer-in-residence at Indiana University and Purdue. From 1971 to 1976, she was an assistant professor teaching black literature at Indiana University in Bloomington. At that time she also produced and directed a television program, *The Black Experience*. From 1969 to 1970, Evans was a consultant to the Discovery Grant Program for the National Endowment for the Arts. Recognized as an outstanding poet, novelist, and essayist, Evans also wrote several children's books. One of the more popular ones was the witty and poetic *Jim Flying High*, illustrated by Ashley Bryan. Her collection of poems, *I Am a Black Woman*, was among the first Coretta Scott King honor books cited in 1971. Critics have said that Evans's writing "subtly interweaves private and public black frustration and dignity with an infectious perception."

Shane Evans 1972–

Shane Evans grew up in Buffalo, New York. Evans studied at Syracuse University School of Visual and Performing Arts, graduated in 1993, and began traveling extensively. His work is influenced by his travels to Africa, South America, Asia, Europe, the Caribbean, and throughout the United States. He currently lives in Kansas City, Missouri, where he runs Dream Studio, a community art space. In addition to contract work in illustration, graphic design, and web design for major companies, Evans has conceptualized and illustrated more than thirty children's books, including *The Way a Door Closes* by Hope Anita Smith, a Coretta Scott King/John Steptoe Award winner. He has also been honored at the 2002 National Book Festival by First Lady Laura Bush and won the the *Boston Globe-Horn* Book Award and the Orbis Pictus Award for Outstanding Nonfiction for Children.

William J. Faulkner 1891–1987

William Faulkner might be called a person with a head just full of stories. He was born in 1891 in Society Hill, South Carolina. In his youth, Faulkner doubted that he would be able to fulfill his educational ambitions. His mother, widowed while her seven children were quite young, had to struggle to keep the family together. But William Faulkner's ambition became known to an itinerant minister—an African prince who helped Faulkner earn his room and board—and his education began to take shape. Starting with training at the Mayesville Educational Institute, he went on to earn a doctorate in theology from Chicago Theological Seminary in 1946.

During his long life, Faulkner worked with young people in many different capacities and in many parts of the world. He was the first Negro lecturer for the Quaker Schools and student counselor at Fisk University. Faulkner established the first "summer camps for colored boys" in Philadelphia and in Atlanta, where he pastored the First Congregational Church.

Faulkner stated that he had heard stories just about all of his life. Many of the stories in his award-winning *The Days When the Animals Talked* (1977) were learned from a former slave, Simon Brown, a sharecropper who worked on the family homesite.

Until his death in 1987, Faulkner continued his scholarly study of African American folklore, including the lore of the Edisto and Sea Islanders living off the coast of South Carolina. The islanders spoke Gullah, a language that fascinated Faulkner and interested him academically. The study he was working on at his death was to be a major publication in the field of African American folklore.

Elton Fax 1909–1993

Elton Fax was born in Baltimore, Maryland. His educational pursuits included a B.F.A. degree from Syracuse University in 1931 and study in Bellagio, Italy, on a Rockefeller Foundation Research Center grant in 1976.

Fax taught at Claflin College in Orangeburg, South Carolina, and A&T College in Greensboro, North Carolina, before taking a position with the Harlem Art Center in New York City.

With oil as his special medium, Fax illustrated several children's books, including Georgiana Faulkner's Melindy series, *Melindy's Medal* (1945) and *Melindy's Happy Summer* (1949), and Florence Hayes's *Skid* (1948). His book of biographical sketches, *17 Black Artists*, received the Coretta Scott King Book Award in 1972.

Fax lived on Long Island and at one time served as writer-in-residence at the Langston Hughes branch library in the Queens public library system.

Tom Feelings 1933–2003

The world of literature was saddened in August 2003 by the news of the death of artist Tom Feelings. At the time of his passing, Feelings was working on a sequel to his masterpiece, *Middle Passage*.

Tom Feelings was born in Brooklyn, New York. A part of his early education included two years at the School of Visual Arts. He served a stint in the United States Air Force, where he was a staff artist for the graphic division of the Third Air Force. Feelings began drawing his Brooklyn neighbors in the 1950s, but his drive to depict the African American experience took on a new urgency during the turmoil of the civil rights movement.

In 1964, he moved to Ghana, then in the vanguard of the struggles for African independence. Feelings wrote that living there for two years as an illustrator for the Government Publishing House "reaffirmed much that was positive that I had deep inside me about black people." He returned to the United States, where he began to illustrate children's books. In 1971, he was invited to Guyana to train textbook illustrators in that newly independent country.

Feelings spent the twenty years after his return from Guyana developing his monumental work *The Middle Passage: White Ships/Black Cargo*, for which he received the 1996 Coretta Scott King Book Award. He also received the Coretta Scott King Book Award for the illustrations in *Something on My Mind* and *Soul Looks Back in Wonder* and the Brooklyn Arts Award for *Jambo Means Hello*. *Jambo Means Hello* and *Moja Means One* were both selected as Caldecott honor books, the first two Caldecott honors for a black artist.

Feelings once said, "When I am asked what kind of work I do, my answer is that I am a storyteller in picture form who tries to reflect and interpret the lives and experiences of the people who gave me life." Formerly a member of the faculty at the University of South Carolina, Feelings made his home in Columbia, South Carolina.

Carol Fenner
1929–2002

Carol Fenner, the oldest of five children, was born in Almond, New York. Most of her childhood was spent between Brooklyn and rural Connecticut. She recalled the hours of pleasure she spent listening to stories told by her aunt, the noted young adult author Phyllis Fenner.

Carol Fenner's early ambition was to become a poet, but her writings were mainly storybooks for young readers, including the 1979 Coretta Scott King honor book *Skates of Uncle Richard*.

Amos Ferguson
1920–2009

Amos Ferguson was born in Exuma, the Bahamas. As a young man, he moved to Nassau and took a job polishing furniture to support his family. Ferguson had sketched and drawn since he was a boy but did not attempt painting until he was an adult. He found that he loved making pictures. His paintings cover a wide range of subjects.

Ferguson's first one-person show was held at the Wadsworth Atheneum in Hartford, Connecticut, in March 1985, and it traveled for two years across the United States. A thirty-minute documentary made by Connecticut Public Television on Ferguson and his work received an Emmy nomination.

After viewing some of Ferguson's paintings set in his tropical homeland, Eloise Greenfield wrote the lyrical poetry that accompanies the 1989 Coretta Scott King honor-winning paintings in *Under the Sunday Tree*.

Sharon G. Flake
1955–

Sharon G. Flake, a native of Philadelphia, Pennsylvania, and a graduate of the University of Pennsylvania, began her writing career with contributions to popular magazines. In 1992, she won the August Wilson Short Story Contest with her submission to the "multicultural enlightenment periodical" *AIM*. Flake was also the winner of a Highlights for Children's Writer's Conference scholarship.

Named a Publisher's Weekly Flying Start Author to Watch in 1998, Flake has focused on issues within the African American community. This interest is illustrated by her 1999 Coretta Scott King/John Steptoe New Talent Award for *The Skin I'm In*, a challenge to stereotyped ideals of beauty and physical perfection. Flake's "upfront writing style" won her Coretta Scott King honors for *Money Hungry* (2002) and *Who Am I without Him?* (2005). The latter honor title was also selected as a 2005 ALA Best Book for Young Adults. Her additional books for young adults include *Bang!* and *Begging for Chanoe*. Flake and her daughter Brittney Banks live in Pittsburgh.

George Ford
1936–

George Ford was born in Brooklyn, New York, but spent his early years in Barbados, West Indies. It was there that his early love for art and illustration was nurtured. Ford remembers that his grandmother "could draw like an angel" and encouraged him in his youthful efforts.

On his return to New York, Ford studied art at such varied centers as the Art Students League, Pratt Institute, the School of Visual Arts, and Cooper Union. He also earned a bachelor of science degree from City College of New York. Exhibits of Ford's work were viewed at the Brooklyn Museum in the 1971 exhibition "Black Artists in Graphic Communications." While working as an art director in the advertising field, Ford turned his talents to illustrating books for children. He received the very first Coretta Scott King Book Award for illustrations in 1974 for his drawings in Sharon Bell Mathis's *Ray Charles*. That historic book was reissued by Lee & Low publishers in 2001.

Ford's current focus in illustrating children's books seems to reflect once again the influence of his grandmother: "Her interest in social concerns and in portraying human characters with dignity rubbed off on me." He proudly shares as examples of this philosophy the books he has done for Just Us Books, such as *Bright Eyes, Brown Skin*.

Ford, his wife, Bernette, and their daughter live in Brooklyn.

Sundee T. Frazier
1969–

Perhaps Sundee T. Frazier should have known she would find her calling in writing for young people. At age nine, she told her mom she wanted to publish a book and, although she graduated with a degree in broadcast journalism from the University of Southern California, her favorite course there was children's literature. Her final project—to write and illustrate a children's book—energized her so much that she did not even need caffeine to pull the all-nighter it took to complete it. Several years later, her husband asked the question that sparked her commitment to pursue writing as a career: "If you could do anything, without regard to money, what would you do?" "I'd be a children's writer" shot from her mouth. A couple of years later, she told the guests at her thirtieth birthday party that she planned to have a children's book published by the time she was forty.

She was ecstatic (and quite relieved) when her first novel, *Brendan Buckley's Universe and Everything in It*, was released the week of her thirty-ninth birthday.

Over the ten years that she was honing her craft, Frazier had several mentors, but she is especially grateful for those who guided her as she was working for a master of fine arts in the Writing for Children program at Vermont College. Carolyn Coman (author of *What Jamie Saw* and *Many Stones*) was particularly instrumental in the shaping of *Brendan Buckley's Universe*. Frazier also found inspiration in the work of Christopher Paul Curtis. Before working on her own novel, she would read parts of *Bud, Not Buddy* to remind her of the quality to which she aspired. At the 2008 Coretta Scott King awards breakfast, the recipient of the 2008 Coretta Scott King/John Steptoe New Talent Award mused that, in her wildest dreams, she never could have imagined she would be "sitting on the same dais as Curtis to receive a Coretta Scott King award." The fact that she was made the experience all the more incredible.

Frazier was born and raised in Seattle and still lives in that area with her husband and one daughter. Thinking of her home she remarks, "I find the mountains, water, trees, and even gray skies hugely nurturing to my creative soul."

Jan Spivey Gilchrist 1949-

The artist Jan Spivey Gilchrist was born in Chicago, Illinois, and in early childhood developed an interest in painting. Her graduate education was at Eastern Illinois University, where in 1973 she earned a bachelor of science degree in art education. She holds a master's degree in painting from Northern Iowa University, where she completed her work in 1979. Gilchrist summarizes her philosophy by stating, "I wish always to portray a positive and sensitive image for all children, especially the African American children." In keeping with that position, Gilchrist has many times collaborated with the noted poet Eloise Greenfield in producing fine books of poetry and prose that speak with a positive force for and about the African American family. These include *Nathaniel Talking*, for which Gilchrist received a Coretta Scott King Book Award for illustrations in 1990, and *Night on Neighborhood Street*, whose illustrations received a Coretta Scott King honor in 1992.

Gilchrist has won many awards for her paintings, including recognition from the National Academic Artists Association and the Du Sable Museum, which is in charge of the Purchase Award.

The Gilchrist family—husband, wife, and two children—lives in a suburb of Chicago.

Berry Gordy Sr. 1888-1978

Berry Gordy Sr. was enormously successful as a businessman and a family man. From his birth to his death he was a living example of the level of achievement that is possible when one sets high goals and works to meet them. Berry Gordy Sr. recorded his life story for his children as he approached the ninetieth year of his life. And this exemplary life was not lost on his family, as represented by one of his sons, Berry Gordy Jr. Gordy Jr., one-time Golden Gloves boxer and later the owner of a small record store, made the Gordy name famous to many Americans. As an entrepreneur in Detroit, Gordy Jr. started the recording dynasty known as Motown. From an eight-hundred-dollar loan he developed the venture into a fifty-million-dollar business that launched the musical careers of such greats as Smoky Robinson, the Supremes, Martha and the Vandellas, and the Jackson 5. As a musician himself, Gordy Jr. composed several pieces, one of the most popular being "You Made Me So Very Happy."

Lorenz Graham 1902-1989

Lorenz Graham may well be called a pioneer in any review of African Americans in the world of publishing. He is credited with being the first African American to have a book published by a major publishing house. Nine years after the novel was completed and after many rejections, Follett accepted the manuscript for *South Town*, an outspoken criticism of racism in the South. This was the beginning of the author's many years of writing in a variety of literary genres.

Graham, who was born in New Orleans, Louisiana, received his higher education at the University of California, Los Angeles, and at the New York School of Social Work.

It appears that some of the themes of Graham's early writing were inspired by the stories told by his minister father. This is reflected in Graham's biblical series *How God Fix Jonah*, written in the language of the natives of Liberia, where he served for many years as a U.S. ambassador. His *Every Man Heart Lay Down* was among the first Coretta Scott King honor books named in 1971. Later books were written in protest of racism in the United States. A prolific writer, Graham contributed to the literary field until a few years before his death at age eighty-seven. His last work was a biography of John Brown, completed in 1980.

Shirley Graham 1907–1977

Shirley Graham was born in Indianapolis, Indiana, the daughter of a Methodist minister and a homemaking mother. She was educated at Oberlin College, where she received both her B.A. and M.A. With highly regarded musical talent, Graham studied further at New York University, Yale Drama School, and the Sorbonne in Paris, France. She later taught music at both Morgan State University and Tennessee State University.

Graham recalled that her love of books started early in childhood. She describes books and music as her childhood partners. Out of this partnership, she wrote a children's opera, *Little Black Sambo*, as well as the opera *Tom Tom*, which was performed by the Cleveland Opera Company in 1937.

Graham's writing shows a focus on historical themes and includes many biographies for young readers. In discussing this, Graham once said that she hoped to inspire young people of minority groups to achieve the same greatness that her heroes did. Certain factors seem to have had a negative effect on Graham's writing career. For example, due to the controversy concerning Paul Robeson's loyalty to the United States, the U.S. State Department in 1953 had all copies of Graham's biography of Robeson withdrawn from the shelves of overseas libraries. Some critics believe, too, that her writing career was shortened by her marriage in 1951 to her mentor and friend, the civil rights activist W. E. B. Du Bois, who often criticized the treatment of racial minorities in the United States. Graham and Du Bois spent several years in Ghana in the company of political, social, and educational leaders. Among the educators she met was the teacher Julius Nyerere, about whom she wrote in *Julius K. Nyerere: Teacher of Africa*, a 1976 Coretta Scott King honor book.

Graham and her husband, W. E. B. Du Bois, traveled widely in Africa, Russia, and China. It was in Peking, China, that she died in 1977.

Eloise Greenfield 1929–

Eloise Little Greenfield was born on May 17, 1929, in Parmele, North Carolina, but was raised in Washington, D.C., where she continues to live. Her family moved to the D.C. area in 1930, just as the Depression was beginning to grip the country. Life was a struggle for the family. They lived with and shared their home with relatives and friends until they were accepted to live in Langston Terrace, one of the first housing projects. Greenfield was a shy and quiet child, scared of moving. The fact that everyone was new at Langston made the newness easier for her. Her family had a whole house (upstairs and down) to themselves, and in the neighborhood a community began to slowly form. This community provided her with a good place to grow up. She studied piano and joined a singing group called the Langston Harmonettes.

Music reverberates in Greenfield's books and poetry, which have won many awards. She began to write as a young wife and mother while working at the U.S. Patent Office. But it wasn't until 1963 that her first work, a poem, was published. Several of her picture books started out as poetry, but she has also produced excellent nonfiction and novels. She was a member of the District of Columbia's Black Writer's Workshop, in which she held positions of leadership, and also belongs to several other writing groups. Sharon Bell Mathis inspired Greenfield to use her artistic talents to help build a collection of literature for children. Greenfield's many books in this field attest to her continuing contribution and dedication to providing the best for today's and future generations of African American children. Eloise Greenfield received the Coretta Scott King Book Award in 1978 for *Africa Dream* and earned Coretta Scott King honors for *Night on Neighborhood Street* (1992), *Nathaniel Talking* (1990), *Mary McLeod Bethune* (1978), and *Paul Robeson* (1976), and with coauthor Lessie Jones *Little for Childtimes: A Three Generation Memoir* (1980). In 1998, Eloise Greenfield received the Hope S. Dean Award for her body of work. The award is sponsored by the Foundation for Children's Books in Boston. In 2003, she was named Poet of the Year by the National Council of Teachers of English, an honor that recognizes a poet whose works speak to children and young adults.

Nikki Grimes 1950–

Nikki Grimes, a native of New York, majored in English and studied African languages at Livingston College, a division of Rutgers University. Following graduation, she was the recipient of a Ford Foundation grant that enabled her to spend a year in Tanzania, where she researched and collected African folktales and poetry.

Grimes's interests are many and varied. In the field of journalism she has written numerous articles for *Essence*, and as a dramatist she recently led a performing troupe to many areas of China. Her poetry has been published in anthologies for both children and adults, and she has conducted poetry readings and lectures in Russia, Sweden, Tanzania, and Haiti as well as in scores of cities in the United States.

A talented photographer, Grimes has had her work exhibited in the United States and abroad. Many of her books for children have received national recognition. The Coretta Scott King Book Award was given to *Bronx Masquerade* in 2003, and Coretta Scott King honors were bestowed on *Talkin' About Bessie* (2003) and *Jazmin's Notebook* (1999). *Come Sunday* was named an ALA Notable Book in 1997, and *Malcolm X: A Force for Change* was nominated for an NAACP Image Award. Nikki Grimes was honored in 2003 with the Kerlan Award, which is given in recognition of "singular attainments in creation of children's literature and in appreciation for generous donations of unique resources to the Kerlan Collection." The collection is housed at the University of Minnesota in Minneapolis, Minnesota.

In 2005, Nikki Grimes was the recipient of the National Council of English Poetry Award. When not traveling, lecturing, or writing, Grimes relaxes with needlework and reading. She makes her home in Los Angeles, California.

Virginia Hamilton 1936–2002

Virginia Hamilton was born in Yellow Springs, Ohio, in 1936. Her first book for children, *Zeeley*, was published in 1967 and remains in print. Since that time her books have won every major award accorded to American writers, including the Newbery Medal, the *Boston Globe–Horn Book* Award, the National Book Award, and the Coretta Scott King Book Award. In fact, three of Hamilton's books received Coretta Scott King awards: *Her Stories: African American Folktales, Fairy Tales, and True Tales* (1996), *The People Could Fly: American Black Folktales* (1986), and *Sweet Whispers, Brother Rush* (1983). And six of her books received Coretta Scott King honors: *The Bells of Christmas* (1990), *Anthony Burns: The Defeat and Triumph of a Fugitive Slave* (1989), *Junius over Far* (1986), *A Little Love* (1985), *The Magical Adventures of Pretty Pearl* (1984), and *Justice and Her Brothers* (1979).

Hamilton is often credited with having raised the standards for excellence in children's fiction, folklore, and biography. In 1992, she gained international recognition when she was awarded the Hans Christian Andersen Medal for her lifetime contributions to the world of children's literature, making her the fifth American to have received this illustrious award since its inception in 1958. In addition, in 1995, Hamilton was named a MacArthur Fellow, making her the very first author of children's literature to receive that prestigious "genius" award. The last of Virginia Hamilton's literacy legacy is the novel *Time Pieces*, completed just before her death in February 2002. She is survived by her poet husband, Arnold Adoff, and two children, Leigh and Jamie.

Joyce Hansen 1942–

Born October 18, 1942, in New York City, Joyce Hansen attended Pace University and earned her M.A. in English from New York University. Before her retirement, she taught reading and language arts in the New York City public schools.

Hansen's love of books and writing developed at an early age, nurtured by a mother who wanted to be a journalist and a photographer father, the late Austin Hansen, who shared with her the stories of his West Indian boyhood and Harlem youth. From her father's photography, Hansen came to see "the beauty and poetry" in everyday scenes, which is reflected in her first novels, *The Gift Giver*, *Home Boy*, and *Yellow Bird and Me*. Her works, both fiction and nonfiction, also exemplify her interest in the Civil War and Reconstruction. Her storytelling skill was recognized with Coretta Scott King honors in 1987 for *Which Way Freedom?*; in 1995 for *The Captive*; in 1998 for *I Thought My Soul Would Rise and Fly: The Diary of Patsy, a Freed Girl*; and in 1999, after her continued scholarly research, for *Breaking Ground, Breaking Silence: The Story of New York's African Burial Ground*. In that book, working in partnership with the archaeologist Gary McGowan, the author documents the history of the Negro burial ground established in New York City during the colonial period.

Now retired, Hansen and her husband live in Columbia, South Carolina.

James Haskins 1941–2005

James Haskins was born in Montgomery, Alabama, but received most of his schooling elsewhere. He attended high school in Boston, Massachusetts, and he went on to receive degrees from Georgetown University in Washington, D.C., Alabama State University, and the University of New Mexico. Early in his career Haskins taught music in the public schools of New York City, which led him to write one of his early publications, *Diary of a Public School Teacher* (1969). The success of that work sparked invitations from publishers to write books for young people.

Haskins wrote or edited more than one hundred books for children and young adults—all of them nonfiction. Commenting on that preference, the author stated, "It seems to me that the more you know about the real world, the better off you are, and since there is so much in the real world to talk about, you are better off concentrating on fact rather than fiction." His books for both youth and adults have been acclaimed for their careful research and their lucid, understated, and straightforward writing style. The author received many awards and honors for his work related to African American cultural history. He was given the Coretta Scott King Book Award in 1977 for *The Story of Stevie Wonder* and earned Coretta Scott King honors for *Barbara Jordan* (1978), *James Van DerZee: The Picture Takin' Man* (1980), *Andrew Young: Young Man with a Mission* (1980), *Lena Horne* (1984), *Black Dance in America: A History through Its People* (1991), and *Bayard Rustin: Behind the Scenes of the Civil Rights Movement* (1998).

Barbara Hathaway 1944–

Barbara Hathaway was born in Harlem. *Missy Violet and Me* is based on the recollections of her mother, who often spoke gloriously of a relative who served as a midwife in her southern community in the 1930s. Hathaway, a retired healthcare worker, was also inspired by the nurse-midwives at the Columbia Presbyterian Medical Center with whom she was privileged to work for several years. *Missy Violet and Me* was originally planned as a picture book, but with encouragement from Houghton Mifflin it was expanded a year and a half later into this novella. The story is based on the real life of a community midwife, who Hathaway remembers as being hardworking and underappreciated. The John Steptoe New Talent Award winner states, "I have tried to shine a spotlight on a unique but seldom recognized group of women who provide a valuable service to our communities." This goal was duly recognized by the Coretta Scott King awards jury in 2005. Hathaway lives in Westchester County with her family.

Kristin Hunter 1931–2008

Kristin Hunter was born in Philadelphia during the Depression but grew up in New Jersey. Both of her parents were in education—her father an elementary school principal and her mother a music teacher. However, after Hunter's birth, due to a rigid state statute, her mother was no longer eligible to teach. Thus, Hunter explained, her only-child status was based on economics rather than on biology or choice. Hunter attended the University of Pennsylvania, where she earned a B.S. in education in 1951. However, her writing career started much earlier than that: at the age of fourteen she was writing a weekly column for the local black newspaper.

Hunter's first novel, *God Bless the Child*, was written in 1964. But the author stated that her greatest inspiration for writing came after her return to Philadelphia, where she drew her themes from observing the life of the people in the area of South Street. It was in this setting that she wrote her award-winning *Soul Brothers and Sister Lou*, which was recognized by the Council on Interracial Books for Children and the National Conference of Christians and Jews and has been translated into the Dutch language. Hunter received Coretta Scott King honors for *Guests in the Promised Land* (1974) and *Lou in the Limelight* (1982).

Hunter was married to photographer John Lattany and lived in Magnolia, New Jersey.

JoeSam. 1939–

Anyone who talks to JoeSam. can hear his interest in and empathy for underprivileged children, and anyone who reads his biographical notes will quickly discover the roots of those feelings. JoeSam. was born and raised in Harlem, New York. In spite of what he describes as a difficult childhood, JoeSam. persevered, and after high school he attended Columbia University and later earned a doctorate in education and psychology from the University of Massachusetts at Amherst.

JoeSam. is described as a mixed-media painter and sculptor. His style has been characterized as independent, employing simple elements and bright colors, and at times it's clear that he uses his work to make serious social commentary.

The colors, simple elements, and rhythmically angular lines of the illustrations in *The Invisible Hunters: A Legend from the Miskito Indians of Nicaragua* were surely among the factors that motivated the Coretta Scott King awards jury to bestow an honor on JoeSam. in 1988.

Angela Johnson 1961–

Angela Johnson, who attended Kent State University and served as a VISTA worker in the early 1980s, is now a freelance writer. One observer noted that her "narrators are feisty, intelligent, and sensitive African-Americans struggling with the . . . challenges of growing up; Johnson's stories retain a universality that resonates with both young readers and adults." In recognition of those qualities in her literature and of the range of her works, from prose to poetry to simple text for picture books, Angela Johnson was named a 2003 MacArthur Fellow. That prestigious five-year grant, given by the John D. and Catherine T. MacArthur Foundation to individuals who show "exceptional merit and promise for continued and enhanced creative work," is "a monetary award with no strings attached."

Johnson has received Coretta Scott King awards for *Toning the Sweep* (1994), *Heaven* (1999), and *The First Part Last* (2004), and Coretta Scott King honors for *When I Am Old with You* (1991) and *The Other Side: Shorter Poems* (1999).

This talented writer continues to live and work in Kent, Ohio.

Traci L. Jones 1965–

In her online biography, Jones makes it clear that reading and writing have been twin passions since childhood. She remembers always having a book in hand, and one of her fondest Christmas memories centers on the manual typewriter she received from her mother. The present seemed to cement her desire to pursue a writing career. Unfortunately, when an insensitive college English instructor told her "in brutal terms" that she was a terrible writer, she backed off, turning her attention to research and acquiring a degree in psychology. Lucky for young readers, however, Jones was never able to completely abandon her first love. Ten years after her confidence-shattering blow, she took up writing once again. Her debut novel, *Standing against the Wind*, which she began as an exercise for a writing class at the University of Denver, garnered her the 2007 Coretta Scott King/John Steptoe New Talent Award. She continues to write for middle graders and young teens, her favorite audiences. For more about Jones, visit her website: www.tracibjones.com.

June Jordan 1936–2002

June Jordan was born in Harlem, New York. Her parents were immigrants from the British West Indies. Jordan attributed her interest in words to religious influences. As a member of the Universal Truth faith, she was taught what was almost a mantra—"declare the truth"—and believed that she could do that effectively through words.

As her writing career developed, Jordan's major interest was in writing poetry for children because, she said, "children are the most vulnerable and the most beautiful." One of her early books, *Who Look at Me*, was part of a project started by Milton Meltzer and Langston Hughes. Jordan was asked by the Academy of Poets to complete this blend of art and poetry after Hughes's untimely death in 1967.

Jordan attended Barnard College and taught English at City College in New York, Connecticut College, and Sarah Lawrence. With Terri Bush she directed the Voice of the Children Workshop "mainly for black and Puerto Rican children in Brooklyn, New York." She and Bush received a Coretta Scott King honor in 1971 for *The Voice of the Children*.

Jerome Lagarrigue 1973–

Living in Brooklyn and serving on the faculty of Parsons School of Design, Jerome Lagarrigue is immersed in the New York art world. He graduated from the Rhode Island School of Design in 1996.

He grew up in France, the son of a French father and an African American mother. His childhood was spent between schools in France and summer vacations in New York. This dual cultural heritage was greatly enriched by the creative backgrounds of his parents. His mother was a journalist and writer, and his father was a painter and illustrator. They both encouraged their son's interest in art.

Lagarrigue won many awards for his art, both as a child and as an adult. He received the Lefevre Memorial Award for excellence in illustration and was the featured artist for the Sixth Biennale Film Festival in Paris.

Lagarrigue has said, "My paintings are a reaction to the static quality of a face and the aging quality of a façade. I want to paint faces as landscapes and landscapes as faces. Walls and faces have something in common. They tell their own story. I am trying to reveal and express that story." After winning the Coretta Scott King/John Steptoe New Talent Award in 2002 for *Freedom Summer*, Lagarrigue feels he is well on the way to exploring the world of children's books as an avenue for his illustrator talents.

Julius Lester 1939–

Julius Lester was born in St. Louis, Missouri, and grew up in Nashville, Tennessee. It was in Tennessee that he later received a bachelor's degree in English from Fisk University. He grew up hearing stories from his minister father, and his love of story is reflected in such titles as *How Many Spots Does a Leopard Have?*

Lester moved on to other topics as he increasingly realized the need for sharing with his children and with other children an accurate record of the lives and contributions of African Americans. The power of this concept was recognized in 1969 when Lester's *To Be a Slave* was selected as a Newbery honor book and in 1983 when *This Strange*

New Feeling received a Coretta Scott King honor. This imaginative author received a Coretta Scott King honor again in 1988 for *The Tales of Uncle Remus: The Adventures of Brer Rabbit*, in which he interprets the Brer Rabbit stories in a language that imparts new dignity and makes an important piece of literary history accessible and acceptable to a much wider audience.

Although best known for his writing, Lester is a well-respected photographer whose works are on permanent exhibit at Howard University. He is also a talented guitarist.

Lester lives in Amherst, Massachusetts, and teaches Judaic and Near Eastern studies at Amherst College.

E. B. Lewis 1956–

Earl Bradley Lewis comes from a family of artists. In elementary school, where he was known as the class clown, he was ridiculed for saying that he wanted to be a lawyer when he grew up. Taking the ridicule seriously, he became a dedicated student. Inspired by his two uncles, who were artists, he showed early artistic talent. After completing sixth grade, he attended Saturday morning classes at the Temple University School Art League, run by his uncle, where he studied with the noted Philadelphia painter Clarence Wood. At the Temple University Tyler School of Art, he majored in graphic design, illustration, and art education, and began working with watercolors. This remains his favorite medium.

Following graduation, Lewis taught and worked as a freelance artist. Some fifteen years after graduating from Temple, he illustrated his first children's book, *Fire on the Mountain*, written by Jane Kurtz. Five years and eighteen books later, Lewis received his first Coretta Scott King honor for the illustrations in *The Bat Boy and His Violin*. He won further Coretta Scott King honors for illustrating *My Rows and Piles of Coins* (2000) and *Virgie Goes to School with Us Boys* (2001). In 2003, he won the Coretta Scott King Book Award for the watercolor paintings in Nikki Grimes's *Talkin' About Bessie*.

Lewis, now teaching illustration in Philadelphia, is a member of the Society of Illustrators in New York City and has served on the board of the Philadelphia Watercolor Club. His watercolors, many of which are widely exhibited, are a part of the permanent collection of the Pew Charitable Trust and First Pennsylvania Bank.

The Lewis family, including two sons, Aaron and Joshua, lives in New Jersey.

John Lewis 1940–

Born in Troy, Alabama, John Lewis is a U.S. congressman from Georgia. A key figure in the civil rights movement, Lewis served as the chairman of the Student Nonviolent Coordinating Committee, participated in the Selma to Montgomery marches, and was a member of the freedom riders. Lewis published his autobiography, *Walking with the Wind: A Memoir of the Movement*, in 1999 and the first in a planned trilogy of graphic novels co-written with Andrew Aydin, *March: Book One*, in 2013. He has received many honors, including the Profile in Courage Award from the John F. Kennedy Library Foundation, the Spingarn Medal from the NAACP, and the Presidential Medal of Freedom. Lewis currently lives in Atlanta, Georgia, with his wife.

Lessie Jones Little 1906–1986

Lessie Jones Little was born in Parmele, North Carolina. The daughter of William Jones and Pattie Francis Ridley Jones, all her life Little recalled long hours working in tobacco fields and hating the lingering pungent smell of the plants. Her education included attendance at Higgs Roanoke Seminary near Parmele, where she had in-depth studies in black history. After graduation from high school, Little spent two years at North Carolina State Normal School, then taught elementary subjects in a school in rural North Carolina.

After a move to Washington, D.C., Little worked as a clerk–typist in the U.S. Surgeon General's office. Although always an avid reader, Little did not embark on a writing career until she was sixty-seven years old. Her first book, *Childtimes: A Three-Generation Memoir*, is a family story written in collaboration with her daughter, the author Eloise Greenfield. This title was selected as both a 1979 *Boston Globe–Horn Book* Award honor book in the nonfiction category and a 1980 Coretta Scott King honor book.

Little, the mother of five children, died in 1986.

Kekla Magoon 1980–

Kekla Magoon was born in Michigan and grew up in Fort Wayne, Indiana. She graduated from Northwestern University, where she majored in history; she earned a master of fine arts in writing from Vermont College of Fine Arts. Currently, she lives and writes in New York City and works as a full-time author, writing teacher, and speaker. Magoon is the author of four young adult novels: *Camo Girl*, *37 Things I Love*, *Fire in the Streets*, and *The Rock and the River*, which received the ALA Coretta Scott King New Talent Award and an NAACP Image Award nomination. She also writes history books, including *Today the World Is Watching You: The Little Rock Nine and the Fight for School Integration, 1957* and a forthcoming book on the Black Panthers.

Peter Magubane 1932–

Peter Magubane was born in Johannesburg, South Africa. He began his outstanding career as a photographer by working for the magazine *Drum* and as a staff member for the *Rand Daily Mail*, the Johannesburg newspaper. Over the years he has been recognized as the foremost black South African news photographer. *Black Child*, for which he won the 1983 Coretta Scott King Book Award, was a follow-up to the more adult-oriented photographic essay *Magubane's South Africa*. His photographs were outspoken criticisms against apartheid. Magubane's latest recorded residence is in Dupkloof, in the black township of Soweto, South Africa.

After a long period of silence it was welcome to find that Peter Magubane is still active in his chosen field of photography. As late as March 2008, it was recorded that he was the photographer at the celebration of Nelson Mandela's ninetieth birthday at the Schomburg Center for Research in Black Culture, New York City.

Donald F. Martin 1944–

Donald Martin was born in Baltimore, Maryland. His early education took place in North Carolina, where he graduated from Dudley High School in 1962. After receiving a master of arts degree from the University of Akron, he earned a Ph.D. from Ohio State University in Columbus, Ohio, in 1973.

Martin's interest in sharing learning experiences with young people is a strong motivating factor as he teaches and is involved in administrative duties at the University of North Carolina at Chapel Hill. His concern for extending student knowledge of African American history prompted him to collaborate with Dr. Clarence Blake in writing *Quiz Book on Black America*, a 1977 Coretta Scott King honor book of challenging questions and answers on a variety of topics related to black history.

Sharon Bell Mathis 1937–

Sharon Bell Mathis was born in Atlantic City, New Jersey. Her extensive education includes a bachelor's degree from Morgan State University in Baltimore, Maryland, a master's in library science from Catholic University of America, and a fellowship for further study at Wesleyan University. During her career she has worked as a special education teacher, an instructor in a Washington, D.C., parochial school, a writer-in-residence at Howard University, and a media specialist at the Friendship Educational Center.

During her distinguished writing career, Mathis has been cited for her contributions to *Ebony Jr.* magazine; earned the Council on Interracial Books for Children writers' award for the still popular *Teacup Full of Roses* (1982); and received a Newbery honor for *The Hundred Penny Box* (1975). Her young readers' biography of Ray Charles, the 1974 Coretta Scott King award winner for writing, also received the first Coretta Scott King Book Award for illustrations. That award went to the artist George Ford.

With an endless interest in helping children expand their creativity, Mathis has been a member of the D.C. Black Writers Workshop, where she was designated writer-in-charge of the children's literature division.

Mathis currently resides just outside Washington, D.C.

Janet McDonald 1954–2007

Janet McDonald, one of seven siblings, grew up in the public housing projects of Brooklyn, New York. Recognized as academically gifted, McDonald earned degrees from Vassar College, New York University School of Law, and Columbia Graduate School of Journalism. She was a member of Mensa, the international high-IQ society.

McDonald often called on her recollections of life in the projects when setting her stories. Her characters show with sincere honesty that "not everyone is made for college. We should have the opportunity to go where our talents and inclinations lead us." She received the 2003 Coretta Scott King/John Steptoe New Talent Award for *Chill Wind*, the story of a "project girl" who overcomes many obstacles to find and succeed at what is right for her.

Gary McGowan 1961–

Gary McGowan has spent the major part of his professional life in preserving history through the study and documentation of archaeological findings. At the present time he is the principal conservator for Cultural Preservation and Restoration, Inc., located in Hackettstown, New Jersey.

Since 1992, McGowan has developed and directed the Foley Square laboratory that focuses on the conservation of cultural material recovered from the eighteenth century African burial ground in New York City. These initial findings became the subject of a 1999 Coretta Scott King honor book, *Breaking Ground, Breaking Silence: The Story of New York's African Burial Ground*, which McGowan coauthored with Joyce Hansen.

McGowan holds a master's of museum studies with a major in conservation from the State University of New York. He is currently the president of the New York Regional Association for Conservation and has been named a professional associate within the American Institute for Conservation of Historic and Artistic Works.

McGowan lives in Washington Township, New Jersey, with his wife, Alice, and their two children, Adam and Noah.

Fredrick McKissack Jr. 1965-

Fredrick McKissack Jr., a noted journalist, started his writing career as a stringer for suburban newspapers in his hometown of St. Louis, Missouri. He says of his first assignment—to cover his high school's homecoming football game, "I thought I was 'Joe Cool,' with my steno pad and pen." McKissack moved on to write for an African American newspaper, the *St. Louis American*, where he covered topics from politics to art. Working for the *Edwardsville Intelligencer* in Edwardsville, Illinois, McKissack gained reporting experience as he covered everything from movies to the flood of 1993. Formerly a writer and editor of political feature articles for the *Progressive Media Project* in Madison, Wisconsin, McKissack now continues in journalism in Chicago, where he lives with his wife, Lisa.

McKissack, the son of noted authors Patricia C. and Fredrick L. McKissack, coauthored his first book with his mother. The 1995 Coretta Scott King honor book *Black Diamond: The Story of the Negro Baseball Leagues* grew out of a love the mother and son share for the game of baseball, and their admiration and respect for the stalwart members of the early Negro baseball leagues. The coauthors felt strongly that this story needed to be told to today's youth, who take the multicultural ball scene for granted.

Patricia C. McKissack 1944-
Fredrick L. McKissack 1939-2013

Patricia and Fredrick McKissack, both natives of Nashville, Tennessee, lived and worked in St. Louis, Missouri, since becoming a writing team in 1982.

Patricia McKissack (nee Carwell) was educated at Tennessee State University, where she majored in English. Continued study led to a master's degree in children's literature from Webster University. Fred McKissack was also a graduate of Tennessee State University, where the two writers met and married in 1964. One of the most significant things that drew them together was a common love of literature. However, in their early years together, this talented writing team's careers were on entirely different tracks. Fredrick McKissack worked as a civil engineer, while Patricia McKissack taught school. However, books were always important, and out of their love for reading grew their realization that there was a need to put history in its proper perspective and to give positive messages to all readers about aspects of the black experience.

As a writing team, the McKissacks concentrated on bringing to light the productive lives of notable African Americans and on writing biographical and historical books at various reading levels. Patricia reports that "Fred did most of the research and I wrote it up.... Fred fact-checked it and messed around with it... and we kept doing that until the text was refined."

Patricia and Fred McKissack worked on a regular schedule in a home office, writing, reading, and completing books while making preparations to travel for research as well as for enjoyment.

Mary E. Mebane 1933-1992

Born in 1933 in Durham, North Carolina, Mary Mebane graduated from North Carolina College in 1955. She taught English first at the high school level and then at the college level while she earned her doctorate in American literature from the University of North Carolina. Most of Mebane's writing deals with African American life in the South prior to 1960. She wrote poetry and plays and is best known for her *Mary: An Autobiography*, which was a Coretta Scott King honor book in 1982. In 1983, she wrote a sequel to that book, *Mary, Wayfarer* (Viking).

Daniel Minter 1961–

Born in Ellaville, a small rural community in southern Georgia, in 1963, Daniel Minter loved art at an early age. After high school he moved to Atlanta and graduated from The Art Institute of Atlanta. Since then he has worked professionally as an illustrator, arts educator, painter, and sculptor. He currently lives in Portland, Maine, with his wife and son.

Minter has illustrated nine children's books, including *Ellen's Broom*, written by Kelly Starling Lyons, which won the 2013 Coretta Scott King honor for illustration, *Seven Spools of Thread: A Kwanzaa Story*, winner of a Best Book Award from the Oppenheim Toy Portfolio, and *The Riches of Oseola McCarty*, named an Honor Book by the Carter G. Woodson Awards. He has also created the markers for the Portland Freedom Trail, which identifies significant sites related to the abolitionist movement and the Underground Railroad in Portland, Maine, and he created the 2004 Kwanzaa stamp and the 2011 Kwanzaa stamp for the U.S. Postal Service.

Frank Morrison 1971–

Frank Morrison was born in Massachusetts but his family soon moved to New Jersey. He grew up during the early days of rap music, graffiti, and break dancing. Within this culture, he became well known as a graffiti artist, an accomplished break dancer, and a member of the Sugar Hill Gang dance entourage. It was during one of this group's European tours that Morrison got a chance to visit the Louvre. Intrigued by the magnificent art that surrounded him, he decided, at that moment, to return to his roots and become an artist. Today, Morrison's lively art, mostly watercolor and acrylics, enjoys the attention of art galleries nationwide. Among his exhibitions is a one-man show at the Schomburg Center for Research in Black Culture sponsored by *Essence* magazine. Winner of the 2005 Coretta Scott King/John Steptoe New Talent Award for *Jazzy Miz Mozetta*, Morrison makes his home in Georgia with his wife, three sons, and one daughter.

Toni Morrison 1931–

Toni Morrison was born Chloe Anthony Wofford in Lorrain, Ohio. Her parents, from migrant and sharecropping families, had moved there to escape the more virulent racism of the South. Her father, a shipyard welder, shared with her the African American folktales that would later become the foundation for her work as a writer. Morrison earned a bachelor of arts degree from Howard University and a master's degree from Cornell University. She taught English for two years at Texas Southern University before returning to teach at Howard. In D.C., she married architect Harold Morrison, and the couple had two sons.

While working at Howard, Morrison joined an informal writers group. On one occasion this budding author shared with the group a short story based on an African American girl she had known as a child who yearned to have blue eyes. This would later develop into her first published novel. After a divorce, Morrison worked as a textbook editor and, while her sons slept, she crafted her novel, *The Bluest Eye*. This first novel was finally published in 1970. Recognition for her work soon followed. *Sula*, published in 1973, was nominated for a National Book Award. *Song of Solomon* won the National Book Critics Circle Award in 1977. *Beloved*, a 1987 title, was awarded the prestigious Pulitzer Prize for fiction. When this gifted writer was awarded the Nobel Prize for Literature, it was headlined that Morrison was the first African American and only the eighth woman to be so honored. Morrison also edited the works of such prominent African American authors as Toni Cade Bambara and Angela Davis, under the Random House imprint. Until her retirement in 2006, Morrison held the Robert F. Goheen Chair in the College of Humanities at Princeton University.

In testament to her contributions to the world of literature, in May 2006 the *New York Times* Book Review cited Toni Morrison's *Beloved* as the best American novel published in the previous twenty-five years. Young readers will share in this gifted writer's talents as they read the 2005 Coretta Scott King author award winner *Remember: The Journey to School Integration*.

Shelia P. Moses 1961–

Poet, playwright, and author of several adult books, including a *New York Times* best seller about civil rights activist and performer Dick Gregory, Moses wrote her first book for young readers, *The Legend of Buddy Bush*, in 2004. The following year the novel was selected as a Coretta Scott King author honor book and was a National Book Award finalist. Other youth titles followed, including *I, Dred Scott*, *The Return of Buddy Bush*, *The Baptism*, and *Joseph*, which was nominated for an NAACP Image Award in 2008. Moses now lives in Atlanta, but she notes that her youth in a rural North Carolina hamlet shaped her early books for young people. "I was raised on a place in the middle of no place," she told Sheryl Cannady in an interview that took place during the 2007 National Book Festival in Washington, D.C., going on to explain how her mother and grandmother encouraged her to read, love stories, and, eventually, tell them in her writing.

Christopher Myers 1974-

Christopher Myers is a native New Yorker who was born in Queens. He is a graduate of Brown University, where he majored in American civilization and art semiotics. After graduation he did further study as a participant in the Whitney Museum of American Art's Independent Study Program, which is designed for emerging artists. In addition to children's book illustration, Myers's current work includes sculpture and installation art.

When asked about those whose art has had an influence on him, Myers lists Romare Bearden, Jacob Lawrence, William H. Johnson, the photographer Roy DeCarava, and the multimedia sculptor and performance artist David Hammons.

Myers received Coretta Scott King honors for illustration in 1998 for *Harlem*, which was written by his father, Walter Dean Myers, and in 2000 for *Black Cat*, which Christopher both wrote and illustrated. He currently resides in Brooklyn, New York.

Walter Dean Myers 1937-2014

Born in Martinsburg, West Virginia, Walter Dean Myers was informally adopted by family and friends after his mother's death. At age three he moved to Harlem with foster parents. There he attended plays for children at Columbia University, listened to stories at the local public library, and attended summer Bible school at St. James Church. (This church was to become the first home of the Dance Theater of Harlem.) Myers learned stories told by his adoptive father and grandfather. The talented writer describes school as frustrating because he had a severe speech problem. Fortunately, an understanding teacher observed his talent for writing poetry and short stories and encouraged him to express himself on paper, where the "words came out more easily." In spite of that encouragement, Myers dropped out of high school and joined the Army on his seventeenth birthday.

After a stint in the Army, Myers returned to civilian life with few skills, little formal education, but a passion for writing. While he was working as an employment supervisor for the New York State Department of Labor, he wrote his first short work for children, *Where Does the Day Go?* He entered the manuscript in a competition sponsored by the Council on Interracial Books for Children and won. From 1970 to 1977, Myers was a trade book editor for Bobbs-Merrill. During that time he expanded a short story into his first young adult novel, *Fast Sam, Cool Clyde, and Stuff*. When that work was named a 1976 Coretta Scott King honor book, Myers received important confirmation of his commitment to writing as a career.

Since 1977, Myers has worked full-time as a freelance writer. In addition to earning five Coretta Scott King awards and four Coretta Scott King honors, he has received a Newbery honor for *Somewhere in the Darkness* (1993), two National Endowment for the Arts grants, and a MacDowell fellowship. Myers also received the 1994 Margaret A. Edwards Award in recognition of his outstanding contribution to literature for young adults and the 1997 Virginia Hamilton Writer's Award. For his 2003 book *Blue Journey*, which was illustrated by his son, Christopher Myers, Walter Dean Myers received an honor from the judges of the Lee Bennett Hopkins Poetry Award.

Myers was the first recipient of the Printz Award, established by the Young Adult Library Services Association in 2000 to honor the late Michael L. Printz, an ardent supporter of youth. That "annual award for the finest book for young adults, based solely on literary quality," was given to Myers's dramatic novel *Monster*. Recognition for this multitalented writer continued when in 2007 he received the Lee Bennett Hopkins Poetry Award and in 2008 was selected to present the Mae Hill Arbuthnot Lecture at the Children's Defense Fund, Langston Hughes Library on the Haley Farm, Clinton, Tennessee.

When not writing, Myers relaxed playing the flute and browsing through rare bookstores. A skilled photographer, he was also a noted collector of photographic images of African Americans, many of which found their way into beautiful books with Myers's original poetry. Most recently, as a father-and-son team, Walter Dean and Christopher were lauded for their words and pictures, particularly in books with music as the theme.

John Nagenda 1938-

John Nagenda was born and educated in Uganda. He worked in book publishing until 1965, when he became a full-time freelance writer. His short stories, articles, and poetry have been published in Africa, Europe, and the United States. *Mukasa*, a 1974 Coretta Scott King honor book, was his first book for children. He is somewhat fanatical about games and even played cricket for Uganda. He has made his home in England since 1966.

Kadir Nelson 1974-

Kadir Nelson was born in Washington, D.C., and grew up in Atlantic City, New Jersey, and San Diego, California. He began drawing at the age of three, and at age eleven he came under the tutelage of his uncle, an artist and teacher. As a high school student, he began entering his paintings in art competitions and was awarded a scholarship to Pratt Institute.

Nelson's work has been widely exhibited at such places as the Simon Weisenthal Center Museum of Tolerance, the Museum of African American History (Detroit, Michigan), the Society of Illustrators (New York), the Citizen's Gallery (Yokohama, Japan), and the Center for Culture (Tijuana, Mexico). His paintings have decorated the sets of television shows and feature films, and he was the conceptual artist for the Steven Spielberg film *Amistad*. *Just the Two of Us*, by Will Smith with illustrations by Kadir Nelson, won a 2002 NAACP Image Award as an Outstanding Literary Work for Children. His dramatic depictions of the Negro Leagues, originally painted for *Sports Illustrated*, were included in an exhibit of artwork about the Negro Baseball Leagues experience in 2004. Nelson received a 2004 Coretta Scott King illustrator honor for *Thunder Rose*, by Jerdine Nolen, and a 2005 illustrator award for *Ellington Was Not a Street*, by Ntozake Shange. His 2007 illustrator award–winning *Moses: When Harriet Tubman Led Her People to Freedom*, by Carole Boston Weatherford, was also a Caldecott honor book. In 2009, Nelson received the Coretta Scott King Book Award for *We Are the Ship*, which was also selected as a CSK illustrator honor book.

Nelson lives with his wife and two daughters in San Diego, California.

Marilyn Nelson 1946-

Marilyn Nelson was born in Cleveland, Ohio, the daughter of a schoolteacher and a career Air Force officer. Growing up on a succession of military bases, she developed an interest in writing, particularly poetry, while still in elementary school. She later earned a bachelor of arts degree from the University of California, Davis, a master of science degree from the University of Pennsylvania, and a doctorate from the University of Minnesota. In 2002, she was named professor emeritus at the University of Connecticut, Storrs, where she taught creative writing and Aframerican and American ethnic literature. From 2001 to 2006, she served as poet laureate of the State of Connecticut. Marilyn Nelson has lent her work and extraordinary voice to the Poetry Foundation's podcasts, which introduce poetry as an oral art form to young people. She received Coretta Scott King author honors in 2005 for *A Wreath for Emmett Till* and in 2006 for the haunting manumission manuscript *Fortune's Bones*. Among her many other honors, she has been a National Book Award finalist for *The Home Place*, *The Field of Praise*, and *Carver: A Life in Poems*.

Vaunda Micheaux Nelson 1953-

Vaunda Micheaux Nelson loves bringing books and children together and feels lucky to have two careers that foster this. The children's librarian and author says, "It was destined from the day I was born. My mother found my name in a novel she was reading." Vaunda's first book, *Always Gramma*, was selected by the Children's Book Council as a Notable Children's Trade Book in the Field of Social Studies. *Mayfield Crossing* won the Georgia Children's Book in 1995, and *Beyond Mayfield* received a 1999 Parents' Choice Gold Award. *Almost to Freedom*, her most recent title, received a Coretta Scott King honor for illustration in 2004. In addition, Vaunda's poetry has been published in *Cricket* and *Cicada* magazines.

Vaunda has been a teacher, newspaper reporter, bookseller, school librarian, and twice a member of the Newbery Award Committee. She holds master's degrees from the Bread Loaf School of English at Middlebury College, Vermont, and from the University of Pittsburgh School of Library and Information Science. Her memberships include the SCBWI, the American Library Association, and the Association for Library Service to Children.

The Pennsylvania native is currently the young adult librarian at a public library in New Mexico, where she lives with her husband, Drew, and two cats.

Greg Neri, G. Neri 1963-

Greg Neri, who writes under the pen name G. Neri, was raised in Los Angeles, California, and currently lives in Tampa, Florida. Initially pursuing a career as a filmmaker, he began writing and illustrating for kids in 1999, before switching to writing for teens in 2004. Neri's 2010 book, *Yummy: The*

Last Days of a Southside Shorty, earned him a Coretta Scott King author honor. His work has also been honored by the Museum of Tolerance and the Simon Wiesenthal Center, Antioch University, the International Reading Association, the American Library Association, the Junior Library Guild, and the National Council for Teachers of English.

Lillie Patterson 1917–1999

Lillie Patterson was raised by her grandmother in Hilton Head, South Carolina. She once said that her grandmother, a singer, gave her a sense of the power of words. As a storyteller, Patterson used her command of words in developing educational radio and television programs for children. During a long career in the field of education, Patterson served as a library service specialist and the chair of the Elementary School Book Reviewing Committee in the Baltimore public school system.

In her writing career, which started in 1962, Patterson concentrated on creating nonfiction material for young readers, especially simple biographies of noted African Americans. Lillie Patterson earned Coretta Scott King honors for *Coretta Scott King* (1978), *Benjamin Banneker: Genius of Early America* (1979), and *Martin Luther King, Jr., and the Freedom Movement* (1990), but she will be most remembered as the first person to receive the Coretta Scott King Book Award, given in 1970 in recognition of her *Dr. Martin Luther King, Jr.: Man of Peace.*

Margaret Peters 1936–

Margaret Peters was born in Dayton, Ohio, in 1936. Inspired by her parents to dedicate her life to work in the church and in education, she earned bachelor's and master's degrees and a supervisor's certificate from the University of Dayton. As a high school teacher of English and history, she was troubled by the lack of adequate, accurate information about African American history for young people. The goal of her career from that time onward was to enrich the curriculum with information that children needed about the black experience.

Peters inaugurated after-school classes in black history, became a resource teacher in black history in the Dayton public schools, conducted a weekly radio program on African American culture, and introduced the only course in the Dayton schools that focused on black history. Peters retired in June 1993 and now volunteers in the schools and continues to write and speak about African American culture. She has served on the board of the Dayton chapter of the Southern Christian Leadership Conference and has chaired the Dr. Martin Luther King Jr. scholarship competition, which has helped twenty-six African American students attend college.

Over the years, Peters has been the recipient of numerous local and national awards for her contributions to education, including the Dr. Carter G. Woodson Book Award from the National Council for the Social Studies and the National Council of Negro Women's Award for Excellence in Teaching. Her *Ebony Book of Black Achievement* was named a Coretta Scott King honor book in 1971. Peters has served on the Executive Council of the Association for the Study of Afro-American Life and History and is still very involved in volunteer work, stressing the importance of sharing information on African American history.

Jeanne Whitehouse Peterson 1939–

Jeanne Whitehouse Peterson was born in Walla Walla, Washington. She earned a bachelor's degree from Washington State University before traveling to New York to study at Columbia University, where she earned a master's degree. After further study Peterson received her Ph.D. in American studies from the University of New Mexico in Albuquerque. She taught in public schools and served in Malaysia in the Peace Corps.

Peterson has said that she had long felt the urge to write but that it was the desire to tell about her sister that ultimately prompted her to write *I Have a Sister, My Sister Is Deaf,* which was named a Coretta Scott King honor book in 1979.

Peterson is a lecturer in children's literature at the University of New Mexico and is actively concerned with Native American affairs in the New Mexico area. She spends as much time as possible caring for and enjoying her string of horses.

Andrea Davis Pinkney 1963–

Andrea Davis Pinkney was born in Washington, D.C., to parents deeply involved in the civil rights movement. She spent many of her summer vacations at the national conferences of the National Urban League.

Planning to become a magazine writer, Pinkney majored in journalism at Syracuse University. After a stint as senior editor of *Essence* magazine, she began editing books for young people at Simon & Schuster, and later at Scholastic.

At Hyperion Books for Children she launched the Jump at the Sun imprint to publish "books celebrating the beauty of black culture for every child's pleasure."

Pinkney was promoted to editorial director at Hyperion and in 2002 became vice president and publisher of children's books at Houghton Mifflin. In addition to her executive responsibilities, she continues to write both fiction and nonfiction books for young readers. Among the titles she has done in collaboration with her husband, the illustrator Brian Pinkney, is *Duke Ellington: The Piano Prince and His Orchestra*, which was named a 1999 Coretta Scott King honor book for illustration. In 2001, this talented writer received a Coretta Scott King honor for the text of *Let It Shine*, a collective biography of ten African American woman freedom fighters.

Andrea and Brian Pinkney and their two children live in Brooklyn, New York.

Brian Pinkney 1961-

Brian Pinkney continues to gain wider and wider recognition for his work in the field of children's book illustration. Born and raised in New York, Pinkney studied at the Philadelphia College of Art, where he earned a B.A. in fine arts. After further study at the School of Visual Arts in New York City, he received a master's degree in fine arts. While accepting the value of his formal education, Pinkney credits much of his artistic strength to growing up in a family where creativity was the norm. When evaluating his early works, he states that he wanted to be "just like my father," the noted illustrator Jerry Pinkney.

With the ever more distinctive honing of his unique scratchboard technique, Brian Pinkney produced the vibrant and musical illustrations for *Duke Ellington: The Piano Prince and His Orchestra*, with text written in "classic jazz talk" by his wife, Andrea Davis Pinkney. For the artwork in this outstanding tribute to the creator of great jazz music, Brian Pinkney received a 1999 Coretta Scott King honor. The book was also named a Caldecott honor book by the ALA Association for Library Service to Children.

Among the places where Pinkney's works have been exhibited are the Schomburg Center for Research in Black Culture and the National Coalition of 100 Black Women Art Show. His illustrations have appeared in publications such as the *New York Times Magazine*, *Woman's Day*, *Business Tokyo*, and *Ebony*.

Brian Pinkney lives in Brooklyn, New York, with his author-editor wife, Andrea, and their two children.

Jerry Pinkney 1939-

Jerry Pinkney describes his world as a "world full of color" that reflects the people, the activities, and the neighborhood connections he experienced while growing up in a black community. Out of this philosophical background, the artist states that one of his goals is to "depict black folks as naturally and with as much respect as possible." Pinkney's illustrations typically portray the individuality of the characters within a group—their uniqueness in clothing, hairstyle, skin tone, and community background.

Pinkney was born in Philadelphia and studied at the Philadelphia Museum College of Art. Over the years his works have been honored by the Art Director's Show, the American Institute of Graphic Arts, the Council on Interracial Books for Children, and the National Conference of Christians and Jews. In addition to earning Coretta Scott King awards in 1986, 1987, 1989, 1999, and 2002 and CSK honors in 1981, 1990, and 2009, Pinkney has received the Carter G. Woodson Book Award and recognition from the New England Book Show.

Pinkney may be best noted for his book illustration, but he also designed several U.S. postage stamps for the Black Heritage Commemorative Series and later served on the U.S. Postal Service Stamp Advisory Committee. He has designed many record album covers, and his art has been exhibited in many galleries throughout the United States. Pinkney and his wife, Gloria, a writer of children's literature, live in Croton-on-Hudson, New York. During the 2001 holiday season, Jerry Pinkney enjoyed a singular honor: owing to his masterful art skills, he was selected to design that year's White House Christmas brochure. The theme came from the Christmas tree decorations, which were representations of the homes of all the former presidents. Mr. and Mrs. Pinkney enjoyed a visit with First Lady Laura Bush when the brochure was presented.

Sean Qualls 1969-

Sean Qualls was born in Cocoa Beach, Florida. His father worked for NASA at the time. Shortly after he was born, he moved with his mother, grandmother, and sister to Bordentown, New Jersey. Bordentown is small, with a population just under five thousand people. His days as a child were spent playing in the woods, walking along train tracks, and listening to music (mostly Kiss records), and his earliest memories of making art were of coloring in coloring books with his older sister, Angela. His favorite book when he was seven years old was an illustrated Bible that he had received for Christmas. After graduating from high school, he moved to Brooklyn to attend Pratt Institute and study fine arts. He dropped out after a year and half and took a few night courses at the School of Visual Arts. He considers himself to be mostly self-educated. He has created illustrations for a variety of publications, and his works have been exhibited in galleries across the country. His website lists fairy tales, outsider art, African art, and memorabilia as influences on his work, but he says, "I get most inspired when listening to music, reading, going for long walks, or visiting museums." He lives with his wife, Selina Alko (who is also an illustrator), and two children, Ginger and Isaiah, in a little house in Park Slope, Brooklyn, where he also makes his art.

James E. Ransome 1961–

James E. Ransome was born in Rich Square, North Carolina, where he spent his early years under the guidance of a nurturing and loving grandmother. Although the illustrator cannot remember when his interest in art began, he does remember creating his own drawings based on what he saw in comic strips and Mad magazine. It was in high school in Bergen, New Jersey, that Ransome began to hone his skills in filmmaking and cinematography. An observant teacher who noticed Ransome's skills in animation suggested that he take drawing and painting classes, and his interest in art and painting grew from that encouragement.

Ransome earned a bachelor of fine arts in illustration from Pratt Institute in Brooklyn, New York. Among the major influences on Ransome were his introduction in art history to such artists as Mary Cassatt, John Singer Sargent, Winslow Homer, and Edward Degas, and his meeting with the renowned artist Jerry Pinkney, who lectured and taught senior art illustration at Pratt. Ransome states, "I had always been given the impression that there were virtually no African American artists, so meeting Jerry Pinkney and discovering his large body of work was very encouraging." A warm relationship between the two artists continues to this day.

Ransome says of his illustrating, "What makes illustrating so exciting is that because each book has a special voice, my approach toward each is different. Whether it be through choice of palette, design, or perspective, there is always a desire to experiment and explore what makes each book unique."

Ransome, currently a member of the Society of Illustrators, has been named by the Children's Book Council among the seventy-five authors and illustrators everyone should know. His 1994 Coretta Scott King honor book Uncle Jed's Barbershop was featured on the popular children's television program Reading Rainbow. His illustrations for The Creation, which won the Coretta Scott King Book Award in 1995, also won an International Board on Books for Young People Award that year.

As his schedule allows, Ransome shares his talent and his time by doing school visitations during which he demonstrates his drawing processes, shows slides of his works in progress, and explains how he got into the field of children's book illustration. Ransome lives in upstate New York with his wife, Lesa, two daughters, Jaime and Maya, and Clinton, the ever-present family Dalmatian.

Jewell Parker Rhodes 1954–

Jewell Parker Rhodes has always loved reading and writing stories. Born in Pittsburgh, Pennsylvania, she received her doctor of arts from Carnegie Mellon University and now teaches creative writing at Arizona State University. She is the author of two children's books, six novels, and three nonfiction books. Her writing has won numerous awards, including the American Book Award, the National Endowment for the Arts Award in Fiction, the Black Caucus of the American Library Award for Literary Excellence, the PEN Oakland/Josephine Miles Award for Outstanding Writing, the Jane Addams Children's Book Award, and the Coretta Scott King Author Honor Award.

Faith Ringgold 1930–

Faith Ringgold was born in New York City and was educated in the schools of upper Harlem. Even during the Depression, her family saw to it that Faith and her brother and sister enjoyed cultural experiences. As a young child, Faith showed artistic ability, and her interest in art was stimulated by frequent trips to the city's art museums.

In high school, along with the usual academic subjects, Ringgold studied art, and she continued her art studies in the school of education at City College of New York, where she earned her bachelor's degree. She spent years teaching art in the city schools, but deep down she felt a call to express something more of her African American heritage and to encourage museum curators to give greater exposure to the art of African American women. From flat paintings, the artist moved to soft sculpture, remembering the faces of her family and the people of her Harlem childhood. With time came another change in her technique: picture stories in acrylic on canvas bordered by quilt squares, with details that engrossed the viewer into "reading" each story very carefully. This unique art style has brought renown to Ringgold, and she has transposed some of her historical quilt stories into picture books for young readers. Her first picture book, *Tar Beach*, received both the 1992 Coretta Scott King Book Award for illustration and a Caldecott honor.

Ringgold presently lives in New Jersey within sight of the George Washington Bridge.

Dorothy Robinson 1929–

Dorothy Robinson was one of the earliest winners of the Coretta Scott King Book Award, which she received in 1975 for *The Legend of Africania*. Then a librarian in the Chicago Public Library system, the author recalls that she conceived the idea for her book during the civil rights movement of the 1960s. It was one of many books that she believed were needed to help children of the civil rights era understand what was being seen on television and her "way of explaining to them who they were and the beauty of their history as African Americans."

Dorothy Robinson retired from the Chicago Public Library system in the mid-1980s. In 1990, she founded a program, "The Genie in Every Child," designed to help parents and teachers use books and reading to raise children's self-esteem.

Robinson was born in Waycross, Georgia, went to Fisk University, and earned her master's in library science from Atlanta University. She now lives in Laurel, Maryland, a suburb of Baltimore.

Charlemae Rollins 1897–1979

Charlemae Rollins was born in Yazoo, Mississippi, and spent her early childhood in Oklahoma with her grandmother, a former slave. After teaching in Oklahoma, Rollins moved to Chicago, where she began her career as a librarian in the public library system. It was the start of an outstanding career as a children's librarian during which she developed programs that moved beyond the traditional story hours and reading-guidance activities. In circulating books to children, she became acutely aware of the shortage of cultural material that spoke positively of the black experience. Rollins thus turned her talents to writing both criticisms decrying racial stereotyping and quality biographies about blacks who overcame tremendous obstacles to make outstanding contributions to American culture.

Rollins was one of the first editors of the National Council of Teachers of English bibliography "Reading Ladders of Human Relations," which addressed the importance of cultural diversity.

For this pioneer in services for children, the awards were many. Rollins was the first black to be given life membership in the American Library Association, after she became the first black to serve as president of the then Children's Services Division. In 1971, she received the Coretta Scott King Book Award for her biography of a friend, *Black Troubadour: Langston Hughes*. She also earned the American Brotherhood Award of the National Conference of Christians and Jews, the Grolier Foundation Award, and the National Centennial Award, to name a few.

Within the American Library Association, the Association for Library Service to Children has created a permanent memorial to Charlemae Rollins in its annual Charlemae Rollins President's Program.

Reynold Ruffins 1930–

Reynold Ruffins was born in New York City and grew up in Queens. He attended the High School of Music and Art in Manhattan and Cooper Union. A graphic designer and illustrator for commercial ads and magazines, Ruffins has taught art subjects at the School of Visual Arts and Parsons School of Design in New York City and at the Syracuse University College of Visual and Performing Arts.

Among his many awards, Ruffins has received the Saint-Gaudens Medal, the highest honor given to a Cooper Union alumnus. Ruffins's early activity in the field of illustration was the result of meeting Jane Sarnoff at a civil rights protest march in 1976, and the two collaborated on at least fourteen books. He has also illustrated children's folktales, including Verna Aardema's *Misoso: Once upon a Time Tales from Africa* and *Koi and the Kola Nuts*, an edition of which is available on tape, read by Whoopi Goldberg. In 1997, Ruffins received a Coretta Scott King honor for his illustrations in Denizé Lauture's *Running the Road to ABC*.

Ruffins and his wife, Joan, live in Sag Harbor, New York.

Sonia Lynn Sadler 1958–2013

Sonia Lynn Sadler, artist and designer, was born at Fort Riley, an Army base in Kansas. Sadler attended the Maryland Institute College of Art in Baltimore and received a bachelor of fine arts degree in fashion design from Parsons School of Design in New York. Originally working in fashion at houses that included Anne Klein, Jones of New York, and Liz Claiborne, she began to pursue a career as a professional artist. Her art has been featured in the *Washington Post*, *Valentine New York*, *Washington Woman*, and the *Daily News*. She was also the illustrator of three children's books: *The Goat Goes to Town* by Phyllis Gershator, *Ma Dear's Old Green House* by Denise Lewis Patrick, and *Seeds of Change* by Jen Cullerton Johnson, which won her the Coretta Scott King/John Steptoe Award from the American Library Association, the Green Earth Award from the Newton Morassco Foundation, the Best Children's Book of the Year Award from Access Africa presented at the Smithsonian, and the Sigurd Olson Nature Writing Award for Children's Literature by the Sigurd Environmental Institute of Wisconsin. She was also selected as one of ten acclaimed illustrators to contribute to Scholastic's *America the Beautiful: Together We Stand*.

Synthia Saint James 1949–

Synthia Saint James was born in Los Angeles but spent her formative, early years in New York City. She attributes the development of her "creative self" to this New York environment, surrounded by an extended family. She says New York was where she learned to color and to draw and where she sold her first original oil paintings.

Now an internationally recognized fine artist, Saint James had her first one-woman exhibit in 1977 and later exhibited in Paris, Canada, Korea, and several cities in the United States. She has designed cover art for books by such noted authors as Alice Walker, Terry Macmillan, and Iyanla Vanzant. Her distinguished style can be seen on greeting cards (including those for UNICEF), calendars, and T-shirts. In 1997, the United States Postal Service issued the Kwanzaa stamp created by Saint James.

This talented artist has illustrated six picture books for children, including *Neeny Coming, Neeny Going*, which was named a Coretta Scott King honor book in 1997. She says of *Neeny Coming, Neeny Going*, "This is a very special story to me. This is not only because I enjoyed researching and painting beautiful Daufuskie Island, where the story is set, but also because the story deals with issues that changes can create, even among family."

Saint James lives in Los Angeles with her cat, Chisai.

Terea Shaffer 1969–

Terea Shaffer is a native of Brooklyn, New York. Her formal art training includes an associate degree in applied science and a bachelor of fine arts degree from the Fashion Institute of Technology in New York City. While pursuing her studies, Shaffer received the Howland Clark Quinby honor from the National Arts Club. She enjoys music, collecting artwork from various artists in various formats, and art history books.

Shaffer is the illustrator of several children's books, including the 1995 Coretta Scott King honor title *The Singing Man*. She makes her home in Brooklyn, New York.

Tayna R. Simon 1966–

Tayna Simon is a literary agent and lives in New York. Simon has an M.A. in anthropology. Her debut novel, *Zora and Me*, coauthored with Victoria Bond, is a fictional account of the childhood of Zora Neale Hurston, a canonical Harlem Renaissance writer, imagining her as a girl detective. The book has received several honors, including the Coretta Scott King/John Steptoe Award for New Talent.

Charles R. Smith Jr. 1969–

Born and raised in California, Charles R. Smith Jr. "spent many hours with characters in books traveling the world, solving mysteries, or living in a different time in history." From early on, he wrote stories and poems, played sports, especially basketball, and developed a serious interest in photography. Smith has combined these interests and experiences to create several books for children and young people. After graduating from photography school, Smith moved to New York, where he continued his writing.

With more than twenty books to his credit, his *Rimshots: Basketball Pix, Rolls and Rhythms* was a 2006 ALA Notable Children's Book. In discussing the Coretta Scott King honor citation in 2008 for his book *Twelve Rounds to Glory: The Story of Muhammad Ali*, he noted that he wanted to tell the story of Ali's life "in a way that hadn't been done before." He wanted the book "to represent every part of this remarkable man." Since the book is about boxing, he explained, "I wanted it to feel like a boxing match, so to do the fight scenes, I watched old movies of the actual fights and wrote down what I saw." With his books, he wants "to show students, particularly boys, that there are many ways to pursue their interests, no matter what they may be." The influence of rap music is evident in his poetry.

Smith lives in Poughkeepsie, New York, with his wife and three children.

Hope Anita Smith 1962–

Hope Anita Smith is a native of Akron, Ohio, and now lives in Los Angeles, California.

At the age of four, Hope Anita was already reading, and as she read she became totally connected with the characters in the stories. Her love of storytelling and performing dramatic orations grew as she read the poetry of such greats as James Weldon Johnson and Paul Laurence Dunbar. In later years she became immersed in the words of such poets as Nikki Giovanni, Maya Angelou, and Edna St. Vincent Millay. By the age of eight, she was creating poems. As the writer describes it, "a sheet of paper became her canvas and words were her palette."

Among her projects for sharing her love of creative writing with young people, Smith has developed a poetry-writing program that she presents in schools to children of all ages. She has also created a program called Bookmarked for Poetry, in which winning student poems are made into bookmarks and distributed in the school library.

Smith received the 2004 Coretta Scott King/John Steptoe New Talent Award for the poetic prose in her debut novel *The Way a Door Closes*, and she is now working on a sequel. *The Way a Door Closes* also received honors from the judges of the Lee Bennett Hopkins Poetry Award. In 2009, she received a Coretta Scott King author honor for *Keeping the Night Watch*.

Ellease Southerland 1943–

Ellease Southerland, a native New Yorker, was born in Brooklyn. She attended Queens College and later earned a master's of fine arts degree from Columbia University. Growing up as the oldest of fifteen brothers and sisters in a close-knit family, Southerland recalls a household organized on the religious principles of her minister father. She remembers it, too, as a house filled with music.

Southerland's first novel, *Let the Lion Eat Straw*, was named a Coretta Scott King honor book in 1980. The author relates that the religious motifs that permeate that book are based loosely on the home life she knew and that the mother figure is a bittersweet reflection of her mother. The sequel, *A Feast of Fools*, appeared in *Breaking Ice: An Anthology of Contemporary African-American Fiction* (1990).

Southerland's primary focus has been on writing poetry. Her works have been published in several periodicals, including *Black World*, *Massachusetts Review*, and the *Journal of Black Poetry*. The high quality of her work won her the Gwendolyn Brooks Poetry Award in 1972.

Southerland is an adjunct professor at Pace University and lives in Jamaica, New York.

Martha Southgate 1960–

Martha Southgate's early writing career includes eleven years as a journalist for, among others, the *New York Daily News*, *Essence*, and *Premiere*. After graduating from Smith College with a bachelor of science degree, Southgate continued her studies and received a master of fine arts degree from Goddard College. Her interest in and knowledge of ballet, which she studied as a teenager, is evident in the accurate details of her first novel, *Another Way to Dance*. That novel not only received the 1997 New Talent Award but also was named an ALA Best Book for Young Adults and is listed in the 1997 New York Public Library bibliography "Books for the Teen Age."

Southgate, born and raised in Cleveland, Ohio, now lives in New York City with her husband, Jeff Phillips, and son, Nathaniel.

Javaka Steptoe 1974–

Javaka Steptoe was born and raised in Brooklyn, New York. The son of the famous artist and illustrator John Steptoe, he states that he always thought about illustrating children's books. To further his goal, Steptoe studied art and graduated from Cooper Union in New York City. To share his personal bent for creativity, Steptoe teaches art to children in the Bedford-Stuyvesant area of Brooklyn. When this talented artist speaks of Brooklyn, his eyes light up with infectious pleasure and love of the place he calls home. He received the 1998 Coretta Scott King Book Award for illustrating *In Daddy's Arms I Am Tall*, a collection of poems celebrating fathers and fatherhood.

When not seriously involved in an art-related project, Steptoe enjoys reading, rollerblading, and sharing time with his sisters and twin nieces.

John Steptoe 1950–1989

John Steptoe was born in Brooklyn, New York, and from the time he was an art student in high school, he knew that he wanted to create picture books for African American children. His first book, *Stevie* (Harper & Row, 1969), was published when he was just nineteen. It met with immediate success when it was reprinted in its entirety in *Life* magazine, and its talented young artist was called to national attention. Steptoe's early style was often compared to that of the French painter Rouault, and through the years his picture books showed the development of his painting style as he experimented with abstraction, expressionism, and surrealism.

Steptoe's tragic death in 1989 cut short a career filled with vision and promise. In his brief lifetime he won numerous awards and distinctions, including two Caldecott honors; the Boston Globe–Horn Book Award; Coretta Scott King awards for *Mother Crocodile / Maman-Caiman* in 1982 and *Mufaro's Beautiful Daughters: An African Tale* in 1988; and a Coretta Scott King honor for *All the Colors of the Race* in 1983. In 1999, the New Talent Award was officially renamed the Coretta Scott King/John Steptoe New Talent Award. It symbolizes the task force's wish to recognize the talent of emerging artists and authors, just as Steptoe's early works were recognized as "only the beginning."

The legacy John Steptoe left to children and to children's literature is perhaps best summed up in a statement he made about his work in 1988: "In my picture books I put all the things I never saw when I was a child."

Ruth Ann Stewart 1942–

Ruth Ann Stewart was born in Chicago. She attended the University of Chicago but completed her studies at Wheaton College in Massachusetts, where she earned a bachelor of arts degree in 1963. After earning a master of science degree from Columbia University in New York, she did further study at Harvard University and, in 1987, at the Kennedy School of Government.

Stewart has served on several advisory boards, including the board of visitors at the Pittsburgh School of Library and Information Science, the board of trustees at Wheaton College, and the District of Columbia Historical Records Advisory Board.

Of *Portia*, the book for which she won a 1978 Coretta Scott King honor, Stewart said:

> It was my intention to tell the story in an interesting and lively manner of a woman whose life also provided a previously unknown perspective on an important chapter in African American history. . . . Even though Portia was the daughter of a famous man [Booker T. Washington], her career and personal struggles are common to the stories yet to be written of many black women. . . . It is my hope that this literary shortcoming will be vigorously addressed and there will be many Portias (including a few more of mine) taking their place on shelves of libraries and bookstores in the near future.

Stewart lives in Washington, D.C., and has one daughter.

Shadra Strickland 1977–

Shadra Strickland was born in Nashville, Tennessee, and grew up in Atlanta, Georgia. As a child, her favorite things to do were spending time with family, playing outdoors, and reading. "My mom was a teacher," says Strickland, "and I spent a lot of time around her high school students. Education and learning has always played a big role in my family's life." After graduating from college, Strickland taught art for several years, but she ultimately decided to pursue her dream of creating children's books. "I decided that making children's books was my creative calling," she says. "Looking at the work of Pat Cummings, Christopher Myers, Jerry Pinkney, Jon Muth, Jan Ormerod, and Kadir Nelson fueled my desire even more." Strickland moved to New York City and enrolled in the School of Visual Art's Illustration as Visual Essay program. "I sought out many of the people whose work I had admired from afar for so long. Through many meetings, promotional postcards, and emails, my dreams slowly started to come true." Strickland's first picture book, *Bird*, was released in October 2008. The book received a starred review from *Kirkus* Reviews and was named an Editor's Favorite of 2008 in both the *Bloomsbury Review* and *Kirkus*. *Publisher's Weekly* called *Bird* "a promising debut" and said of Strickland's illustrations, "A complicated weaving of impressive watercolor, gouache, charcoal, and ink drawings amplifies the metaphors and action of the poetic text." A freelance designer as well as an illustrator, Strickland holds a B.A. from Syracuse University and an M.F.A. from the School of Visual Arts. She loves to read, write, and travel, especially to visit friends.

Strickland currently lives in Brooklyn, New York.

Mildred D. Taylor 1943–

Mildred Taylor was born in 1943 in Jackson, Mississippi, but her father soon moved his young family north because he did not want his daughters to grow up in the segregated South.

Taylor showed early promise as a writer by winning first prize in the 1973 Council on Interracial Books for Children contest with a fictionalized story from her father's childhood in rural Mississippi. The award-winning manuscript,

Song of the Trees, was published by Dial in 1975 and became the first in a series of books Taylor would write about the Logan family. It was also awarded the first of many honors she would receive from the Coretta Scott King Task Force. Her second novel, *Roll of Thunder, Hear My Cry*, won the Newbery Medal, was a National Book Award finalist, was a *Boston Globe–Horn Book* honor book, and was a Coretta Scott King honor book.

Taylor has continued the Logan family saga in subsequent books, firmly establishing herself as one of the premiere writers of American historical fiction for children and adolescents. She focuses almost exclusively on her father's era because she wants to bring to life for contemporary children the previous generation's experiences and work in laying the groundwork for the civil rights movement of the fifties and sixties.

Taylor has received Coretta Scott King awards for *Let the Circle Be Unbroken* (1982), *The Friendship* (1988), *The Road to Memphis* (1991), and *The Land* (2002), which is the prequel to *Roll of Thunder, Hear My Cry*.

Mildred Taylor and her family make their home in the Rocky Mountains.

Theodore Taylor III 1986–

Theodore Taylor III was born in Roanoke, Virginia, and currently lives in Washington, D.C. He received a bachelor of fine arts degree in communication arts from Virginia Commonwealth University's School of the Arts, where he studied drawing, graphic design, web design, and photography. His illustrations can be found in *When the Beat Was Born: DJ Kool Herc and the Creation of Hip Hop*, his first outing in the children's book field. He draws inspiration from a variety of sources such as animation, graphic novels, street art, video games, and especially music.

Joyce Carol Thomas 1938–

Joyce Carol Thomas was born in Ponca City, Oklahoma, one of nine children. Among her childhood memories is one of picking cotton in fields near her home. A less backbreaking job came later, when she worked as a telephone operator by day while attending night classes at San Jose University in California. At San Jose she earned a bachelor's degree in Spanish. Her master's in education came from Stanford University.

Thomas has taught in middle schools, high schools, and universities. She was an associate professor in the English department at Purdue University and taught classes in creative writing at the University of California, Santa Cruz. In addition to her teaching, Thomas has traveled as a lecturer in Africa, Haiti, and the United States.

Thomas has earned many awards for her writing in a variety of genres, including poetry, short stories, novels, and plays for both adults and young adults. *Marked by Fire*, one of her earliest novels for young adults, was named one of the American Library Association's Best Books for Young Adults in 1982. Two of her works were named Coretta Scott King honor books: the novel *Bright Shadow* in 1984 and the poetry collection *Brown Honey in Broomwheat Tea* in 1994. When asked about *Brown Honey in Broomwheat Tea*, Thomas recalls, "In just about all my novels, broomwheat tea is steeped, poured, sipped. When I had a headache or caught chicken pox . . . my mother would go into the weed fields and pick the tea leaves and serve me a steaming cup from the crushed blossoms." Readers of this book of lyrical poetry will take comfort in Thomas's mother's assertion as the tea is being sipped, "Good for what ails you."

Thomas, currently a professor of English at the University of Tennessee, is the mother of four. She lives just outside Knoxville, Tennessee.

Demetria Renee Tucker 1950–

Demetria Tucker was born in Greenville, North Carolina. The daughter of William Alfred and Helen Hemby Tucker, she was a military brat who lived in Tokyo, Japan, for four and a half years, returning to Hampton, Virginia. After graduating from Hampton High School she graduated from North Carolina A&T State University and later received her master of science degree in library science from the University of North Carolina at Chapel Hill. Demetria began her career as a branch manager at the City of Roanoke Public Libraries and later served and retired as the coordinator of youth services.

She also worked as a library media specialist for the City of Roanoke Public Schools at Forest Park Elementary. Demetria moved back to Hampton, Virginia, and currently works as the senior family and youth services librarian at the Pearl Bailey Library in Newport News, Virginia. In 2013, Pearl Bailey Library's youth programs was the recipient of the 2013 President's Committee of the Arts and the Humanities Youth Afterschool Program Award. She was also named by the University of North Carolina's SILS Alumni Association to receive the 2014 Distinguished Alumni Award. She is a member of Alpha Kappa Alpha Sorority, Incorporated.

Janice May Udry 1928–

Janice May Udry was born in Jacksonville, Illinois, a small town that, she says, earned a place on the map because it was the center for the construction of Ferris wheels. Udry, who wanted to write "ever since I learned how to read," earned a B.S. from Northwestern University. After her marriage she moved to Chapel Hill, North Carolina. The writer got some of the ideas for her books while working as an assistant in a nursery school, where she was inspired by the spontaneous excitement the young children showed when she shared quality picture books with them. Udry is the author of the 1957 Caldecott-winning book *A Tree Is Nice* and of the 1960 Caldecott honor book *The Moon Jumpers*. In 1971, she received a Coretta Scott King honor for *Mary Jo's Grandmother*.

Eric Velasquez 1961–

Eric Velasquez is a native New Yorker, born in Spanish Harlem to parents of Afro–Puerto Rican descent. His interest in art involves "a passion for jazz music and a fascination with the African-American experience in the arts."

Velasquez received the 1999 Coretta Scott King/John Steptoe New Talent Award for his illustrations in *The Piano Man*. Although this was his first foray into children's book illustration, he has illustrated book jackets for both young people's and adult novels. His work was based on serious preparation. In addition to researching photo references in the Schomburg picture collection at the New York Public Library, he studied details in the movie *The Exile*, by the pioneering African American filmmaker Oscar Micheaux.

Eric Velasquez and his wife, Deborah, make their home in Hartsdale, New York.

Mildred Pitts Walter 1922–

Mildred Pitts Walter, born in De Ridder, Louisiana, received her bachelor's degree in English from Southern University in New Orleans. She earned a master's degree in education after studying in California and completing her work at the Antioch extension in Denver. Walter taught school in California, served as a consultant at Western Interstate Commission of Higher Education in Denver, and later was a consultant teacher and lecturer at Metro State College, also in Denver.

Walter closed her teaching career in 1969 to devote all of her time to writing. Her dedication to sharing African American history with young readers can be seen in two of her Coretta Scott King honor books: *Because We Are* (1984), which takes a provocative look at school integration, and *Mississippi Challenge* (1993), a scholarly study of that state's history from the African American perspective. *Her Trouble's Child* (1986) also received a Coretta Scott King honor.

Walter has been active in a variety of civil rights movements and the pursuit of world peace. She accepted her 1987 Coretta Scott King Book Award for *Justin and the Best Biscuits in the World* in absentia because she was on a peace mission to Russia. Before her husband's death, the couple traveled widely for civil rights causes around the United States and abroad, including to Africa and China.

Mildred Pitts Walter, the mother of two sons, makes her home in Denver, Colorado.

Carole Boston Weatherford 1956–

New York Times best-selling writer Carole Boston Weatherford doesn't limit herself to one type of book or one audience. She has written historical fiction, informational books, picture books, even board books, winning numerous accolades for her work. Poetry, however, is her real passion, and as she often tells her young fans, she wrote her first poem when she was in the first grade. Her 2009 Coretta Scott King author honor book, a fictional verse memoir of the legendary Billie Holiday, illustrates that she has no intention of setting poetry aside. Like Holiday, Carole lived in Baltimore, and over the years she developed a deep appreciation of Lady Day's music and a fascination with her history. As she's said in an interview, "Billie whispered in my ear." She couldn't decide, however, if the singer's life and art would resonant with young people today. An encounter with a teenage Holiday fan finally convinced her that it would, and *Becoming Billie Holiday* was born. Carole holds an M.A. in publications design from the University of Baltimore and an M.F.A. in creative writing from the University of North Carolina. She's an associate professor at Fayetteville State University in North Carolina, and she enjoys conducting programs that connect teachers and students with historical events and people. She lives with her family in High Point, North Carolina.

Rita Williams-Garcia 1957–

Rita Williams-Garcia was born in Jamaica, New York, and spent her growing years in Seaside, California, and in

Georgia. She experienced her first great writing success at age fourteen, when *Highlights for Children* purchased one of her stories. A graduate of Hofstra University, Williams-Garcia continued her education and later earned a master's degree in creative writing from Queens College, New York.

Williams-Garcia's novels are noted for their realistic and compassionate portrayals of contemporary, urban, African American teenagers. The author attests that many of her books are inspired by the young people she met while working with a remedial group. The first title from this experience, *Blue Tights* (1987), was followed by *Fast Talk on a Slow Track* (1991). Her short stories have appeared in a number of anthologies, including *No Easy Answers*, edited by Donald Gallo; *Twelve Shots: Outstanding Short Stories about Guns*, edited by Harry Mazer; and *Stay True: Short Stories for Strong Girls*, compiled by Marilyn Singer.

In addition to receiving a 1996 Coretta Scott King honor for *Like Sisters on the Home Front*, this talented writer's works have been included in the American Library Association's *Best Books for Young Adults* and *Quick Picks for Reluctant Young Adult Readers* and in the New York Public Library's annual bibliography, "Books for the Teen Age." She is also the recipient of the PEN/Norma Klein Citation for Children's Literature.

Williams-Garcia is a resident of Queens, New York. When her writing schedule allows, she tells stories and gives book talks to area youth.

Kathleen Atkins Wilson
1950–

Kathleen Wilson grew up in Ypsilanti, Michigan, and received her formal art training at Pepperdine University and the Otis Art Institute in Los Angeles.

Wilson's art reflects her philosophy of sharing her heritage through "artistic symbolism." The winner of the 1993 Coretta Scott King Book Award for *The Origin of Life on Earth: An African Creation Myth* typically uses silhouette figures set against luminous backgrounds to celebrate some aspect of her African American heritage and to invite others to join in the celebration. She works in a combination of watercolor, wax crayon, oil, and opaque black, the results of which have been described as magical.

Soft-spoken and serious, yet warm and friendly, Wilson speaks of the spirituality that drives all she does. The parents of two children, Kathleen and her business-manager husband live in California.

Michele Wood
1964–

A native of Indianapolis, Indiana, Michele Wood graduated from the American College in Atlanta, Georgia, and continued her studies under the internationally acclaimed Nigerian sculptor Lamidi Olande Fakeye. The artist, who works in a variety of art forms, was commissioned in 1993 to create the Black History Month Jazz Series poster, which was unveiled by the mayor of Atlanta in the High Museum of Art. Her 1995 Black History Month commemorative poster was featured on NBC's *Today* show.

In 1999, Wood received the Coretta Scott King Book Award for her illustrations in *I See the Rhythm*. That book was also cited by *Publishers Weekly* and the *San Francisco Chronicle* as one of the best books of 1998 for both its art and its text, which was written by Toyomi Igus.

Wood's travels include what she terms her "personal journey to the American South," the fruits and lasting influence of which were expressed in the book *Going Back Home* (1997), which was honored with the prestigious American Book Award. In defining her art Wood says, "My art is my way of looking back and documenting my history and of creatively expressing who I am."

Michele Wood lives and works in Atlanta, Georgia.

Jacqueline Woodson
1963–

Jacqueline Woodson was born in Columbus, Ohio, but spent her growing years in Greenville, South Carolina, and Brooklyn, New York. After graduating from college with a bachelor of arts in English, Woodson began a career as a drama therapist, working with runaways and homeless children in New York City.

Woodson's interest in becoming a writer was sparked in the fifth grade, when she was elected the editor of a magazine. Three books subsequently convinced her that writing should be her career: Toni Morrison's *The Bluest Eye*, Louise Meriweather's *Daddy Was a Number Runner*, and Rosa Guy's *Ruby*. After reading these titles, Woodson realized that "books could be written about people like her—people who were different from the mainstream characters in most novels."

In her critically acclaimed writing the author, who describes herself as strong and independent, tackles difficult issues and seeks to change readers' attitudes about racial issues, sexual abuse, sexual orientation, and class tension. Woodson received the 2001 Coretta Scott King Book Award for *Miracle's Boys* and earned Coretta Scott King honors for *I Hadn't Meant to Tell You This* (1995),

From the Notebooks of Melanin Sun (1996), and *Locomotion* (2004).

Woodson spends much of her time traveling to schools and talking to young people. She considers this work necessary so that "her readers will be more aware of different types of people and better equipped to effect change when they get older." When not writing or traveling, Woodson relaxes by making scarves and quilts for her friends. The writer and her daughter live in Brooklyn, New York.

Contributors

Contributors to the Current Edition

Lana Adlawan is currently the Supervising Librarian for Teen Services for Oakland Public Library. She began her career as a paraprofessional with Oakland Public Library and moved to Brooklyn to attend Pratt Institute, where she received her master's degree in library and information science. Ms. Adlawan became a children's librarian for Brooklyn Public Library, where she worked a number of years and then returned to California to work for Sacramento Public Library as a youth services librarian, as well as a manager for several locations. An advocate for teens and literature for young people, Ms. Adlawan was a member on the 2010 and 2011 Young Adult Library Association (YALSA) Alex Awards Committee and chaired the 2012 Asian Pacific American Librarians Association (APALA) Young Adult Literature Committee. Ms. Adlawan is also a 2011 California Eureka! Fellow and a 2008 ALA Emerging Leader. In 2013–2014, she served a two-year term on the Coretta Scott King awards jury.

Eunice Anderson is Chief of Neighborhood Library Services and has enjoyed working at Enoch Pratt Free Library for many years. Customer service has always been her top priority. Reader's advisory, assisting patrons with research projects, developing library programs, and providing other information needs have kept her challenged and excited to come to work each day. She served on the Coretta Scott King awards jury, 2009–2010.

Therese Bigelow, now retired, spent many years working in public libraries. She has both a master's degree in library science and in children's literature. She is a past president of the Association for Library Service to Children and has served on many children's book award committees including Notable Children's Books, the Newbery Award, the USBBY Outstanding International Books, and the Coretta Scott King awards jury.

Rudine Sims Bishop is professor emerita at The Ohio State University, where she taught courses in children's literature and co-directed an annual children's literature conference. She is the author of *Free Within Ourselves: The Development of African American Children's Literature* (2007). She served on the Coretta Scott King Book Awards Committee, 2014.

Lesley Colabucci is an associate professor at Millersville University of Pennsylvania, where she teaches graduate and undergraduate children's literature courses. She most recently has served on NCTE's Excellence in Poetry award. She served on the Coretta Scott King awards jury, 2011–2012.

Eboni Curry is a graduate of the University of Michigan, School of Information, and has been a youth services librarian for nine years at the District of Columbia Public Libraries. She is an active member of the American Library Association (ALA) and an active member of the Ethnic Multicultural Information Exchange Roundtable (EMIERT), Association of Library Services to Children (ALSC), Public Library Association (PLA), and the Black Caucus of the American Library Association (BCALA), where she served as secretary. Ms. Curry was a member of the Coretta Scott King awards jury, 2010–2012.

Rose Timmons Dawson has held the position of Director of the Alexandria Library in Alexandria, Virginia, for five years. Prior to working there, Ms. Dawson held a number of progressively responsible positions for the District of Columbia Public Library from the Coordinator for Community Youth Services to the head of the Children's Division of the Martin Luther King, Jr. Memorial Library. She holds a master's degree from the University of North Carolina at Chapel Hill. She is a life member of the American Library Association and an active member of the Ethnic Multicultural Information Exchange Roundtable, Association of Library Services to Children (ALSC), Public Library Association, and the Black Caucus of the American Library Association (BCALA). Within the Coretta Scott King (CSK) Committee, she has served on the Virginia Hamilton Lifetime Achievement Award (2011–2013), the CSK Book Award jury. And as an ALSC member, she served on the Theodor Geisel Award (2007), Robert F. Sibert Award (2005), and the Andrew Carnegie Award (1999). She is the 2010 recipient of the BCALA Distinguished Service to the Library Profession Award.

Dr. Cora Phelps Dunkley is an associate professor in the School of Information at the University of South Florida, where she teaches school media and youth services courses. Her research interests include multicultural literature for children and young adults and the impact of the school librarian and school library on the academic success of students. Dr. Dunkley is an active member of the American Library Association (ALA), the Black Caucus of ALA and the Association for Library Service to Children. She has served as a member of the Notable Children's Video Committee, the Coretta Scott King awards jury and the Caldecott Committee. A former school librarian, Dr. Dunkley is the Immediate Past President of the Florida Association for Media in Education.

Diane Foote is assistant dean at Dominican University's Graduate School of Library and Information Science in River Forest, Illinois. She is a former associate editor of *Book Links* magazine, and a former executive director of the Association for Library Service to Children (ALSC), a division of the American Library Association. She served on the 2010 John Newbery Award Selection Committee and the Coretta Scott King awards juries (2011–2012), and has reviewed children's and parenting books for *Booklist* magazine and *Kirkus Reviews*. She lives in Chicago with her family.

Debby Gold has been a children's librarian at Cuyahoga County Public Library for thirty years and served on the Coretta Scott King awards jury, 2011–2012.

Karen Lemmons is a library media specialist at Detroit School of Arts. She was also a member of the 2011 Coretta Scott King awards jury.

Martha Ruff received her M.L.S. degree from the University of Chicago. Ms. Ruff is a performing storyteller and a librarian at Maryland's Prince George's County Public Library. She is the former librarian for the NAACP national headquarters' library and the Sojourner Truth African American Research Collection. Ms. Ruff received the ALSC Melcher scholarship and was a contributing writer for the ALA book *Venture into Culture*. She has served on the Caldecott Award Jury and the Coretta Scott King awards jury.

Sue Sherif, currently the head of library development for the Alaska State Library, worked for most of her career in public and school libraries in Alaska and North Carolina. Her graduate studies in library and information sciences were at the University of Wisconsin Madison and the University of California Berkeley. She has taught children's literature and public library services at the University of Alaska and the University of Iceland. She has served on a number of ALA committees, most recently on the 2013–2014 Coretta Scott King awards jury.

Henrietta M. Smith is professor emerita with the School of Library and Information Science, University of South Florida, Tampa, and teaches the youth-oriented courses in the library school's East Coast program. Her service to ALA includes membership on Newbery, Caldecott, Batchelder, Carnegie, and Notable Film committees and chairing the Wilder Award Committee. Smith has served as chair of the Coretta Scott King Task Force, been both a member and chair of the awards jury, and edited the four previous editions of *The Coretta Scott King Awards*. For her services to youth in many arenas, Smith received the ALSC 2008 Distinguished Service Award, and the CSK Virginia Hamilton Lifetime Achievement Award.

Robin Smith is a second grade teacher in Nashville, Tennessee. In addition to teaching, she is a reviewer for the following professional journals: *The Horn Book*, *Kirkus Reviews* and *BookPage*. She also served on the Coretta Scott King awards jury, 2009–2010.

Contributors to Previous Editions

- **Rita Auerbach**
- **Carol Edwards**
- **Dorothy Evans**
- **Darwin Henderson, Ed.D.**
- **Kathleen Horning**
- **Hilda Weeks Kuter**
- **Carole J. McCollough, PhD**
- **Ann Miller**
- **Sandra Payne**
- **Adelaide Poniatowski Phelps**
- **Susan Pines**
- **Deborah D. Taylor**

Coretta Scott King Award-Winning Authors, 1970–2014

WEB *Readers can download a printable copy of this list at alaeditions.org/webextras.*

Adoff, Jaime. *Jimi & Me.* New Talent, 2006.

Angelou, Maya. *I Know Why the Caged Bird Sings.* Honor, 1971.

Bailey, Pearl. *Duey's Tale.* Winner, 1976.

Berry, James. *A Thief in the Village and Other Stories.* Honor, 1989.

Blake, Clarence N. *Quiz Book on Black America.* Honor, 1977.

Bolden, Tonya. *Maritcha: A Nineteenth-Century American Girl.* Honor, 2006.

Bond, Victoria, and T. R. Simon. *Zora and Me.* John Steptoe, 2011.

Boyd, Candy Dawson. *Circle of Gold.* Honor, 1985.

Bryan, Ashley. *Lion and the Ostrich Chicks: And Other African Folk Tales.* Honor, 1987.

Bush, Terri. *The Voice of the Children.* Honor, 1971.

Childress, Alice. *Rainbow Jordan.* Honor, 1982.

———. *A Hero Ain't Nothin' but a Sandwich.* Honor, 1974.

Chisholm, Shirley. *Unbought and Unbossed.* Honor, 1971.

Clifton, Lucille. *Everett Anderson's Goodbye.* Winner, 1984.

———. *Everett Anderson's Friend.* Honor, 1977.

———. *Don't You Remember?* Honor, 1974.

Crane, Louise. *Ms. Africa: Profiles of Modern African Women.* Honor, 1974.

Curtis, Christopher Paul. *Elijah of Buxton.* Winner, 2008.

———. *Bud, Not Buddy.* Winner, 2000.

———. *The Watsons Go to Birmingham—1963.* Honor, 1996.

Davis, Ossie. *Escape to Freedom: A Play about Young Frederick Douglass.* Winner, 1979.

Davis, Tanita S. *Mare's War.* Honor, 2010.

De Veaux, Alexis. *An Enchanted Hair Tale.* Honor, 1988.

———. *Don't Explain: A Song of Billie Holiday.* Honor, 1981.

Draper, Sharon M. *November Blues.* Honor, 2008.

———. *Copper Sun.* Winner, 2007.

———. *The Battle of Jericho.* Honor, 2004.

———. *Forged by Fire.* Winner, 1998.

———. *Tears of a Tiger.* New Talent, 1995.

Duckett, Alfred. *I Never Had It Made: The Autobiography of Jackie Robinson.* Winner, 1973.

English, Karen. *Francie.* Honor, 2000.

Evans, Mari. *I Am a Black Woman.* Honor, 1971.

Faulkner, William J. *The Days When the Animals Talked: Black American Folktales and How They Came to Be.* Honor, 1978.

Fax, Elton. *17 Black Artists.* Winner, 1972.

Fenner, Carol. *The Skates of Uncle Richard.* Honor, 1979.

Flake, Sharon G. *Who Am I without Him?* Honor, 2005.

———. *Money Hungry.* Honor, 2002.

———. *The Skin I'm In.* New Talent, 1999.

Frazier, Sundee T. *Brendan Buckley's Universe and Everything in It.* New Talent, 2008.

Glass, Frankcina. *Marvin and Tige.* Honor, 1978.

Gordy, Berry, Sr. *Movin' on Up: Pop Gordy Tells His Story.* Honor, 1980.

Graham, Lorenz. *Every Man Heart Lay Down.* Honor, 1971.

Graham, Shirley. *Julius K. Nyerere: Teacher of Africa.* Honor, 1976.

Greenfield, Eloise. *The Great Migration: Journey to the North.* Honor, 2012.

———. *Night on Neighborhood Street.* Honor, 1992.

———. *Nathaniel Talking.* Honor, 1990.

———. *Childtimes: A Three-Generation Memoir.* Honor, 1980.

———. *Africa Dream.* Winner, 1978.

———. *Mary McLeod Bethune.* Honor, 1978.

———. *Paul Robeson.* Honor, 1976.

Grimes, Nikki. *Words with Wings.* Honor, 2014.

———. *The Road to Paris.* Honor, 2007.

———. *Dark Sons.* Honor, 2006.

———. *Bronx Masquerade.* Winner, 2003.

———. *Talkin' About Bessie: The Story of Aviator Elizabeth Coleman.* Honor, 2003.

———. *Jazmin's Notebook.* Honor, 1999.

Groom, Gladys. *Black Means . . .* Honor, 1971.

Grossman, Barney. *Black Means . . .* Honor, 1971.

Hamilton, Virginia. *Her Stories: African American Folktales, Fairy Tales, and True Tales.* Winner, 1996.

———. *The Bells of Christmas.* Honor, 1990.

———. *Anthony Burns: The Defeat and Triumph of a Fugitive Slave.* Honor, 1989.

———. *The People Could Fly: American Black Folktales.* Winner, 1986.

———. *Junius over Far.* Honor, 1986.

———. *A Little Love.* Honor, 1985.

———. *The Magical Adventures of Pretty Pearl.* Honor, 1984.

———. *Sweet Whispers, Brother Rush.* Winner, 1983.

———. *Justice and Her Brothers.* Honor, 1979.

Hansen, Joyce. *Breaking Ground, Breaking Silence: The Story of New York's African Burial Ground.* Honor, 1999.

———. *I Thought My Soul Would Rise and Fly: The Diary of Patsy, a Freed Girl.* Honor, 1998.

———. *The Captive.* Honor, 1995.

———. *Which Way Freedom?* Honor, 1987.

Haskins, James. *Bayard Rustin: Behind the Scenes of the Civil Rights Movement.* Honor, 1998.

———. *Black Dance in America: A History through Its People.* Honor, 1991.

———. *Lena Horne.* Honor, 1984.

———. *Andrew Young: Young Man with a Mission.* Honor, 1980.

———. *James Van DerZee: The Picture Takin' Man.* Honor, 1980.

———. *Barbara Jordan.* Honor, 1978.

———. *The Story of Stevie Wonder.* Winner, 1977.

Hathaway, Barbara. *Missy Violet and Me.* New Talent, 2005.

Hunter, Kristin. *Lou in the Limelight.* Honor, 1982.

———. *Guests in the Promised Land.* Honor, 1974.

Johnson, Angela. *The First Part Last.* Winner, 2004.

———. *Heaven.* Winner, 1999.

———. *The Other Side: Shorter Poems.* Honor, 1999.

———. *Toning the Sweep.* Winner, 1994.

———. *When I Am Old with You.* Honor, 1991.

Jones, Traci L. *Standing against the Wind.* New Talent, 2007.

Jordan, June. *The Voice of the Children.* Honor, 1971.

Lester, Julius. *Day of Tears: A Novel in Dialogue.* Winner, 2006.

———. *The Tales of Uncle Remus: The Adventures of Brer Rabbit.* Honor, 1988.

———. *This Strange New Feeling.* Honor, 1983.

Lewis, John, Andrew Aydin, and Nate Powell. *March: Book One.* Honor, 2014.

Little, Lessie Jones. *Childtimes: A Three-Generation Memoir.* Honor, 1980.

Magoon, Kekla. *The Rock and the River.* John Steptoe, 2010.

Martin, Donald F. *Quiz Book on Black America.* Honor, 1977.

Mathis, Sharon Bell. *Ray Charles.* Winner, 1974.

McDonald, Janet. *Chill Wind.* New Talent, 2003.

McGowan, Gary. *Breaking Ground, Breaking Silence: The Story of New York's African Burial Ground.* Honor, 1999.

McKissack, Patricia C. *Never Forgotten.* Honor, 2012.

———. *The Dark-Thirty: Southern Tales of the Supernatural.* Winner, 1993.

McKissack, Patricia C., and Fredrick L. McKissack. *Days of Jubilee: The End of Slavery in the United States.* Honor, 2004.

———. *Black Hands, White Sails: The Story of African-American Whalers.* Honor, 2000.

———. *Rebels Against Slavery: American Slave Revolts.* Honor, 1997.

———. *Christmas in the Big House, Christmas in the Quarters.* Winner, 1995.

———. *Sojourner Truth: Ain't I a Woman?* Honor, 1993.

———. *A Long Hard Journey: The Story of the Pullman Porter.* Winner, 1990.

McKissack, Patricia C., and Fredrick McKissack Jr. *Black Diamond: The Story of the Negro Baseball Leagues.* Honor, 1995.

Mebane, Mary E. *Mary: An Autobiography.* Honor, 1982.

Morrison, Toni. *Remember: The Journey to School Integration.* Winner, 2005.

Moses, Shelia P. *The Legend of Buddy Bush.* Honor, 2005.

Myers, Walter Dean. *Darius & Twig.* Honor, 2014.

———. *Lockdown.* Honor, 2011.

———. *Monster.* Honor, 2000.

———. *Slam!* Winner, 1997.

———. *Malcolm X: By Any Means Necessary.* Honor, 1994.

———. *Somewhere in the Darkness.* Honor, 1993.

———. *Now Is Your Time! The African American Struggle for Freedom.* Winner, 1992.

———. *Fallen Angels.* Winner, 1989.

———. *Motown and Didi: A Love Story.* Winner, 1985.

———. *The Young Landlords.* Winner, 1980.

———. *Fast Sam, Cool Clyde, and Stuff.* Honor, 1976.

Nagenda, John. *Mukasa.* Honor, 1974.

Nelson, Kadir. *Heart and Soul: The Story of America and African Americans.* Winner, 2012.

———. *We Are the Ship: The Story of Negro League Baseball.* Winner, 2009.

Nelson, Marilyn. *A Wreath for Emmett Till.* Honor, 2006.

———. *Fortune's Bones: The Manumission Requiem.* Honor, 2005.

———. *Carver: A Life in Poems.* Honor, 2002.

Nelson, Vaunda Micheaux. *No Crystal Stair: A Documentary Novel of the Life and Work of Lewis Michaux, Harlem Bookseller.* Honor, 2013.

———. *Bad News for Outlaws: The Remarkable Life of Bass Reeves, Deputy U.S. Marshal.* Winner, 2010.

Neri, Greg. *Yummy: The Last Days of a Southside Shorty.* Honor, 2011.

Patterson, Lillie. *Martin Luther King, Jr., and the Freedom Movement.* Honor, 1990.

———. *Benjamin Banneker: Genius of Early America.* Honor, 1979.

———. *Coretta Scott King.* Honor, 1978.

———. *Dr. Martin Luther King, Jr.: Man of Peace.* Winner, 1970.

Peters, Margaret. *The Ebony Book of Black Achievement.* Honor, 1971.

Peterson, Jeanne Whitehouse. *I Have a Sister, My Sister Is Deaf.* Honor, 1979.

Pinkney, Andrea Davis. *Hand in Hand: Ten Black Men Who Changed America.* Winner, 2013.

———. *Let It Shine! Stories of Black Women Freedom Fighters.* Honor, 2001.

Poitier, Sidney. *This Life.* Winner, 1981.

Rhodes, Jewell Parker. *Ninth Ward.* Honor, 2011.

Robinson, Dorothy. *The Legend of Africania.* Winner, 1975.

Rollins, Charlemae. *Black Troubadour: Langston Hughes.* Winner, 1971.

Smith, Charles R., Jr. *Twelve Rounds to Glory: The Story of Muhammad Ali.* Honor, 2008.

Smith, Hope Anita. *Keeping the Night Watch.* Honor, 2009.

———. *The Way a Door Closes.* New Talent, 2004.

Southerland, Ellease. *Let the Lion Eat Straw.* Honor, 1980.

Southgate, Martha. *Another Way to Dance.* New Talent, 1997.

Stewart, Ruth Ann. *Portia: The Life of Portia Washington Pittman, the Daughter of Booker T. Washington.* Honor, 1978.

Taylor, Mildred D. *The Land.* Winner, 2002.

———. *The Road to Memphis.* Winner, 1991.

———. *The Friendship.* Winner, 1988.

———. *Let the Circle Be Unbroken.* Winner, 1982.

———. *Roll of Thunder, Hear My Cry.* Honor, 1977.

———. *Song of the Trees.* Honor, 1977.

Taylor, Theodore III. *When the Beat Was Born: DJ Kool Herc and the Creation of Hip Hop.* John Steptoe, 2014.

Thomas, Joyce Carol. *The Blacker the Berry: Poems.* Honor, 2009.

———. *Brown Honey in Broomwheat Tea.* Honor, 1994.

———. *Bright Shadow.* Honor, 1984.

Udry, Janice May. *Mary Jo's Grandmother.* Honor, 1971.

Walter, Mildred Pitts. *Mississippi Challenge.* Honor, 1993.

———. *Justin and the Best Biscuits in the World.* Winner, 1987.

———. *Trouble's Child.* Honor, 1986.

———. *Because We Are.* Honor, 1984.

Weatherford, Carole Boston. *Becoming Billie Holiday.* Honor, 2009.

Williams-Garcia, Rita. *P.S. Be Eleven.* Winner, 2014.

———. *One Crazy Summer.* Winner, 2011.

———. *Like Sisters on the Home Front.* Honor, 1996.

Woods, Brenda. *The Red Rose Box.* Honor, 2003.

Woodson, Jacqueline. *Each Kindness.* Honor, 2013.

———. *Locomotion.* Honor, 2004.

———. *Miracle's Boys.* Winner, 2001.

———. *From the Notebooks of Melanin Sun.* Honor, 1996.

———. *I Hadn't Meant to Tell You This.* Honor, 1995.

Coretta Scott King Author Award and Honor Books by Title

WEB *Readers can download a printable copy of this list at alaeditions.org/webextras.*

Africa Dream, by Eloise Greenfield. Winner, 1978.

Andrew Young: Young Man with a Mission, by James Haskins. Honor, 1980.

Another Way to Dance, by Martha Southgate. New Talent, 1997.

Anthony Burns: The Defeat and Triumph of a Fugitive Slave, by Virginia Hamilton. Honor, 1989.

Bad News for Outlaws: The Remarkable Life of Bass Reeves, Deputy U.S. Marshal, by Vaunda Micheaux Nelson. Winner, 2010.

Barbara Jordan, by James Haskins. Honor, 1978.

The Battle of Jericho, by Sharon M. Draper. Honor, 2004.

Bayard Rustin: Behind the Scenes of the Civil Rights Movement, by James Haskins. Honor, 1998.

Because We Are, by Mildred Pitts Walter. Honor, 1984.

Becoming Billie Holiday, by Carole Boston Weatherford. Honor, 2009.

The Bells of Christmas, by Virginia Hamilton. Honor, 1990.

Benjamin Banneker: Genius of Early America, by Lillie Patterson. Honor, 1979.

Black Dance in America: A History through Its People, by James Haskins. Honor, 1991.

Black Diamond: The Story of the Negro Baseball Leagues, by Patricia McKissack and Fredrick McKissack Jr. Honor, 1995.

Black Hands, White Sails: The Story of African-American Whalers, by Patricia C. McKissack and Fredrick L. McKissack. Honor, 2000.

Black Means . . . , by Barney Grossman with Gladys Groom. Honor, 1971.

Black Troubadour: Langston Hughes, by Charlemae Rollins. Winner, 1971.

The Blacker the Berry: Poems, by Joyce Carol Thomas. Honor, 2009.

Breaking Ground, Breaking Silence: The Story of New York's African Burial Ground, by Joyce Hansen and Gary McGowan. Honor, 1999.

Brendan Buckley's Universe and Everything in It, by Sundee T. Frazier. New Talent, 2008.

Bright Shadow, by Joyce Carol Thomas. Honor, 1984.

Bronx Masquerade, by Nikki Grimes. Winner, 2003.

Brown Honey in Broomwheat Tea, by Joyce Carol Thomas. Honor, 1994.

Bud, Not Buddy, by Christopher Paul Curtis. Winner, 2000.

The Captive, by Joyce Hansen. Honor, 1995.

Carver: A Life in Poems, by Marilyn Nelson. Honor, 2002.

Childtimes: A Three-Generation Memoir, by Eloise Greenfield and Lessie Jones Little. Honor, 1980.

Chill Wind, by Janet McDonald. New Talent, 2003.

Christmas in the Big House, Christmas in the Quarters, by Patricia C. McKissack and Fredrick L. McKissack. Winner, 1995.

Circle of Gold, by Candy Dawson Boyd. Honor, 1985.

Copper Sun, by Sharon M. Draper. Winner, 2007.

Coretta Scott King, by Lillie Patterson. Honor, 1978.

Darius & Twig, by Walter Dean Myers. Honor, 2014.

Dark Sons, by Nikki Grimes. Honor, 2006.

The Dark–Thirty: Southern Tales of the Supernatural, by Patricia C. McKissack. Winner, 1993.

Day of Tears: A Novel in Dialogue, by Julius Lester. Winner, 2006.

Days of Jubilee: The End of Slavery in the United States, by Patricia C. McKissack and Fredrick L. McKissack. Honor, 2004.

The Days When the Animals Talked: Black American Folktales and How They Came to Be, by William J. Faulkner. Honor, 1978.

Don't Explain: A Song of Billie Holiday, by Alexis De Veaux. Honor, 1981.

Don't You Remember? by Lucille Clifton. Honor, 1974.

Dr. Martin Luther King, Jr.: Man of Peace, by Lillie Patterson. Winner, 1970.

Duey's Tale, by Pearl Bailey. Winner, 1976.

Each Kindness, by Jacqueline Woodson. Honor, 2013.

The Ebony Book of Black Achievement, by Margaret Peters. Honor, 1971.

Elijah of Buxton, by Christopher Paul Curtis. Winner, 2008.

An Enchanted Hair Tale, by Alexis De Veaux. Honor, 1988.

Escape to Freedom: A Play about Young Frederick Douglass, by Ossie Davis. Winner, 1979.

Everett Anderson's Friend, by Lucille Clifton. Honor, 1977.

Everett Anderson's Goodbye, by Lucille Clifton. Winner, 1984.

Every Man Heart Lay Down, by Lorenz Graham. Honor, 1971.

Fallen Angels, by Walter Dean Myers. Winner, 1989.

Fast Sam, Cool Clyde, and Stuff, by Walter Dean Myers. Honor, 1976.

The First Part Last, by Angela Johnson. Winner, 2004.

Forged by Fire, by Sharon M. Draper. Winner, 1998.

Fortune's Bones: The Manumission Requiem, by Marilyn Nelson. Honor, 2005.

Francie, by Karen English. Honor, 2000.

The Friendship, by Mildred D. Taylor. Winner, 1988.

From the Notebooks of Melanin Sun, by Jacqueline Woodson. Honor, 1996.

The Great Migration: Journey to the North, by Eloise Greenfield. Honor, 2012.

Guests in the Promised Land, by Kristin Hunter. Honor, 1974.

Hand in Hand: Ten Black Men Who Changed America, by Andrea Davis Pinkney. Winner, 2013.

Heart and Soul: The Story of America and African Americans, by Kadir Nelson. Winner, 2012.

Heaven, by Angela Johnson. Winner, 1999.

Her Stories: African American Folktales, Fairy Tales, and True Tales, by Virginia Hamilton. Winner, 1996.

A Hero Ain't Nothin' but a Sandwich, by Alice Childress. Honor, 1974.

I Am a Black Woman, by Mari Evans. Honor, 1971.

I Hadn't Meant to Tell You This, by Jacqueline Woodson. Honor, 1995.

I Have a Sister, My Sister Is Deaf, by Jeanne Whitehouse Peterson. Honor, 1979.

I Know Why the Caged Bird Sings, by Maya Angelou. Honor, 1971.

I Never Had It Made: The Autobiography of Jackie Robinson, by Alfred Duckett. Winner, 1973.

I Thought My Soul Would Rise and Fly: The Diary of Patsy, a Freed Girl, by Joyce Hansen. Honor, 1998.

James Van DerZee: The Picture Takin' Man, by James Haskins. Honor, 1980.

Jazmin's Notebook, by Nikki Grimes. Honor, 1999.

Jimi & Me, by Jaime Adoff. New Talent, 2006.

Julius K. Nyerere: Teacher of Africa, by Shirley Graham. Honor, 1976.

Junius over Far, by Virginia Hamilton. Honor, 1986.

Justice and Her Brothers, by Virginia Hamilton. Honor, 1979.

Justin and the Best Biscuits in the World, by Mildred Pitts Walter. Winner, 1987.

Keeping the Night Watch, by Hope Anita Smith. Honor, 2009.

The Land, by Mildred D. Taylor. Winner, 2002.

The Legend of Africania, by Dorothy Robinson. Winner, 1975.

The Legend of Buddy Bush, by Shelia P. Moses. Honor, 2005.

Lena Horne, by James Haskins. Honor, 1984.

Let It Shine! Stories of Black Women Freedom Fighters, by Andrea Davis Pinkney. Honor, 2001.

Let the Circle Be Unbroken, by Mildred D. Taylor. Winner, 1982.

Let the Lion Eat Straw, by Ellease Southerland. Honor, 1980.

Like Sisters on the Home Front, by Rita Williams-Garcia. Honor, 1996.

Lion and the Ostrich Chicks: And Other African Folk Tales, by Ashley Bryan. Honor, 1987.

A Little Love, by Virginia Hamilton. Honor, 1985.

Lockdown, by Walter Dean Myers. Honor, 2011.

Locomotion, by Jacqueline Woodson. Honor, 2004.

A Long Hard Journey: The Story of the Pullman Porter, by Patricia C. McKissack and Fredrick L. McKissack. Winner, 1990.

Lou in the Limelight, by Kristin Hunter. Honor, 1982.

The Magical Adventures of Pretty Pearl, by Virginia Hamilton. Honor, 1984.

Malcolm X: By Any Means Necessary, by Walter Dean Myers. Honor, 1994.

March: Book One, by John Lewis, Andrew Aydin, and Nate Powell. Honor, 2014.

Mare's War, by Tanita S. Davis. Honor, 2010.

Maritcha: A Nineteenth-Century American Girl, by Tonya Bolden. Honor, 2006.

Martin Luther King, Jr., and the Freedom Movement, by Lillie Patterson. Honor, 1990.

Marvin and Tige, by Frankcina Glass. Honor, 1978.

Mary: An Autobiography, by Mary E. Mebane. Honor, 1982.

Mary Jo's Grandmother, by Janice May Udry. Honor, 1971.

Mary McLeod Bethune, by Eloise Greenfield. Honor, 1978.

Miracle's Boys, by Jacqueline Woodson. Winner, 2001.

Mississippi Challenge, by Mildred Pitts Walter. Honor, 1993.

Missy Violet and Me, by Barbara Hathaway. New Talent, 2005.

Money Hungry, by Sharon G. Flake. Honor, 2002.

Monster, by Walter Dean Myers. Honor, 2000.

Motown and Didi: A Love Story, by Walter Dean Myers. Winner, 1985.

Movin' on Up: Pop Gordy Tells His Story, by Berry Gordy Sr. Honor, 1980.

Ms. Africa: Profiles of Modern African Women, by Louise Crane. Honor, 1974.

Mukasa, by John Nagenda. Honor, 1974.

Nathaniel Talking, by Eloise Greenfield. Honor, 1990.

Never Forgotten, by Patricia C. McKissack. Honor, 2012.

Night on Neighborhood Street, by Eloise Greenfield. Honor, 1992.

Ninth Ward, by Jewell Parker Rhodes. Honor, 2011.

No Crystal Stair: A Documentary Novel of the Life and Work of Lewis Michaux, by Vaunda Micheaux Nelson. Honor, 2013.

November Blues, by Sharon M. Draper. Honor, 2008.

Now Is Your Time! The African American Struggle for Freedom, by Walter Dean Myers. Winner, 1992.

One Crazy Summer, by Rita Williams-Garcia. Winner, 2011.

The Other Side: Shorter Poems, by Angela Johnson. Honor, 1999.

Paul Robeson, by Eloise Greenfield. Honor, 1976.

The People Could Fly: American Black Folktales, by Virginia Hamilton. Winner, 1986.

Portia: The Life of Portia Washington Pittman, the Daughter of Booker T. Washington, by Ruth Ann Stewart. Honor, 1978.

P.S. Be Eleven, by Rita Williams-Garcia. Winner, 2014.

Quiz Book on Black America, by Clarence N. Blake and Donald F. Martin. Honor, 1977.

Rainbow Jordan, by Alice Childress. Honor, 1982.

Ray Charles, by Sharon Bell Mathis. Winner, 1974.

Rebels Against Slavery: American Slave Revolts, by Patricia C. McKissack and Fredrick L. McKissack. Honor, 1997.

The Red Rose Box, by Brenda Woods. Honor, 2003.

Remember: The Journey to School Integration, by Toni Morrison. Winner, 2005.

The Road to Memphis, by Mildred D. Taylor. Winner, 1991.

The Road to Paris, by Nikki Grimes. Honor, 2007.

The Rock and the River, by Kekla Magoon. John Steptoe, 2010.

Roll of Thunder, Hear My Cry, by Mildred D. Taylor. Honor, 1977.

17 Black Artists, by Elton Fax. Winner, 1972.

The Skates of Uncle Richard, by Carol Fenner. Honor, 1979.

The Skin I'm In, by Sharon G. Flake. New Talent, 1999.

Slam! by Walter Dean Myers. Winner, 1997.

Sojourner Truth: Ain't I a Woman? by Patricia C. McKissack and Fredrick L. McKissack. Honor, 1993.

Somewhere in the Darkness, by Walter Dean Myers. Honor, 1993.

Song of the Trees, by Mildred D. Taylor. Honor, 1977.

Standing against the Wind, by Traci L. Jones. New Talent, 2007.

The Story of Stevie Wonder, by James Haskins. Winner, 1977.

Sweet Whispers, Brother Rush, by Virginia Hamilton. Winner, 1983.

The Tales of Uncle Remus: The Adventures of Brer Rabbit, by Julius Lester. Honor, 1988.

Talkin' About Bessie: The Story of Aviator Elizabeth Coleman, by Nikki Grimes. Honor, 2003.

Tears of a Tiger, by Sharon M. Draper. New Talent, 1995.

A Thief in the Village and Other Stories, by James Berry. Honor, 1989.

This Life, by Sidney Poitier. Winner, 1981.

This Strange New Feeling, by Julius Lester. Honor, 1983.

Toning the Sweep, by Angela Johnson. Winner, 1994.

Trouble's Child, by Mildred Pitts Walter. Honor, 1986.

Twelve Rounds to Glory: The Story of Muhammad Ali, by Charles R. Smith Jr. Honor, 2008.

Unbought and Unbossed, by Shirley Chisholm. Honor, 1971.

The Voice of the Children, by June Jordan and Terri Bush. Honor, 1971.

The Watsons Go to Birmingham—1963, by Christopher Paul Curtis. Honor, 1996.

The Way a Door Closes, by Hope Anita Smith. New Talent, 2004.

We Are the Ship: The Story of Negro League Baseball, by Kadir Nelson. Winner, 2009.

When I Am Old with You, by Angela Johnson. Honor, 1991.

Which Way Freedom? by Joyce Hansen. Honor, 1987.

Who Am I without Him? by Sharon G. Flake. Honor, 2005.

Words with Wings, by Nikki Grimes. Honor, 2014.

A Wreath for Emmett Till, by Marilyn Nelson. Honor, 2006.

The Young Landlords, by Walter Dean Myers. Winner, 1980.

Yummy: The Last Days of a Southside Shorty, by Greg Neri. Honor, 2011.

Zora and Me, by Victoria Bond and T. R. Simon. John Steptoe, 2011.

Coretta Scott King Award-Winning Illustrators, 1974–2014

WEB *Readers can download a printable copy of this list at alaeditions.org/webextras.*

Andrews, Benny. *Langston Hughes.* Honor, 2007.
Bootman, Colin. *Almost to Freedom.* Honor, 2004.
Brown, Elbrite. *My Family Plays Music.* New Talent, 2004.
Bryan, Ashley. *Let It Shine: Three Favorite Spirituals.* Winner, 2008.
———. *Beautiful Blackbird.* Winner, 2004.
———. *Ashley Bryan's ABC of African American Poetry.* Honor, 1998.
———. *All Night, All Day: A Child's First Book of African-American Spirituals.* Honor, 1992.
———. *What a Morning! The Christmas Story in Black Spirituals.* Honor, 1988.
———. *Lion and the Ostrich Chicks: And Other African Folk Tales.* Honor, 1987.
———. *I'm Going to Sing: Black American Spirituals.* Honor, 1983.
———. *Beat the Story-Drum, Pum-Pum.* Winner, 1981.
Byard, Carole. *Working Cotton.* Honor, 1993.
———. *Grandma's Joy.* Honor, 1981.
———. *Cornrows.* Winner, 1980.
———. *Africa Dream.* Winner, 1978.
Christie, R. Gregory. *Brothers in Hope: The Story of the Lost Boys of Sudan.* Honor, 2006.
———. *Only Passing Through: The Story of Sojourner Truth.* Honor, 2001.
———. *The Palm of My Heart: Poetry by African American Children.* Honor, 1997.
Clay, Wil. *Little Eight John.* Honor, 1993.
Collier, Bryan. *Knock Knock: My Dad's Dream for Me.* Winner, 2014.
———. *I, Too, Am America.* Winner, 2013.
———. *Dave the Potter: Artist, Poet, Slave.* Winner, 2011.
———. *Rosa.* Winner, 2006.
———. *Visiting Langston.* Honor, 2003.
———. *Martin's Big Words: The Life of Dr. Martin Luther King, Jr.* Honor, 2002.
———. *Uptown.* Winner, 2001.
———. *Freedom River.* Honor, 2001.
Cooper, Floyd. *The Blacker the Berry: Poems.* Winner, 2009.
———. *I Have Heard of a Land.* Honor, 1999.
———. *Meet Danitra Brown.* Honor, 1995.
———. *Brown Honey in Broomwheat Tea.* Honor, 1994.
Cummings, Pat. *Storm in the Night.* Honor, 1989.
———. *C.L.O.U.D.S.* Honor, 1987.
———. *My Mama Needs Me.* Winner, 1984.
———. *Just Us Women.* Honor, 1983.
Devard, Nancy. *The Secret Olivia Told Me.* Honor, 2008.
Diakité, Baba Wagué. *The Hunterman and the Crocodile: A West African Folktale.* Honor, 1998.
Dillon, Leo, and Diane Dillon. *Jazz on a Saturday Night.* Honor, 2008.
———. *The People Could Fly: The Picture Book.* Honor, 2005.
———. *Rap a Tap Tap: Here's Bojangles—Think of That!* Honor, 2003.
———. *Her Stories: African American Folktales, Fairy Tales, and True Tales.* Honor, 1996.
———. *Aïda.* Winner, 1991.
———. *The People Could Fly: American Black Folktales.* Honor, 1986.

DuBurke, Randy. *The Moon Ring*. New Talent, 2003.

Evans, Shane W. *Underground*. Winner, 2012.

Feelings, Tom. *The Middle Passage: White Ships/Black Cargo*. Winner, 1996.

———. *Soul Looks Back in Wonder*. Winner, 1994.

———. *Daydreamers*. Honor, 1982.

———. *Something on My Mind*. Winner, 1979.

Ferguson, Mr. Amos. *Under the Sunday Tree*. Honor, 1989.

Ford, George. *Ray Charles*. Winner, 1974.

Gilchrist, Jan Spivey. *Night on Neighborhood Street*. Honor, 1992.

———. *Nathaniel Talking*. Winner, 1990.

JoeSam. *The Invisible Hunters: A Legend from the Miskito Indians of Nicaragua / Los Cazadores Invisibles: Una Leyenda de los Indios Miskitos de Nicaragua*. Honor, 1988.

Lagarrigue, Jerome. *Freedom Summer*. New Talent, 2002.

Lewis, E. B. *The Negro Speaks of Rivers*. Honor, 2010.

———. *Talkin' About Bessie: The Story of Aviator Elizabeth Coleman*. Winner, 2003.

———. *Virgie Goes to School with Us Boys*. Honor, 2001.

———. *My Rows and Piles of Coins*. Honor, 2000.

———. *The Bat Boy and His Violin*. Honor, 1999.

Magubane, Peter. *Black Child*. Winner, 1983.

Minter, Daniel. *Ellen's Broom*. Honor, 2013.

Morrison, Frank. *Jazzy Miz Mozetta*. New Talent, 2005.

Myers, Christopher. *H.O.R.S.E.* Honor, 2013.

———. *Jazz*. Honor, 2007.

———. *Black Cat*. Honor, 2000.

———. *Harlem*. Honor, 1998.

Nelson, Kadir. *Nelson Mandela*. Honor, 2014.

———. *I Have a Dream*. Honor, 2013.

———. *Heart and Soul*. Honor, 2012.

———. *We Are the Ship: The Story of Negro League Baseball*. Honor, 2009.

———. *Moses: When Harriet Tubman Led Her People to Freedom*. Winner, 2007.

———. *Ellington Was Not a Street*. Winner, 2005.

———. *Thunder Rose*. Honor, 2004.

Pinkney, Brian. *In the Time of the Drums*. Winner, 2000.

———. *Duke Ellington: The Piano Prince and His Orchestra*. Honor, 1999.

———. *The Faithful Friend*. Honor, 1996.

———. *Sukey and the Mermaid*. Honor, 1993.

Pinkney, Jerry. *The Moon Over Star*. Honor, 2009.

———. *God Bless the Child*. Honor, 2005.

———. *Goin' Someplace Special*. Winner, 2002.

———. *Minty: A Story of Young Harriet Tubman*. Winner, 1997.

———. *The Talking Eggs*. Honor, 1990.

———. *Mirandy and Brother Wind*. Winner, 1989.

———. *Half a Moon and One Whole Star*. Winner, 1987.

———. *The Patchwork Quilt*. Winner, 1986.

———. *Count on Your Fingers African Style*. Honor, 1981.

Qualls, Sean. *Before John Was a Jazz Giant: A Song of John Coltrane*. Honor, 2009.

Ransome, James E. *The Creation*. Winner, 1995.

———. *Uncle Jed's Barbershop*. Honor, 1994.

Ringgold, Faith. *Tar Beach*. Winner, 1992.

Ruffins, Reynold. *Running the Road to ABC*. Honor, 1997.

Sadler, Sonia Lynn. *Seeds of Change*. John Steptoe, 2011.

Saint James, Synthia. *Neeny Coming, Neeny Going*. Honor, 1997.

Shaffer, Terea. *The Singing Man*. Honor, 1995.

Smith, Charles R., Jr. *My People*. Winner, 2010.

Steptoe, Javaka. *Jimi: Sounds Like a Rainbow*. Honor, 2011.

———. *In Daddy's Arms I Am Tall: African Americans Celebrating Fathers*. Winner, 1998.

Steptoe, John. *Mufaro's Beautiful Daughters: An African Tale*. Winner, 1988.

———. *All the Colors of the Race*. Honor, 1983.

———. *Mother Crocodile / Maman-Caiman*. Winner, 1982.

Strickland, Shadra. *Bird*. New Talent, 2009.

Taylor, Theodore III. *When the Beat was Born: DJ Kool Herc and the Creation of Hip Hop*. John Steptoe, 2014.

Velasquez, Eric. *The Piano Man*. New Talent, 1999.

Wilson, Kathleen Atkins. *The Origin of Life on Earth: An African Creation Myth*. Winner, 1993.

Wood, Michele. *I See the Rhythm*. Winner, 1999.

Illustrations from Award-Winning Books

PLATE 1 From *Dave the Potter: Artist, Poet, Slave*, by Laban Carrick Hill; illustrated by **Bryan Collier** (Little, Brown and Company, a division of Hachette Book Group, Inc., 2010). Illustration © 2010 by Bryan Collier. Reprinted with permission from Little, Brown and Company. **2011 Illustrator Award**

PLATE 2 From *Seeds of Change*, by Jen Cullerton Johnson; illustrated by **Sonia Lynn Sadler** (Lee & Low Books, Inc., 2010). Illustration © 2010 by Sonia Lynn Sadler. Reprinted with permission from Lee & Low Books, Inc. **2011 John Steptoe Award for New Talent**

PLATE 3 From *Nelson Mandela*, by **Kadir Nelson** (HarperCollins Publishers, 2013). Illustration © 2013 by Kadir Nelson. Reprinted with permission from HarperCollins Publishers. **2014 Illustrator Honor**

PLATE 4 From *Jimi: Sounds Like a Rainbow: A Story of the Young Jimi Hendrix*, by Gary Golio; illustrated by **Javaka Steptoe** (Houghton Mifflin Harcourt, 2010). Illustration © 2010 by Javaka Steptoe. Reprinted with permission from Houghton Mifflin Harcout. **2011 Illustrator Honor**

PLATE 5 From *Underground: Finding the Light to Freedom*, by **Shane W. Evans** (Roaring Brook Press, 2011). Illustration © 2011 by Shane W. Evans. Reprinted with permission from Roaring Brook Press. All rights reserved. **2012 Illustrator Award**

PLATE 6 From *When the Beat Was Born: DJ Kool Herc and the Creation of Hip Hop*, by Laban Carrick Hill; illustrated by **Theodore Taylor III** (Roaring Brook Press, 2013). Illustration © 2013 by Theodore Taylor. Reprinted with permission from Roaring Brook Press. All rights reserved. **2014 John Steptoe Award for New Talent**

PLATE 7 From *I, Too, Am America*, by Langston Hughes; illustrated by **Bryan Collier** (Simon & Schuster Books for Young Readers, 2012). Reprinted with permission from Simon & Schuster Children's Publishing. **2013 Illustrator Award**

PLATE 8 From *Heart and Soul: The Story of America and African Americans*, by **Kadir Nelson** (Balzer + Bray/HarperCollins, 2012). Illustration © 2013 by Kadir Nelson. Reprinted with permission from HarperCollins Publishers. **2012 Illustrator Honor**

I have a dream that one day... little black boys and black girls will be able to join hands with little white boys and white girls as sisters and brothers. I have a dream today.

PLATE 9 From *I Have a Dream: Martin Luther King, Jr.*, by Martin Luther King, Jr.; illustrated by **Kadir Nelson** (Schwartz and Wade Books/Random House Children's Books, 2012). Illustration © 2012 by Kadir Nelson. Reprinted by arrangement with the Heirs to the Estate of Martin Luther King Jr., c/o Writers House as agent for the proprietor, New York, New York. **2013 Illustrator Honor**

PLATE 10 From *H.O.R.S.E.: A Game of Basketball and Imagination*, by **Christopher Myers** (Egmont, 2013). Text and illustrations © 2012. Reprinted with permission from Egmont. **2013 Illustrator Honor**

PLATE 11 From *Ellen's Broom,* by Kelly Starling Lyons; illustrated by **Daniel Minter** (G.P. Putnam's Sons, 2012). Illustration © 2012 by Daniel Minter. Reprinted with permission from G.P. Putnam's Sons Books for Young Readers, a division of Penguin Group (USA) LLC. **2013 Illustrator Honor**

PLATE 12 From *The Negro Speaks of Rivers*, by Langston Hughes; illustrated by **E. B. Lewis** (Disney/Jump at the Sun, 2009). Illustration © 2009 by E. B. Lewis. Reprinted with permission from Disney/Jump at the Sun Books, an imprint of Disney Book Group, LLC. All rights reserved. **2010 Illustrator Honor**

PLATE 13 From *My People*, by Langston Hughes; illustrated by **Charles R. Smith Jr.** (Atheneum Books for Young Readers, 2009). Illustration © 2012 by Charles R. Smith Jr. Reprinted with permission from Atheneum/Simon & Schuster. **2010 Illustrator Award**

PLATE 14 From *Knock Knock: My Dad's Dream for Me,* by Daniel Beaty; illustrated by **Bryan Collier** (Little, Brown, 2013). Illustration © 2013 by Bryan Collier. Reprinted with permission from Little, Brown and Company. **2014 Illustrator Award**

Coretta Scott King Illustrator Award and Honor Books by Title

WEB *Readers can download a printable copy of this list at alaeditions.org/webextras.*

Africa Dream, illus. by Carole Byard. Winner, 1978.

Aïda, illus. by Leo Dillon and Diane Dillon. Winner, 1991.

All Night, All Day: A Child's First Book of African-American Spirituals, illus. by Ashley Bryan. Honor, 1992.

All the Colors of the Race, illus. by John Steptoe. Honor, 1983.

Almost to Freedom, illus. by Colin Bootman. Honor, 2004.

Ashley Bryan's ABC of African American Poetry, illus. by Ashley Bryan. Honor, 1998.

The Bat Boy and His Violin, illus. by E. B. Lewis. Honor, 1999.

Beat the Story-Drum, Pum-Pum, illus. by Ashley Bryan. Winner, 1981.

Beautiful Blackbird, illus. by Ashley Bryan. Winner, 2004.

Before John Was a Jazz Giant: A Song of John Coltrane, illus. by Sean Qualls. Honor, 2009.

Bird, illus. by Shadra Strickland. New Talent, 2009.

Black Cat, illus. by Christopher Myers. Honor, 2000.

Black Child, illus. by Peter Magubane. Winner, 1983.

The Blacker the Berry: Poems, illus. by Floyd Cooper. Winner, 2009.

Brothers in Hope: The Story of the Lost Boys of Sudan, illus. by R. Gregory Christie. Honor, 2006.

Brown Honey in Broomwheat Tea, illus. by Floyd Cooper. Honor, 1994.

C.L.O.U.D.S., illus. by Pat Cummings. Honor, 1987.

Cornrows, illus. by Carole Byard. Winner, 1980.

Count on Your Fingers African Style, illus. by Jerry Pinkney. Honor, 1981.

The Creation, illus. by James E. Ransome. Winner, 1995.

Dave the Potter: Artist, Poet, Slave, illus. by Bryan Collier. Winner, 2011.

Daydreamers, illus. by Tom Feelings. Honor, 1982.

Duke Ellington: The Piano Prince and His Orchestra, illus. by Brian Pinkney. Honor, 1999.

Ellen's Broom, illus. by Daniel Minter. Honor, 2013.

Ellington Was Not a Street, illus. by Kadir Nelson. Winner, 2005.

The Faithful Friend, illus. by Brian Pinkney. Honor, 1996.

Freedom River, illus. by Bryan Collier. Honor, 2001.

Freedom Summer, illus. by Jerome Lagarrigue. New Talent, 2002.

God Bless the Child, illus. by Jerry Pinkney. Honor, 2005.

Goin' Someplace Special, illus. by Jerry Pinkney. Winner, 2002.

Grandma's Joy, illus. by Carole Byard. Honor, 1981.

Half a Moon and One Whole Star, illus. by Jerry Pinkney. Winner, 1987.

Harlem, illus. by Christopher Myers. Honor, 1998.

Heart and Soul: The Story of America and African Americans, illus. by Kadir Nelson. Honor, 2012.

Her Stories: African American Folktales, Fairy Tales, and True Tales, illus. by Leo Dillon and Diane Dillon. Honor, 1996.

H.O.R.S.E.: A Game of Basketball and Imagination, illus. by Christopher Myers. Honor, 2013.

The Hunterman and the Crocodile: A West African Folktale, illus. by Baba Wagué Diakité. Honor, 1998.

I Have a Dream, illus. by Kadir Nelson. Honor, 2013.

I Have Heard of a Land, illus. by Floyd Cooper. Honor, 1999.

I See the Rhythm, illus. by Michele Wood. Winner, 1999.

I, Too, Am America, illus. by Bryan Collier. Winner, 2013.

I'm Going to Sing: Black American Spirituals, illus. by Ashley Bryan. Honor, 1983.

In Daddy's Arms I Am Tall: African Americans Celebrating Fathers, illus. by Javaka Steptoe. Winner, 1998.

In the Time of the Drums, illus. by Brian Pinkney. Winner, 2000.

The Invisible Hunters: A Legend from the Miskito Indians of Nicaragua / Los Cazadores Invisibles: Una Leyenda de los Indios Miskitos de Nicaragua, illus. by JoeSam. Honor, 1988.

Jazz, illus. by Christopher Myers. Honor, 2007.

Jazz on a Saturday Night, illus. by Leo Dillon and Diane Dillon. Honor, 2008.

Jazzy Miz Mozetta, illus. by Frank Morrison. New Talent, 2005.

Jimi: Sounds Like a Rainbow: A Story of the Young Jimi Hendrix, illus. by Javaka Steptoe. Honor, 2011.

Just Us Women, illus. by Pat Cummings. Honor, 1983.

Knock Knock: My Dad's Dream for Me, illus. by Bryan Collier. Winner, 2014.

Langston Hughes, illus. by Benny Andrews. Honor, 2007.

Let It Shine: Three Favorite Spirituals, illus. by Ashley Bryan. Winner, 2008.

Lion and the Ostrich Chicks: And Other African Folk Tales, illus. by Ashley Bryan. Honor, 1987.

Little Eight John, illus. by Wil Clay. Honor, 1993.

Martin's Big Words: The Life of Dr. Martin Luther King, Jr., illus. by Bryan Collier. Honor, 2002.

Meet Danitra Brown, illus. by Floyd Cooper. Honor, 1995.

The Middle Passage: White Ships/Black Cargo, illus. by Tom Feelings. Winner, 1996.

Minty: A Story of Young Harriet Tubman, illus. by Jerry Pinkney. Winner, 1997.

Mirandy and Brother Wind, illus. by Jerry Pinkney. Winner, 1989.

The Moon Over Star, illus. by Jerry Pinkney. Honor, 2009.

The Moon Ring, illus. by Randy DuBurke. New Talent, 2003.

Moses: When Harriet Tubman Led Her People to Freedom, illus. by Kadir Nelson. Winner, 2007.

Mother Crocodile / Maman-Caiman, illus. by John Steptoe. Winner, 1982.

Mufaro's Beautiful Daughters: An African Tale, illus. by John Steptoe. Winner, 1988.

My Family Plays Music, illus. by Elbrite Brown. New Talent, 2004.

My Mama Needs Me, illus. by Pat Cummings. Winner, 1984.

My People, illus. by Charles R. Smith, Jr. Winner, 2010.

My Rows and Piles of Coins, illus. by E. B. Lewis. Honor, 2000.

Nathaniel Talking, illus. by Jan Spivey Gilchrist. Winner, 1990.

Neeny Coming, Neeny Going, illus. by Synthia Saint James. Honor, 1997.

The Negro Speaks of Rivers, illus. by E. B. Lewis. Honor, 2010.

Nelson Mandela, illus. by Kadir Nelson. Honor, 2014.

Night on Neighborhood Street, illus. by Jan Spivey Gilchrist. Honor, 1992.

Only Passing Through: The Story of Sojourner Truth, illus. by R. Gregory Christie. Honor, 2001.

The Origin of Life on Earth: An African Creation Myth, illus. by Kathleen Atkins Wilson. Winner, 1993.

The Palm of My Heart: Poetry by African American Children, illus. by R. Gregory Christie. Honor, 1997.

The Patchwork Quilt, illus. by Jerry Pinkney. Winner, 1986.

The People Could Fly: American Black Folktales, illus. by Leo Dillon and Diane Dillon. Honor, 1986.

The People Could Fly: The Picture Book, illus. by Leo Dillon and Diane Dillon. Honor, 2005.

The Piano Man, illus. by Eric Velasquez. New Talent, 1999.

Rap a Tap Tap: Here's Bojangles—Think of That! illus. by Leo Dillon and Diane Dillon. Honor, 2003.

Ray Charles, illus. by George Ford. Winner, 1974.

Rosa, illus. by Bryan Collier. Winner, 2006.

Running the Road to ABC, illus. by Reynold Ruffins. Honor, 1997.

The Secret Olivia Told Me, illus. by Nancy Devard. Honor, 2008.

Seeds of Change, illus. by Sonia Lynn Sadler. John Steptoe, 2011.

The Singing Man, illus. by Terea Shaffer. Honor, 1995.

Something on My Mind, illus. by Tom Feelings. Winner, 1979.

Soul Looks Back in Wonder, illus. by Tom Feelings. Winner, 1994.

Storm in the Night, illus. by Pat Cummings. Honor, 1989.

Sukey and the Mermaid, illus. by Brian Pinkney. Honor, 1993.

Talkin' About Bessie: The Story of Aviator Elizabeth Coleman, illus. by E. B. Lewis. Winner, 2003.

The Talking Eggs, illus. by Jerry Pinkney. Honor, 1990.

Tar Beach, illus. by Faith Ringgold. Winner, 1992.

Thunder Rose, illus. by Kadir Nelson. Honor, 2004.

Uncle Jed's Barbershop, illus. by James E. Ransome. Honor, 1994.

Under the Sunday Tree, illus. by Mr. Amos Ferguson. Honor, 1989.

Underground, illus. by Shane W. Evans. Winner, 2012.

Uptown, illus. by Bryan Collier. Winner, 2001.

Virgie Goes to School with Us Boys, illus. by E. B. Lewis. Honor, 2001.

Visiting Langston, illus. by Bryan Collier. Honor, 2003.

We Are the Ship: The Story of Negro League Baseball, illus. by Kadir Nelson. Honor, 2009.

What a Morning! The Christmas Story in Black Spirituals, illus. by Ashley Bryan. Honor, 1988.

When the Beat Was Born: DJ Kool Herc and the Creation of Hip Hop, illus. by Theodore Taylor III. John Steptoe, 2014.

Working Cotton, illus. by Carole Byard. Honor, 1993.

Subject Index

Adoption
Heaven (Johnson)

Africa
Africa Dream (Greenfield)
Beat the Story-Drum, Pum-Pum (Bryan)
Beautiful Blackbird (Bryan)
Black Child (Magubane)
Brothers in Hope: The Story of the Lost Boys of Sudan (Christie)
The Captive (Hansen)
Copper Sun (Draper)
Cornrows (Yarbrough)
Count on Your Fingers African Style (Zaslavsky)
The Hunterman and the Crocodile: A West African Folktale (Diakite')
Julius K. Nyerere: Teacher of Africa (Graham)
The Legend of Africania (Robinson)
Lion and the Ostrich Chicks: And Other African Folk Tales (Bryan)
Mother Crocodile: An Uncle Amadou Tale From Senegal (Diop)
Ms. Africa: Profiles of Modern African Women (Crane)
Mufaro's Beautiful Daughters: An African Tale (Steptoe)
Mukasa (Nagenda)
My Rows and Piles of Coins (Mollel)
The Negro Speaks of Rivers (Hughes)
Nelson Mandela (Nelson)
Never Forgotten (McKissack)
The Origin of Life on Earth: An African Creation Myth (Anderson)
Seeds of Change (Johnson)
The Singing Man (Medearis)

African Methodist Episcopal Church
I Thought My Soul Would Rise and Fly: The Diary of Patsy, A Freed Girl (Hansen)

Apartheid
Nelson Mandela (Nelson)

Art
Bird (Elliott)
17 Black Artists (Fax)

Baseball
Black Diamond: The Story of the Negro Baseball Leagues (McKissack & McKissack)
I Never Had It Made: The Autobiography of Jackie Robinson (Duckett)
We Are the Ship: The Story of Negro League Baseball (Nelson)

Biblical Stories
Every Man Heart Lay Down (Graham)

Biography
Andrew Young: Young Man with a Mission (Haskins)
Anthony Burns: The Defeat and Triumph of a Fugitive Slave (Hamilton)
Bad News for Outlaws: The Remarkable Life of Bass Reeves, Deputy U.S. Marshal (Nelson)
Barbara Jordan (Haskins)
Bayard Rustin: Behind the Scenes of the Civil Rights Movement (Haskins)
Becoming Billie Holiday (Weatherford)
Benjamin Banneker: Genius of Early America (Patterson)
Black Troubadour: Langston Hughes (Rollins)
Carver: A Life in Poems (Nelson)
Childtimes: A Three Generation Memoir (Greenfield and Little)
Coretta Scott King (Patterson)
Dave the Potter: Artist, Poet, Slave (Hill)
Don't Explain: A Song of Billie Holiday (De Veaux)
Dr. Martin Luther King, Jr.: Man of Peace (Patterson)
The Ebony Book of Black Achievement (Peters)
Escape to Freedom: A Play About Young Frederick Douglass (Davis)
God Bless the Child (Holiday and Herzog)
Hand in Hand: Ten Black Men Who Changed America (Pinkney)
I Know Why the Caged Bird Sings (Angelou)

Biography (cont'd)
I Never Had It Made: The Autobiography of Jackie Robinson (Duckett)
James Van DerZee: The Picture Takin' Man (Haskins)
Julius K. Nyerere: Teacher of Africa (Graham)
Lena Horne (Haskins)
Let It Shine! Stories of Black Women Freedom Fighters (Pinkney)
Malcolm X: By Any Means Necessary (Myers)
March: Book One (Lewis and Aydin)
Martin Luther King, Jr., and the Freedom Movement (Patterson)
Mary: An Autobiography (Mebane)
Mary McLeod Bethune (Greenfield)
Minty: A Story of Young Harriet Tubman (Schroeder)
Moses: When Harriet Tubman Led Her People to Freedom (Weatherford)
Movin' on Up: Pop Gordy Tells His Story (Gordy)
Ms. Africa: Profiles of Modern African Women (Crane)
Mukasa (Nagenda)
Nelson Mandela (Nelson)
No Crystal Stair: A Documentary Novel of the Life and Work of Lewis Michaux (Nelson)
Only Passing Through: The Story of Sojourner Truth (Rockwell)
Paul Robeson (Greenfield)
Portia: The Life of Portia Washington Pittman, the Daughter of Booker T. Washington (Stewart)
Ray Charles (Mathis)
Rosa (Giovanni)
Seeds of Change (Johnson)
17 Black Artists (Fax)
Sojourner Truth: Ain't I a Woman (McKissack)
The Story of Stevie Wonder (Haskins)
Talkin' about Bessie: The Story of Aviator Elizabeth Coleman (Grimes)
This Life (Poitier)
Unbought and Unbossed (Chisholm)
When the Beat Was Born: DJ Cool Herc and the Creation of Hip-Hop (Carrick)
Yummy: the Last Days of a Southside Shorty (Neri)

Biracial Identity
The Blacker the Berry (Thomas)
Brendan Buckley's Universe and Everything in It (Frazier)
Jimi & Me (Adoff)
The Land (Taylor)
The Road to Paris (Grimes)

Birmingham, Alabama
The Watsons Go to Birmingham—1963 (Curtis)

Black Cowboys
Bad News for Outlaws: The Remarkable Life of Bass Reeves, Deputy U.S. Marshal (Nelson)
Justin and the Best Biscuits in the World (Walter)

Black Panther Party
One Crazy Summer (Williams-Garcia)
The Other Side: Shorter Poems (Johnson)
The Rock and the River (Magoon)

Blindness
The Story of Stevie Wonder (Haskins)

Bullying
An Enchanted Hair Tale (De Veaux)
The Battle of Jericho (Draper)
Circle of Gold (Boyd)
Darius & Twig (Myers)
Each Kindness (Woodson)
Lockdown (Myers)
The Skin I'm In (Flake)
Who Am I Without Him? Short Stories About Girls and the Boys in Their Lives (Flake)

Caribbean
The Friendship (Taylor)
Junius over Far (Hamilton)
Neeny Coming, Neeny Going (English)
Running the Road to ABC (Lauture)
A Thief in the Village and Other Stories (Berry)
Under the Sunday Tree (Greenfield)
When the Beat Was Born: DJ Cool Herc and the Creation of Hip-Hop (Carrick)

Child Abuse
Forged by Fire (Draper)

I Hadn't Meant to Tell You This (Woodson)

Civil Rights Movement
Andrew Young: Young Man with a Mission (Haskins)
Bayard Rustin: Behind the Scenes of the Civil Rights Movement (Haskins)
Coretta Scott King (Patterson)
Ellington Was Not a Street (Shange)
Freedom Summer (Wiles)
Heart and Soul (Nelson)
I Have a Dream: Martin Luther King, Jr. (Nelson)
Let It Shine: Stories of Black Women Freedom Fighters (Pinkney)
Malcolm X: By Any Means Necessary (Myers)
March: Book One (Lewis and Aydin)
Martin Luther King, Jr., and the Freedom Movement (Patterson)
Martin's Big Words: The Life of Dr. Martin Luther King Jr. (Rappaport)
One Crazy Summer (Williams-Garcia)
Paul Robeson (Greenfield)
P.S.: Be Eleven (Williams-Garcia)
Remember: The Journey to School Integration (Morrison)
The Rock and the River (Magoon)
Rosa (Giovanni)
This Life (Poitier)
The Watsons Go to Birmingham—1963 (Curtis)

Colonial America
Breaking Ground, Breaking Silence: The Story of New York's African Burial Ground (Hansen and McGowan)

Coming of Age
Elijah of Buxton (Curtis)
Forged by Fire (Draper)
From the Notebooks of Melanin Sun: A Novel (Woodson)
Jazmin's Notebook (Grimes)
Justice and Her Brothers (Hamilton)
The Land (Taylor)
Let the Lion Eat Straw (Southerland)
Like Sisters on the Homefront (Williams-Garcia)
November Blues (Draper)
The Red Rose Box (Woods)

Common Good
(core democratic value)
The Bells of Christmas (Hamilton)
Black Hands, White Sails: The Story of African-American Whalers (McKissack)
Brothers in Hope: The Story of the Lost Boys of Sudan (Williams)
Circle of Gold (Boyd)
Cornrows (Yarbrough)
Count on Your Fingers African Style (Zaslavsky)
Every Man Heart Lay Down (Graham)
Freedom River (Rappaport)
The Hunterman and the Crocodile: A West African Folktale (Diakite')
I Have Heard of a Land (Thomas)
Justin and the Best Biscuits in the World (Walter)
Mother Crocodile: An Uncle Amadou Tale From Senegal (Diop)
My Mama Needs Me (Walter)
My Rows and Piles of Coins (Mollel)
Neeny Coming, Neeny Going (English)
The Patchwork Quilt (Flournoy)
Seeds of Change (Johnson)
Storm in the Night (Stolz)
The Talking Eggs (San Souci)
Thunder Rose (Nolen)
Uptown (Collier)
Working Cotton (Williams)
The Young Landlords (Myers)

Deafness
I Have A Sister: My Sister Is Deaf (Peterson)

Death
Circle of Gold (Boyd)
Everett Anderson's Goodbye (Clifton)
Fast Sam, Cool Clyde, and Stuff (Myers)
Fortune's Bones (Nelson)
I Hadn't Meant to Tell You This (Woodson)
Jazmin's Notebook (Grimes)
Jimi & Me (Adoff)
Locomotion (Woodson)
Miracle's Boys (Woodson)
The Red Rose Box (Woods)
Tears of a Tiger (Draper)
Toning the Sweep (Johnson)
A Wreath for Emmett Till (Nelson)
Yummy: the Last Days of a Southside Shorty (Neri)

Depression Era
Roll of Thunder, Hear My Cry (Taylor)

Diversity
(core democratic value)
Africa Dream (Greenfield)
Beautiful Blackbird (Bryan)
Black Cat (Myers)
The Blacker the Berry (Thomas)
Brendan Buckley's Universe and Everything In It (Frazier)
Bronx Masquerade (Grimes)
Duey's Tale (Bailey)
The Ebony Book of Black Achievement (Peters)
Everett Anderson's Friend (Clifton)
Her Stories: African American Folktales, Fairy Tales, and True Tales (Hamilton)
Jazz (Myers)
Jimi & Me (Adoff)
The Magical Adventures of Pretty Pearl (Hamilton)
My Family Plays Music (Cox)
The Piano Man (Chocolate)
The Singing Man (Medearis)

Draft Riots
Maritcha: A Nineteenth-Century American Girl (Bolden)

Drugs
Bird (Elliott)
Don't Explain: A Song of Billie Holiday (De Veaux)
Fast Sam, Cool Clyde, and Stuff (Myers)
A Hero Ain't Nothin' but a Sandwich (Childress)
Lou In the Limelight (Hunter)
Motown and Didi: A Love Story (Myers)
Slam! (Myers)

Drunk Driving
Tears of a Tiger (Draper)

Education
Because We Are (Walter)
Bronx Masquerade (Grimes)
Circle of Gold (Boyd)
Count on Your Fingers African Style (Zaslavsky)
Goin' Someplace Special (McKissack)
I Thought My Soul Would Rise and Fly: The Diary of Patsy, a Freed Girl (Hansen)
Mary McLeod Bethune (Greenfield)
Mukasa (Nagenda)
Neeny Coming, Neeny Going (English)
Remember: The Journey to School Integration (Morrison)
The Road to Memphis (Taylor)
Running the Road to ABC (Lauture)
Trouble's Child (Walter)
Virgie Goes to School with Us Boys (Howard)

Emancipation Proclamation
Days of Jubilee: The End of Slavery in the United States (McKissack)
I Thought My Soul Would Rise and Fly: The Diary of Patsy, A Freed Girl (Hansen)

Equality
(core democratic value)
An Enchanted Hair Tale (De Veaux)
Another Way to Dance (Southgate)
Bayard Rustin: Behind the Scenes of the Civil Rights Movement (Haskins)
Because We Are (Walter)
Black Child (Magubane)
Black Means... (Grossman, Barney & Groom)
The Blacker the Berry (Thomas)
Fallen Angels (Myers)
Freedom Summer (Wiles)
The Friendship (Taylor)
From the Notebooks of Melanin Sun: A Novel (Woodson)
Goin' Someplace Special (McKissack)
Guests in the Promised Land (Hunter)
Heart and Soul (Nelson)
I Never Had It Made: The Autobiography of Jackie Robinson (Duckett)
I, Too, Am America (Hughes)
Jazzy Miz Mozetta (Roberts)
The Land (Taylor)
Lena Horne (Haskins)
March: Book One (Lewis and Aydin)
Maritcha: A Nineteenth-Century American Girl (Bolden)
Mississippi Challenge (Walter)
Money Hungry (Flake)
Ms. Africa: Profiles of Modern African Women (Crane)
Nelson Mandela (Nelson)
Rebels Against Slavery: American Slave Revolts (McKissack)
The Red Rose Box (Woods)
The Road to Memphis (Taylor)

Equality
(core democratic value) *(cont'd)*
17 Black Artists (Fax)
The Skin I'm In (Flake)
Somewhere in the Darkness (Myers)
This Strange New Feeling (Lester)
Virgie Goes to School With Us Boys (Howard)
The Watsons Go to Birmingham—1963 (Curtis)
We Are the Ship: The Story of Negro League Baseball (Nelson)
Which Way Freedom? (Hansen)

Family Relationships
All the Colors of the Race (Adoff)
Because We Are (Walter)
Bird (Elliott)
Brendan Buckley's Universe and Everything in It (Frazier)
Bright Shadow (Thomas)
Childtimes: A Three-Generation Memoir (Greenfield and Little)
Chill Wind (McDonald)
Circle of Gold (Boyd)
Coretta Scott King (Patterson)
Cornrows (Yarbrough)
Dark Sons (Grimes)
Don't You Remember? (Clifton)
Duey's Tale (Bailey)
Ellen's Broom (Lyons)
Everett Anderson's Goodbye (Clifton)
Forged by Fire (Draper)
Grandma's Joy (Greenfield)
Heaven (Johnson)
A Hero Ain't Nothin' but a Sandwich (Childress)
I Hadn't Meant to Tell You This (Woodson)
I Have a Sister, My Sister Is Deaf (Peterson)
I Have Heard of a Land (Thomas)
I Know Why the Caged Bird Sings (Angelou)
Jimi & Me (Adoff)
Junius Over Far (Hamilton)
Just Us Women (Caines)
Justice and Her Brothers (Hamilton)
Justin and the Best Biscuits in the World (Walter)
Keeping the Night Watch (Smith)
Knock Knock: My Dad's Dream for Me (Beaty)
The Land (Taylor)
The Legend of Buddy Bush (Moses)
Let the Circle Be Unbroken (Taylor)
Let the Lion Eat Straw (Southerland)
Like Sisters on the Homefront (Williams-Garcia)
A Little Love (Hamilton)
Locomotion (Woodson)
Malcolm X: By Any Means Necessary (Myers)
Mare's War (Davis)
Marvin and Tige (Glass)
Miracle's Boys (Woodson)
Money Hungry (Flake)
Movin' Up: Pop Gordy Tells His Story (Gordy)
My Mama Needs Me (Walter)
Mukasa (Nagenda)
My Family Plays Music (Cox)
Nathaniel Talking (Greenfield)
Neeny Coming, Neeny Going (English)
Night on Neighborhood Street (Greenfield)
November Blues (Draper)
One Crazy Summer (Williams-Garcia)
The Other Side: Shorter Poems (Johnson)
The Patchwork Quilt (Flournoy)
The Piano Man (Chocolate)
P.S.: Be Eleven (Williams-Garcia)
Rainbow Jordan (Childress)
The Red Rose Box (Woods)
The Road to Paris (Grimes)
Roll of Thunder, Hear My Cry (Taylor)
The Skates of Uncle Richard (Fenner)
Sojourner Truth: Ain't I a Woman (McKissack)
Something On My Mind (Grimes)
Somewhere in the Darkness (Myers)
Song of the Trees (Taylor)
Standing against the Wind (Jones)
Sweet Whispers, Brother Rush (Hamilton)
The Talking Eggs (Souci)
Toning the Sweep (Johnson)
Trouble's Child (Walter)
The Watsons Go to Birmingham—1963 (Curtis)
The Way a Door Closes (Smith)
When I Am Old with You (Johnson)
Words with Wings (Grimes)
Working Cotton (Williams)

Fantasy
Bright Shadow (Thomas)
C.L.O.U.D.S. (Cummings)
Duey's Tale (Bailey)
An Enchanted Hair Tale (De Veaux)
The Friendship (Souci)
Justice and Her Brothers (Hamilton)
The Magical Adventures of Pretty Pearl (Hamilton)
The Moon Ring (DuBurke)
Tar Beach (Ringgold)
Zora and Me (Bond and Simon)

Father/Daughter Relationships
The First Part Last (Johnson)
Sukey and the Mermaid (Souci)

Father/Son Relationships
Bud, Not Buddy (Curtis)
Dark Sons (Grimes)
In Daddy's Arms I Am Tall: African Americans Celebrating Fathers (Steptoe)
Keeping the Night Watch (Smith)
Knock Knock: My Dad's Dream for Me (Beaty)
The Land (Taylor)
The Rock and the River (Magoon)
Somewhere in the Darkness (Myers)
The Way a Door Closes (Smith)

Fathers
In Daddy's Arms I Am Tall: African Americans Celebrating Fathers (Steptoe)

Folktales/Folklore
Beat the Story-Drum, Pum-Pum (Bryan)
Beautiful Blackbird (Bryan)
The Dark-Thirty: Southern Tales of the Supernatural (McKissack)
The Days When the Animals Talked: Black American Folktales and How They Came to Be (Faulkner)
Every Man Heart Lay Down (Graham)
The Faithful Friend (San Souci)
Her Stories: African American Folktales, Fairy Tales and True Tales (Hamilton)
The Hunterman and the Crocodile: A West African Folktale (Daikité)
The Invisible Hunters: A Legend from the Miskito Indians of Nicaragua (Rohmer, Chow, and Vidaure)
The Legend of Africania (Robinson)
Lion and the Ostrich Chicks and Other African Folk Tales (Bryan)
Little Eight John (Wahl)
The Magical Adventures of Pretty Pearl (Hamilton)

Mother Crocodile (Diop)
Mirandy and Brother Wind (McKissack)
Mufaro's Beautiful Daughters: An African Tale (Steptoe)
The Origin of Life on Earth: An African Creation Myth (Anderson)
The People Could Fly: American Black Folktales (Hamilton)
The Singing Man (Medearis)
Sukey and the Mermaid (San Souci)
The Tales of Uncle Remus: The Adventures of Brer Rabbit (Lester)
The Talking Eggs (San Souci)
Thunder Rose (Nolen)
Zora and Me (Bond and Simon)

Foster Care
Bud, Not Buddy (Curtis)
Locomotion (Woodson)

Friendship
Darius & Twig (Myers)
Duey's Tale (Bailey)
Each Kindness (Woodson)
Everett Anderson's Friend (Clifton)
The Faithful Friend (San Souci)
Fast Sam, Cool Clyde, and Stuff (Myers)
Francie (English)
Freedom Summer (Wiles)
The Friendship (Taylor)
I Hadn't Meant to Tell You This (Woodson)
Marvin and Tige (Glass)
Meet Danitra Brown (Grimes)
The Secret Olivia Told Me (Joy)
Slam! (Myers)
Standing Against the Wind (Jones)
Tears of a Tiger (Draper)
Toning the Sweep (Johnson)
The Young Landlords (Myers)
Zora and Me (Bond and Simon)

Fugitive Slave Act 1793
Anthony Burns: The Defeat and Triumph of a Fugitive Slave (Hamilton)

Gangs
Monster (Myers)
Yummy: the Last Days of a Southside Shorty (Neri)

Geology
Brendan Buckley's Universe and Everything in It (Frazier)

GLBT
From the Notebooks of Melanin Sun: A Novel (Woodson)

Grandparents
Brendan Buckley's Universe and Everything in It (Frazier)
Grandma's Joy (Greenfield)
Justin and the Best Biscuits in the World (Walter)
A Little Love (Hamilton)
Mare's War (Davis)
Mary Jo's Grandmother (Udry)
The Moon Ring (DuBurke)
The Piano Man (Chocolate)
Storm in the Night (Stolz)
Toning the Sweep (Johnson)
Trouble's Child (Walter)
When I Am Old with You (Johnson)

Graphic Novel
Yummy: the Last Days of a Southside Shorty (Neri)

Great Migration, The
God Bless the Child (Holiday and Herzog)
The Great Migration: Journey to the North (Greenfield)

Green Belt Movement
Seeds of Change (Johnson)

Hip-Hop
When the Beat Was Born: DJ Cool Herc and the Creation of Hip-Hop (Carrick)

History
Bad News for Outlaws: The Remarkable Life of Bass Reeves, Deputy U.S. Marshal (Nelson)
Becoming Billie Holiday (Weatherford)
Black Dance in America: A History through Its People (Haskins)
Black Hands, White Sails: The Story of African-American Whalers (McKissack)
Breaking Ground, Breaking Silence: The Story of New York's African Burial Ground (Hansen and McGowan)
Childtimes: A Three-Generation Memoir (Greenfield and Little)
Copper Sun (Draper)
Dave the Potter: Artist, Poet, Slave (Hill)
Day of Tears (Lester)
Days of Jubilee: The End of Slavery in the United States (McKissack)
The Ebony Book of Black Achievement (Peters)
Elijah of Buxton (Curtis)
Ellen's Broom (Lyons)
The Great Migration: Journey to the North (Greenfield)
Hand in Hand: Ten Black Men Who Changed America (Pinkney)
Heart and Soul (Nelson)
I Thought My Soul Would Rise and Fly: The Diary of Patsy, A Freed Girl (Hansen)
I, Too, Am America (Hughes)
A Long Hard Journey: The Story of the Pullman Porter (McKissack)
Malcolm X: By Any Means Necessary (Myers)
March: Book One (Lewis and Aydin)
Maritcha: A Nineteenth-Century American Girl (Bolden)
The Moon over Star (Aston)
The Negro Speaks of Rivers (Hughes)
Nelson Mandela (Nelson)
Never Forgotten (McKissack)
Now Is Your Time! The African American Struggle for Freedom (Myers)
Quiz Book on Black America (Blake and Martin)
Remember: The Journey to School Integration (Morrison)
Underground: Finding the Light to Freedom (Evans)
We Are the Ship: The Story of Negro League Baseball (Nelson)

Holidays
The Bells of Christmas (Hamilton)
Christmas in the Big House, Christmas in the Quarters (McKissack)
What a Morning! The Christmas Story in Black Spirituals (Langstaff)

Homelessness
Money Hungry (Flake)

Inventors
Carver: A Life in Poems (Nelson)

Jamaica
A Thief in the Village and Other Stories (Berry)

Jamaica (cont'd)
When the Beat Was Born: DJ Cool Herc and the Creation of Hip-Hop (Carrick)

Jim Crow Laws
The Friendship (Taylor)
The Great Migration: Journey to the North (Greenfield)
The Land (Taylor)
The Red Rose Box (Woods)
The Road to Memphis (Taylor)
The Legend of Buddy Bush (Moses)
We Are the Ship: The Story of Negro League Baseball (Nelson)
Wreath for Emmett Till (Nelson)

Justice (core democratic value)
Andrew Young: Young Man with a Mission (Haskins)
Anthony Burns: The Defeat and Triumph of a Fugitive Slave (Hamilton)
Black Diamond: The Story of the Negro Baseball Leagues (McKissack)
The Captive (Hansen)
Don't Explain: A Song of Billie Holiday (De Veaux)
Dr. Martin Luther King, Jr.: Man of Peace (Patterson)
Fast Sam, Cool Clyde, and Stuff (Myers)
Francie (English)
Hand in Hand: Ten Black Men Who Changed America (Pinkney)
I Thought My Soul Would Rise and Fly: The Diary of Patsy, A Freed Girl (Hansen)
I, Too, Am America (Hughes)
Let It Shine: Stories of Black Women Freedom Fighters (Pinkney)
Let the Circle Be Unbroken (Taylor)
Lockdown (Myers)
A Long Hard Journey: The Story of the Pullman Porter (McKissack)
Malcolm X: By Any Means Necessary (Myers)
March: Book One (Lewis and Aydin)
Maritcha: A Nineteenth-Century American Girl (Bolden)
Monster (Myers)
Nelson Mandela (Nelson)
Now Is Your Time! The African-American Struggle for Freedom (Myers)
Paul Robeson (Greenfield)
The People Could Fly: American Black Folktales (Hamilton)
The People Could Fly: The Picture Book (Hamilton)
Remember: The Journey to School Integration (Morrison)
The Rock and the River (Magoon)
Roll of Thunder; Hear My Cry (Taylor)
The Secret Olivia Told Me (Joy)
Something On My Mind (Grimes)
Song of the Trees (Taylor)
Talkin' About Bessie: The Story of Aviator Elizabeth Coleman (Grimes)
Tar Beach (Ringgold)
Unbought and Unbossed (Chisholm)
We Are the Ship: The Story of Negro League Baseball (Nelson)

Juvenile Trials
Monster (Myers)

Kenya
Seeds of Change (Johnson)

Ku Klux Klan
The Legend of Buddy Bush (Moses)

Land Run/Oklahoma
I Have Heard of a Land (Thomas)

Liberty (core democratic value)
Almost to Freedom (Nelson)
The Bat Boy and His Violin (Curtis)
Christmas in the Big House, Christmas in the Quarters (McKissack)
Copper Sun (Draper)
Dave the Potter: Artist, Poet, Slave (Hill)
Day of Tears (Lester)
Days of Jubilee: The End of Slavery in the United States (McKissack)
Escape to Freedom: A Play About Young Frederick Douglass (Davis)
Fortune's Bones: The Manumission Requiem (Nelson)
Heart and Soul (Nelson)
I Have a Dream: Martin Luther King, Jr. (Nelson)
I, Too, Am America (Hughes)
The Land (Taylor)
The Legend of Buddy Bush (Moses)
Martin Luther King, Jr. and the Freedom Movement (Patterson)
Nelson Mandela (Nelson)
Never Forgotten (McKissack)
Sojourner Truth: Ain't I a Woman (McKissack)
Twelve Rounds to Glory: The Story of Muhammad Ali (Smith)
We Are the Ship: The Story of Negro League Baseball (Nelson)
Zora and Me (Bond and Simon)

Life (core democratic value)
Jazmin's Notebook (Grimes)
Sweet Whispers, Brother Rush (Hamilton)
Tears of a Tiger (Draper)
A Wreath for Emmett Till (Nelson)
Yummy: the Last Days of a Southside Shorty (Neri)

Medical Ethics
Fortune's Bones: The Manumission Requiem (Nelson)

Mental Illness
Jazmin's Notebook (Grimes)
Sweet Whispers, Brother Rush (Hamilton)

Midwifery
Missy Violet and Me (Hathaway)

Mother/Daughter Relationships
Like Sisters on the Homefront (Williams-Garcia)
Money Hungry (Flake)
November Blues (Draper)
One Crazy Summer (Williams-Garcia)
P.S.: Be Eleven (Williams-Garcia)
Rainbow Jordan (Childress)
Toning the Sweep (Johnson)
Words with Wings (Grimes)

Mother/Son Relationships
From the Notebooks of Melanin Sun: A Novel (Woodson)

Murder
The Watsons Go to Birmingham—1963 (Curtis)
A Wreath for Emmett Till (Nelson)
Yummy: the Last Days of a Southside Shorty (Neri)

Music
Aïda (Price, adapter)
All Night, All Day: A Child's First Book of African-American Spirituals (Bryan, selector)

The Bat Boy and His Violin (Curtis)
Becoming Billie Holiday (Weatherford)
Before John Was a Jazz Giant (Weatherford)
Don't Explain: A Song of Billie Holiday (De Veaux)
Duke Ellington: The Piano Prince and His Orchestra (Pinkney)
Ellington Was Not a Street (Shange)
God Bless the Child (Holiday and Herzog)
I See the Rhythm (Igus)
I'm Going to Sing: Black American Spirituals (Bryan, selector)
Jazz (Myers)
Jazz on a Saturday Night (Dillon)
Jazzy Miz Mozetta (Morrison)
Jimi & Me (Adoff)
Jimi: Sounds Like a Rainbow: A Story of Young Jimi Hendri (Golio)
Lena Horne (Haskins)
Let It Shine: Three Favorite Spirituals (Bryan)
Let the Lion Eat Straw (Southerland)
Lou in the Limelight (Hunter)
My Family Plays Music (Cox)
Paul Robeson (Greenfield)
The Piano Man (Chocolate)
Rap a Tap Tap: Here's Bojangles—Think of That! (Dillon)
Ray Charles (Mathis)
The Story of Stevie Wonder (Haskins)
What a Morning! The Christmas Story in Black Spirituals (Langstaff, comp.)
When the Beat Was Born: DJ Cool Herc and the Creation of Hip-Hop (Carrick)

Negro Spirituals
All Night, All Day: A Child's First Book of African American Spirituals (Bryan)
I'm Going to Sing: Black American Spirituals (Bryan)
Let It Shine: Three Favorite Spirituals (Bryan)
What a Morning! The Christmas Story in Black Spirituals (Langstaff)

New Orleans
Ninth Ward (Rhodes)

New York City
Breaking Ground, Breaking Silence: The Story of New York's African Burial Ground (Hansen and McGowan)
Ellington Was Not a Street (Shange)
Harlem (Myers)
Maritcha: A Nineteenth-Century American Girl (Bolden)
No Crystal Stair: A Documentary Novel of the Life and Work of Lewis Michaux (Nelson)
Uptown (Collier)

Occupations
Becoming Billie Holiday (Weatherford)
Black Hands, White Sails: The Story of African-American Whalers (McKissack)
A Long Hard Journey: The Story of the Pullman Porter (McKissack)
The Moon Over Star (Aston)
No Crystal Stair: A Documentary Novel of the Life and Work of Lewis Michaux (Nelson)
Talkin' about Bessie: The Story of Aviator Elizabeth Coleman (Grimes)
Twelve Rounds to Glory: The Story of Muhammad Ali (Smith)
Uncle Jed's Barbershop (Mitchell)
We Are the Ship: The Story of Negro League Baseball (Nelson)
Working Cotton (Williams)

Parents/Loss of
Everett Anderson's Goodbye (Clifton)
Knock Knock: My Dad's Dream for Me (Beaty)
Locomotion (Woodson)
Miracle's Boys (Woodson)

Peer Relationships
The Battle of Jericho (Draper)
I Hadn't Meant to Tell You This (Woodson)
November Blues (Draper)
Who Am I Without Him? Short Stories About Girls and the Boys in Their Lives (Flake)

Personal Growth and Development/ Self-Concept
The Blacker the Berry (Thomas)
Chill Wind (McDonald)
Francie (English)
Guests in the Promised Land (Hunter)
Heaven (Johnson)
I Am a Black Woman (Evans)
Meet Danitra Brown (Grimes)
Nathaniel Talking (Greenfield)
Rainbow Jordan (Childress)
The Road to Memphis (Taylor)
The Road to Paris (Grimes)
The Skin I'm In (Flake)
Words with Wings (Grimes)

Personal Freedom (core democratic value)
Becoming Billie Holiday (Weatherford)
I Have a Dream: Martin Luther King, Jr. (Nelson)
I, Too, Am America (Hughes)
March: Book One (Lewis and Aydin)
Nelson Mandela (Nelson)
We Are the Ship: The Story of Negro League Baseball (Nelson)

Photography
James Van DerZee: The Picture Takin' Man (Haskins)

Poetry
All the Colors of the Race (Adoff)
Ashley Bryan's ABC of African American Poetry (Bryan)
Becoming Billie Holiday (Weatherford)
Black Cat (Myers)
The Blacker the Berry (Thomas)
Bronx Masquerade (Grimes)
Brown Honey in Broomwheat Tea (Thomas)
Carver: A Life in Poems (Nelson)
The Creation (Johnson)
Dave the Potter: Artist, Poet, Slave (Hill)
Everett Anderson's Goodbye (Clifton)
Every Man Heart Lay Down (Graham)
Fortune's Bones (Nelson)
The Great Migration: Journey to the North (Greenfield)
Half a Moon and One Whole Star (Dragonwagon)
I Am a Black Woman (Evans)
In Daddy's Arms I Am Tall: African Americans Celebrating Fathers (Steptoe)
Jazz on a Saturday Night (Dillon)
Keeping the Night Watch (Smith)
Langston Hughes (Hughes)
Locomotion (Woodson)
Meet Danitra Brown (Grimes)
My People (Hughes)
The Negro Speaks of Rivers (Hughes)
Night on Neighborhood Street (Greenfield)

Poetry (cont'd)

The Other Side: Shorter Poems (Johnson)
The Palm of My Heart: Poetry by African American Children (Adedjouma, ed.)
Soul Looks Back In Wonder (Feelings)
Under the Sunday Tree (Greenfield)
Visiting Langston (Perdomo)
The Voice of the Children (Jordan and Bush)
Words with Wings (Grimes)
A Wreath for Emmett Till (Nelson)

Politics

Barbara Jordan (Haskins)
Julius K. Nyerere: Teacher of Africa (Graham)
Let It Shine: Stories of Black Women Freedom Fighters (Pinkney)
Mississippi Challenge (Walter)
Nelson Mandela (Nelson)
Paul Robeson (Greenfield)
Unbought and Unbossed (Chisholm)

Pregnancy

The First Part Last (Johnson)
Like Sisters on the Home Front (Williams-Garcia)
November Blues (Draper)

Prejudice

Another Way to Dance (Southgate)
Freedom Summer (Wiles)
The Land (Taylor)
The Legend of Buddy Bush (Moses)
Let the Circle Be Unbroken (Taylor)
Mississippi Challenge (Walter)
Roll of Thunder, Hear My Cry (Taylor)
Brendan Buckley's Universe and Everything In It (Frazier)
Darius & Twig (Myers)
Guests in the Promised Land (Hunter)
Lena Horne (Haskins)
March: Book One (Lewis and Aydin)
We Are the Ship: The Story of Negro League Baseball (Nelson)

Pullman Porters

A Long Hard Journey: The Story of the Pullman Porter (McKissack)

Pursuit of Happiness (core democratic value)

The Battle of Jericho (Draper)
Becoming Billie Holiday (Weatherford)
Before John Was a Jazz Giant: A Song of John Coltrane (Weatherford)
Bird (Elliott)
Black Troubadour: Langston Hughes (Rollins)
Bright Shadow (Thomas)
Brown Honey and Broomwheat Tea (Thomas)
Bud, Not Buddy (Curtis)
Carver: A Life in Poems (Nelson)
Chill Wind (McDonald)
The Creation (Johnson)
Dark Sons (Grimes)
Daydreamers (Greenfield)
Each Kindness (Woodson)
Ellen's Broom (Lyons)
The First Part Last (Johnson)
Forged by Fire (Draper)
A Hero Ain't Nothin' but a Sandwich (Childress)
I Have a Dream: Martin Luther King, Jr. (Nelson)
I Know Why the Caged Bird Sings (Angelou)
I, Too, Am America (Hughes)
I'm Going to Sing: Black American Spirituals (Bryan)
Junius Over Far (Hamilton)
Just Us Women (Caines)
Keeping the Night Watch (Smith)
Let It Shine: Three Favorite Spirituals (Bryan)
Like Sisters on the Homefront (Williams-Garcia)
Little Eight John (Wahl)
Locomotion (Woodson)
Lou In the Limelight (Hunter)
Mary Jo's Grandmother (Udry)
Meet Danitra Brown (Grimes)
Miracle's Boys (Woodson)
Mirandy and Brother Wind (McKissack)
The Moon Over Star (Aston)
Motown and Didi (Myers)
Mufaro's Beautiful Daughters: An African Tale (Steptoe)
Nathaniel Talking (Greenfield)
Night on Neighborhood Street (Greenfield)
November Blues (Draper)
The Origin of Life on Earth: An African Creation Myth (Anderson)
The Other Side: Shorter Poems (Johnson)
Rainbow Jordan (Childress)
Ray Charles (Mathis)
The Road to Paris (Grimes)
The Skates of Uncle Richard (Fenner)
Soul Looks Back In Wonder (Feelings)
Standing Against the Wind (Jones)
Tales of Uncle Remus: The Adventures of Brer Rabbit (Lester)
A Thief in the Village and Other Stories (Berry)
Trouble's Child (Walter)
Uncle Jed's Barbershop (Mitchell)
The Way a Door Closes (Smith)
We Are the Ship: The Story of Negro League Baseball (Nelson)
When I Am Old With You (Johnson)
Who Am I Without Him? Short Stories About Girls and the Boys in Their Lives (Flake)
Words With Wings (Grimes)
Yummy: the Last Days of a Southside Shorty (Neri)

Racial Identity

All the Colors of the Race (Adoff)
I Am a Black Woman (Evans)
Zora and Me (Bond and Simon)

Racism

Another Way to Dance (Southgate)
Black Diamond: The Story of the Negro Baseball Leagues (McKissack)
Coretta Scott King (Patterson)
Fast Sam, Cool Clyde, and Stuff (Myers)
Francie (English)
Goin' Someplace Special (McKissack)
I Never Had It Made: The Autobiography of Jackie Robinson (Duckett)
The Land (Taylor)
Lena Horne (Haskins)
Let the Circle Be Unbroken (Taylor)
Malcolm X: By Any Means Necessary (Myers)
Movin' Up: Pop Gordy Tells His Story (Gordy)
The Road to Memphis (Taylor)
Roll of Thunder; Hear My Cry (Taylor)
Song of the Trees (Taylor)
This Life (Poitier)
We Are the Ship: The Story of Negro League Baseball (Nelson)

Reconstruction

Ellen's Broom (Lyons)
I Thought My Soul Would Rise and Fly: The Diary of Patsy, A Freed Girl (Hansen)
The Land (Taylor)

Rituals

The Bells of Christmas (Hamilton)
Christmas in the Big House, Christmas in the Quarters (McKissack)
Mirandy and Brother Wind (McKissack)
Toning the Sweep (Johnson)
Zora and Me (Bond and Simon)

Rivers

The Negro Speaks of Rivers (Hughes)

Rock Collecting

Brendan Buckley's Universe and Everything in It (Frazier)

Romance

A Little Love (Hamilton)
Motown and Didi: A Love Story (Myers)
Who Am I without Him? (Flake)

Rule of Law (core democratic value)

Bad News for Outlaws: The Remarkable Life of Bass Reeves, Deputy U.S. Marshal (Nelson)
Becoming Billie Holiday (Weatherford)
Elijah of Buxton (Curtis)
Nelson Mandela (Nelson)
One Crazy Summer (Williams-Garcia)
The Rock and the River (Magoon)

School Clubs

The Battle of Jericho (Draper)

School Integration

Remember: The Journey to School Integration (Morrison)

School Stories

The Battle of Jericho (Draper)
Because We Are (Walter)
Each Kindness (Woodson)
Locomotion (Woodson)
Tears of a Tiger (Draper)
Virgie Goes to School with Us Boys (Howard)
Words with Wings (Grimes)

Science

Carver: A Life in Poems (Nelson)

Segregation

Freedom Summer (Wiles)
The Friendship (Taylor)
Goin' Someplace Special (McKissack)
I Have a Dream: Martin Luther King, Jr. (Nelson)
March: Book One (Lewis and Aydin)
Mary McLeod Bethune (Greenfield)
Roll of Thunder, Hear My Cry (Taylor)
Rosa (Giovanni)
The Watsons Go to Birmingham—1963 (Curtis)
We Are the Ship: The Story of Negro League Baseball (Nelson)

Self-Concept

Another Way to Dance (Southgate)
The Battle of Jericho (Draper)
Black Means . . . (Grossman)
The Blacker the Berry (Thomas)
Bronx Masquerade (Grimes)
Darius & Twig (Myers)
Daydreamers (Greenfield)
Guests in the Promised Land (Hunter)
Keeping the Night Watch (Smith)
Mare's War (Davis)
Meet Danitra Brown (Grimes)
The Moon over Star (Aston)
One Crazy Summer (Williams-Garcia)
The Other Side: Shorter Poems (Johnson)
My People (Hughes)
The Road to Paris (Grimes)
The Skin I'm In (Flake)
Slam! (Myers)
Something on My Mind (Grimes)
Soul Looks Back in Wonder (Feelings)
Words with Wings (Grimes)

Sexual Orientation

From the Notebooks of Melanin Sun (Woodson)

Single Parenthood

Chill Wind (McDonald)
Forged by Fire (Draper)
From the Notebooks of Melanin Sun: A Novel (Woodson)
Like Sisters on the Homefront (Williams-Garcia)

Slave Revolts

Rebels Against Slavery: American Slave Revolts (McKissack)

Slavery

The Captive (Hansen)
Copper Sun (Draper)
Dave the Potter: Artist, Poet, Slave (Hill)
Day of Tears: A Novel in Dialogue (Lester)
The Days When the Animals Talked: Black American Folktales and How They Came to Be (Faulkner)
Escape to Freedom: A Play About Young Frederick Douglass (Davis)
From the Notebooks of Melanin Sun: A Novel (Woodson)
Heart and Soul (Nelson)
In the Time of the Drums (Siegelson)
The Middle Passage: White Ships Black Cargo (Feelings)
Minty: A Story of Young Harriet Tubman (Schroeder)
Mississippi Challenge (Walter)
Never Forgotten (McKissack)
The People Could Fly: American Black Folktales (Hamilton)
Rebels Against Slavery: American Slave Revolts (McKissack)
Sojourner Truth: Ain't I a Woman (McKissack)
Underground: Finding the Light to Freedom (Evans)

Slavery/Escape From

Almost to Freedom (Nelson)
Anthony Burns: The Defeat and Triumph of a Fugitive Slave (Hamilton)
The Captive (Hansen)
Copper Sun (Draper)
Days of Jubilee: The End of Slavery in the United States (McKissack)
Elijah of Buxton (Curtis)
Escape to Freedom: A Play about Young Frederick Douglass (Davis)
Freedom River (Rappaport)
I Thought My Soul Would Rise and Fly: The Diary of Patsy, a Freed Girl (Hansen)
Moses: When Harriet Tubman Led Her People to Freedom (Weatherford)
Only Passing Through: The Story of Sojourner Truth (Rockwell)
The People Could Fly: American Black Folktales (Hamilton)

Slavery/Escape From (cont'd)
Sojourner Truth: Ain't I a Woman (McKissack)
This Strange New Feeling (Lester)
Underground: Finding the Light to Freedom (Evans)
Which Way Freedom? (Hansen)

South Africa
Nelson Mandela (Nelson)

Sports
The Bat Boy and His Violin (Curtis)
Black Diamond: The Story of the Negro Baseball Leagues (McKissack)
H.O.R.S.E.: A Game of Basketball and Imagination (Myers)
I Never Had It Made: The Autobiography of Jackie Robinson (Duckett)
Slam! (Myers)
Twelve Rounds to Glory: The Story of Muhammad Ali (Smith)
We Are the Ship (Nelson)

Suicide
Tears of a Tiger (Draper)

Tanzania
Julius K. Nyerere: Teacher of Africa (Graham)

Teachers
Julius K. Nyerere: Teacher of Africa (Graham)
The Skin I'm In (Flake)

Teen Pregnancy
The First Part Last (Johnson)

Tuskegee Institute
Portia: The Life of Portia Washington Pittman: The Daughter of Booker T. Washington (Stewart)

Underground Railroad
Underground: Finding the Light to Freedom (Evans)

Urban Stories
Another Way to Dance (Southgate)
Bronx Masquerade (Grimes)
Chill Wind (McDonald)
Darius & Twig (Myers)
Don't Explain: A Song of Billie Holiday (De Veaux)
Fast Sam, Cool Clyde, and Stuff (Myers)
A Hero Ain't Nothin' but a Sandwich (Childress)
James Van DerZee: The Picture Takin' Man (Haskins)
Knock Knock: My Dad's Dream for Me (Beaty)
Lockdown (Myers)
Lou In the Limelight (Hunter)
Marvin and Tige (Glass)
Miracle's Boys (Woodson)
Money Hungry (Flake)
Motown and Didi: A Love Story (Myers)
Night on Neighborhood Street (Greenfield)
No Crystal Stair: A Documentary Novel of the Life and Work of Lewis Michaux (Nelson)
One Crazy Summer (Williams-Garcia)
P.S.: Be Eleven (Williams-Garcia)
The Rock and the River (Magoon)
Slam! (Myers)
Something on My Mind (Grimes)
Who Am I Without Him? Short Stories About Girls and the Boys in Their Lives (Flake)
The Young Landlords (Myers)
Yummy: the Last Days of a Southside Shorty (Neri)

Voting Rights Act
Heart and Soul (Nelson)
Monster (Myers)

War
Brothers In Hope: The Story of the Lost Boys of Sudan (Williams)
Days of Jubilee: The End of Slavery in the United States (McKissack)
Fallen Angels (Myers)
Mare's War (Davis)
The Other Side: Shorter Poems (Johnson)
Which Way Freedom? (Hansen)

Whaling
Black Hands, White Sails: The Story of African-American Whalers (McKissack)

Index

Note: Page numbers in **bold** indicate main discussions for authors, illustrators, and titles.

A

Adedjouma, Davida, 77
Adoff, Arnold, 86
Adoff, Jaime, **16**, 89
Africa Dream, 45, **88**, 92, 102
Aïda, **82**, 97
Alcorn, Stephen, 23–24
All Night, All Day: A Child's First Book of African-American Spirituals, **81**
All the Colors of the Race, **86**, 118
Almost to Freedom, **69**, 91, 111
Anderson, David A., 80
Andrew Young: Young Man with a Mission, **43–44**, 104
Andrews, Benny, 66, **89–90**
Angelou, Maya, 53
Another Way to Dance, **28**, 117
Anthony Burns: The Defeat and Triumph of a Fugitive Slave, **36**, 103
Ashley Bryan's ABC of African American Poetry, **76**, 92
Aston, Dianna Hutts, 64
Aydin, Andrew, **1–2**, 90

B

Bad News for Outlaws: The Remarkable Life of Bass Reeves, Deputy U.S. Marshall, **7–8**
Bailey, Pearl, **48**, 90
Baker, Augusta, 36
Barbara Jordan, **46–47**, 104
The Bat Boy and His Violin, **74–75**, 106

The Battle of Jericho, **19**, 97
Bayard Rustin: Behind the Scenes of the Civil Rights Movement, **27**, 104
Beat the Story-Drum, Pum-Pum, **87**
Beaty, Daniel, 59
Beautiful Blackbird, **68–69**
Because We Are, **40**, 120
Becoming Billie Holiday, **10**, 120
Before John Was a Jazz Giant: A Song of John Coltrane, **64**
The Bells of Christmas, **35**, 103
Benjamin Banneker: Genius of Early America, **45**, 112
Berry, James, **36**, 90
Bible, Charles, 55
Bird, **64–65**, 118
Black Cat, **74**, 110
Black Child, **85**, 107
Black Dance in America: A History through Its People, **34**, 104
Black Diamond: The Story of the Negro Baseball Leagues, **30–31**, 108
Black Hands, White Sails: The Story of African-American Whalers, **24–25**
Black Means . . ., 55
Black Troubadour: Langston Hughes, **53**, 115
The Blacker the Berry: Poems, **10**, **63–64**, 95
Blake, Clarence N., **48**, 90
Bolden, Tonya, **14–15**, **90–91**
Bond, Victoria, **7**, **91**

Bootman, Colin, **69**, **91**
Boyd, Candy Dawson, **39**, **91**
Breaking Ground, Breaking Silence: The Story of New York's African Burial Ground, **26**, 103, 108
Brendan Buckley's Universe and Everything in It, **12–13**, 101
Bright Shadow, **40**, 119
Bronx Masquerade, **20**, 103
Brothers in Hope: The Story of the Lost Boys of Sudan, **67**
Brown, David Scott, 45
Brown, Elbrite, **69**, **91–92**
Brown Honey in Broomwheat Tea, **32**, **79**, 95, 119
Browning, Colleen, 54
Bryan, Ashley, 37, 65, **68–69**, 76, **81**, **83**, **84**, **85–86**, **87**, 92
Bud, Not Buddy, **24**, 95, 101
Bush, Terri, 55
Byard, Carole, 45, **80**, **87**, **88**, **92–93**

C

Caines, Jeannette, 86
The Captive, **30**, 103
Carver: A Life in Poems, **22–23**, 111
Childress, Alice, **41**, **50**, **93**
Childtimes: A Three-Generation Memoir, **43**, 102, 106
Chill Wind, **21**, 107
Chisholm, Shirley, **53–54**, **93**
Chocolate, Debbi, 75

151

Index

Christie, R. Gregory, 7–8, **67**, **72**, **77**, **93**
Christmas in the Big House, Christmas in the Quarters, 29–30
Circle of Gold, 39
Clay, Wil, **80**, **94**
Clifton, Lucille, **39**, **48**, **51**, **94**
C.L.O.U.D.S., **84**, **95**
Collier, Bryan, 12, 59, 60, 62, 66–67, 70, 71–72, 72, 72–73, **94**
Cooper, Floyd, 10, 32, **63–64**, 74, 79, **94–95**
Copper Sun, 13
Coretta Scott King, **47**, 112
Cornrows, **87**, 93
Count on Your Fingers African Style, 87
Cox, Judy, 69
Crane, Louise, **51**
The Creation, **78**, 114
Cummings, Pat, **83**, **84**, **85**, **86**, **95**
Curtis, Christopher Paul, **10–11**, 24, 29, **95**
Curtis, Gavin, 74–75

D

Darius & Twig, 2
Dark Sons, **15**
The Dark-Thirty: Southern Tales of the Supernatural, **32–33**
Dave the Potter, 62
Davis, Lambert, 35
Davis, Ossie, 44, **95–96**
Davis, Tanita S., **8**, **96**
Day of Tears: A Novel in Dialogue, **14**
Daydreamers, **86**
Days of Jubilee: The End of Slavery in the United States, **19**
The Days When the Animals Talked: Black American Folktales and How They Came to Be, **46**, 99
De Veaux, Alexis, **36**, **42**, **96**
Devard, Nancy, **65**, **96**
Diakité, Bab Wagué, **76**, **96**
Dillon, Diane, 5, 28–29, 38, 65–66, **67–68**, **70**, **78**, **82**, **85**, **97**
Dillon, Leo, 5, 28–29, 38, 65–66, **67–68**, **70**, **78**, **82**, **85**, **97**
Diop, Birago, 86
Don't Explain: A Song of Billie Holiday, **42**
Don't You Remember? **51**
Douglas, Gabrielle, **57**
Dr. Martin Luther King, Jr.: Man of Peace, **56**
Dragonwagon, Crescent, 84
Draper, Sharon M., **11**, **13**, **19**, **27**, **31**, **97**
DuBurke, Randy, 7, **71**, **97–98**
Duckett, Alfred, **52**, **98**
Duey's Tale, **48**, 90
Duke Ellington: The Piano Prince and HIs Orchestra, **75**, 113

E

Each Kindness, 3
The Ebony Book of Black Achievement, 55–56
Elijah of Buxton, **10–11**, 95
Ellen's Broom, **60**, 109
Ellington Was Not a Street, **67**, 111
Elliott, Zetta, 64–65
An Enchanted Hair Tale, **36**, 96
English, Karen, **24**, **77**, **98**
Escape to Freedom: A Play about Young Frederick Douglass, 44
Evans, Mari, **54**, **98**
Evans, Shane W., **61**, **98**
Everett Anderson's Friend, **48**, **94**
Everett Anderson's Goodbye, **39**, **94**
Every Man Heart Lay Down, **54**, 101

F

The Faithful Friend, 78
Fallen Angels, 35–36
Fast Sam, Cool Clyde, and Stuff, 49, 110
Faulkner, William J., **46**, **99**
Fax, Elton, 52, 99
Feelings, Tom, 77–78, 79, 86, 88, 99
Fenner, Carol, 44–45, 100
Ferguson, Amos, 83, 100
The First Part Last, 18, 105
Flake, Sharon G., 17, 22, 26, 100
Flournoy, Valerie, 84–85
Forberg, Ati, 44–45
Ford, George, 49, 50, 88, 100
Forged by Fire, **27**, **97**
Fortune's Bones: The Manumission Requiem, 17–18, 111
Francie, **24**, 98
Frazier, Sundee T., **12–13**, **100–101**
Freedom River, **72–73**, **94**
Freedom Summer, 72, 105
The Friendship, 36, 119
From the Notebooks of Melanin Sun, 29, 122

G

Gilchrist, Jan Spivey, 4–5, 34, 35, 81–82, 82, **101**

Ginsburg, Max, 36
Giovanni, Nikki, 66–67
Glass, Frankcina, **46**
God Bless the Child, **68**, 104
Goin' Someplace Special, **71**
Golio, Gary, 62
Gordy, Berry, Sr., **43**, **101**
Graham, Lorenz, **54**, **101**
Graham, Shirley, **49**, **102**
Grandma's Joy, **87**, 93
The Great Migration: Journey to the North, **4–5**
Greenfield, Eloise, **4–5**, **34**, **35**, **43**, **45**, **46**, **49**, 81–82, 82, 83, 86, 87, 88, **102**
Grifalconi, Ann, 39, 48
Grimes, Nikki, **2–3**, **13–14**, **15**, **20**, **25–26**, 70, 79, 88, **102–103**
Groom, Gladys, **55**
Grossman, Barney, **55**
Guests in the Promised Land, **51**, 104
Guy, Rosa, 86

H

Haley, Alex, 43
Half a Moon and One Whole Star, **84**
Hamilton, Virginia, **28–29**, **35**, **36**, **38**, **39**, **40**, **45**, 67–68, 78, 85, **103**
Hand in Hand: Ten Black Men Who Changed America, 3
Hanna, Cheryl, 36
Hansen, Joyce, **26**, **27**, **30**, **37–38**, **103**
Harlem, **76**, 110
Haskins, James, **27**, **34**, **40**, **43–44**, **46–47**, **47–48**, **103–104**
Hathaway, Barbara, **18**, **104**
Heart and Soul: The Story of America and African Americans, **4**, **61**
Heaven, **25**, 105
Her Stories: African American Folktales, Fairy Tales and True Tales, **28–29**, **78**, 97, 103
A Hero Ain't Nothin' but a Sandwich, **50**, **93**
Herzog, Arthur, Jr., 68
Hill, Laban Carrick, 60, 62
Holiday, Billie, 68
H.O.R.S.E.: A Game of Basketball and Imagination, **60–61**
Howard, Elizabeth, 73
Howell, Troy, 46
Hughes, Langston, 60, 63
Hunter, Kristin, **41–42**, **51**, **104**

Index

The Hunterman and the Crocodile: A West African Folktale, **76**, 96

I

I, Too, Am America, **60**
I Am a Black Woman, **54**, 98
I Hadn't Meant to Tell You This, **31**, 121
I Have a Dream: Martin Luther King, Jr., **61**
I Have a Sister, My Sister Is Deaf, **45**, 112
I Have Heard of a Land, **74**, 95
I Know Why the Caged Bird Sings, **53**
I Never Had It Made: The Autobiography of Jackie Robinson, **52**, 98
I See the Rhythm, **74**, 121
I Thought My Soul Would Rise and Fly: The Diary of Patsy, a Freed Girl, **27**, 103
Igus, Toyomi, 74
I'm Going to Sing: Black American Spirituals, **85–86**
In Daddy's Arms I Am Tall: African Americans Celebrating Fathers, **75**, 117
In the Time of the Drums, **73**
The Invisible Hunters: A Legend from the Miskito Indians of Nicaragua/Los Cazadores Invisibles: Una Leyenda de los Indios Miskitos de Nicaragua, **83**, 104

J

James Van DerZee: The Picture Takin' Man, **44**, 104
Jazmin's Notebook, **25–26**, 103
Jazz, **66**
Jazz on a Saturday Night, **65–66**
Jazzy Miz Mozetta, **68**, 109
Jimi & Me, 16
Jimi: Sounds Like a Rainbow: A Story of the Young Jimi Hendrix, **62**
JoeSam, **83**, **104**
Johnson, Angela, 18, 25, 26, 31–32, 34–35, **104–105**
Johnson, James Weldon, 78
Johnson, Jen Cullerton, 62–63
Jones, Traci L., **14**, **105**
Jordan, June, **55**, **105**
Joy, N., 65
Julius K. Nyerere: Teacher of Africa, **49**, 102
Junius over Far, **38**, 103
Just Us Women, **86**, 95
Justice and Her Brothers, **45**, 103

Justin and the Best Biscuits in the World, **37**, 120

K

Keeping the Night Watch, **9–10**, 117
King, Martin Luther, Jr., 61
Knock, Knock: My Dad's Dream for Me, **59**

L

Lagarrigue, Jerome, **72**, **105**
The Land, **22**, 119
Langstaff, John, 83
Langston Hughes: Poetry for Young People series, **66**, 90
Lardy, Philippe, 15–16
Lauture, Denizé, 77
The Legend of Africania, **50**, 115
The Legend of Buddy Bush, **17**
Lena Horne, **40**, 104
Lester, Julius, **14**, **36–37**, **40–41**, **105–106**
Let It Shine! Stories of Black Women Freedom Fighters, **23–24**, 113
Let It Shine: Three Favorite Spirituals, **65**
Let the Circle Be Unbroken, **41**, 119
Let the Lion Eat Straw, **44**, 117
Lewis, E. B., 3, 9–10, 20–21, **63**, **70**, **73**, 73–74, 74–75, **106**
Lewis, John, **1–2**, **106**
Like Sisters on the Home Front, **29**, 121
Lilly, Charles, 51–52
Lion and the Ostrich Chicks: And Other African Folk Tales, **37**, 84
Little, Lessie Jones, **43**, **106**
Little Eight John, **80**, 94
A Little Love, **39**, 103
Lockdown, 6
Locomotion, **19**, 122
A Long Hard Journey: The Story of the Pullman Porter, **35**
Lou in the Limelight, **41–42**
Lyons, Kelly Starling, 60

M

The Magical Adventures of Pretty Pearl, **40**, 103
Magoon, Kekla, **8–9**, **106–107**
Magubane, Peter, **85**, **107**
Malcolm X: By Any Means Necessary, **32**
March: Book One, **1–2**, 90, 106
Mare's War, **8**, 96
Maritcha: A Nineteenth-Century American Girl, **14–15**, 91

Martin, Donald F., **48**, **107**
Martin Luther King, Jr., and the Freedom Movement, **35**, 112
Martin's Big Words: The Life of Dr. Martin Luther King, Jr., **71–72**
Marvin and Tige, **46**
Mary: An Autobiography, **42**, 108
Mary Jo's Grandmother, **56**, 120
Mary McLeod Bethune, **46**, 102
Mathis, Sharon Bell, **50**, 88, **107**
McDonald, Janet, **21**, **107**
McGowan, Gary, **26**, **107–108**
McKissack, Fredrick, Jr., **30**, **108**
McKissack, Fredrick L., **19**, **24–25**, **28**, **29–31**, **33**, **35**, **108**
McKissack, Patricia C., **5**, **19**, **24–25**, **28**, **29–31**, **32–33**, **35**, **71**, **83**, **108**
Mebane, Mary E., **42**, **108**
Medearis, Angela Shelf, 79
Meet Danitra Brown, **79**, 95
The Middle Passage: White Ships/Black Cargo, **77–78**, 99
Mill, Eleanor, 56
Minter, Daniel, **60**
Minty: A Story of Young Harriet Tubman, **76**, **109**
Miracle's Boys, **23**, 121
Mirandy and Brother Wind, **83**
Mississippi Challenge, **33**, 120
Missy Violet and Me, **18**, 104
Mitchell, Margaree King, 80
Mollel, Tololwa, 73–74
Money Hungry, **22**, 100
Monster, **25**, 110
The Moon Over Star, **64**
The Moon Ring, **71**
Morrison, Frank, **68**, **109**
Morrison, Toni, **16**, **109**
Moses, Sheila P., **17**, **109–110**
Moses: When Harriet Tubman Led Her People to Freedom, **66**, 111
Mother Crocodile: An Uncle Amadou Tale from Senegal, **86**, 118
Mother Crocodile/Maman-Caiman, **86**
Motown and Didi: A Love Story, **38–39**
Movin' Up: Pop Gordy Tells HIs Story, **43**
Ms. Africa: Profiles of Modern African Women, **51**
Mufaro's Beautiful Daughters: An African Tale, **83**, 118
Mukasa, **51–52**, **110–111**
My Family Plays Music, **69**
My Mama Needs Me, **85**, 95
My People, **63**

My Rows and Piles of Coins, **73–74**, 106
Myers, Christopher, **60–61**, 66, 74, 76, **110**
Myers, Walter Dean, 2, 6, 25, 28, 32, 33, 34, **35–36**, **38–39**, 43, 49, 66, 76, **110**

N

Nagenda, John, **51–52**, **110–111**
Nathaniel Talking, 35, 82, 101, 102
Neeny Coming, Neeny Going, **77**, 116
The Negro Speaks of Rivers, 63
Nelson, Kadir, 4, 9, 59, **61–62**, 64, 66, 67, 69, **111**
Nelson, Marilyn, **15–16**, **17–18**, **22–23**, **111**
Nelson, Vaunda Micheaux, **3–4**, **7–8**, 69, **111**
Nelson Mandela, 59
Neri, Greg, 7, **111–112**
Ness, Evaline, 51
Never Forgotten, 5
Night on Neighborhood Street, 34, **81–82**, 101, 102
No Crystal Star: A Documentary Novel of the Life and Work of Lewis Michaux, Harlem Bookseller, 3–4
Nolen, Jerdine, 69
November Blues, **11**
Now Is Your Time! The African American Struggle for Freedom, 34

O

One Crazy Summer, **5–6**
Only Passing Through: The Story of Sojourner Truth, **72**, 93
The Origin of Life on Earth: An African Creation Myth, **80**, 121
The Other Side: Shorter Poems, **26**, 105

P

The Palm of My Heart: Poetry by African American Children, **77**, 93
The Patchwork Quilt, **84–85**
Patterson, Lillie, 35, 45, 47, **56**, **112**
Paul Robeson, **49**, 102
The People Could Fly: American Black Folktales, **38**, **85**, 97, 103
The People Could Fly: The Picture Book, **67–68**
Perdomo, Willie, 70
Peters, Margaret, **55–56**, **112**

Peterson, Jeanne Whitehouse, **45**, **112**
The Piano Man, **75**, 120
Pinkney, Andrea Davis, 3, **23–24**, 75, **112–113**
Pinkney, Brian, 3, **32–33**, 73, 75, 78, 81, **113**
Pinkney, Jerry, **36–37**, 64, 68, 71, 76, 82, 83, 84, **84–85**, 87, **113**
Poitier, Sidney, 42
Portia: The Life of Portia Washington Pittman, the Daughter of Booker T. Washington, **47**, 118
Powell, Nate, **1–2**
Price, Leontyne, 82
P.S. Be Eleven, **1**

Q

Qualls, Sean, 64, **113–114**
Quiz Book on Black America, **48**, 90, 107

R

Rainbow Jordan, **41**, 93
Rampersad, Arnold, 66
Ransome, James E., **78**, **80**, **114**
Rap a Tap Tap: Here's Bojangles—Think of That! **70**, 97
Rappaport, Doreen, **71–72**, **72–73**
Ray Charles, **50**, 88, 100
Rebels Against Slavery: American Slave Revolts, **28**
The Red Rose Box, **21**
Remember: The Journey to School Integration, **16**, 109
Rhodes, Jewell Parker, 6, **114**
Ringgold, Faith, 52, 81, **114–115**
The Road to Memphis, **34**, 119
The Road to Paris, **13–14**
Roberts, Brenda C., 68
Robinson, Dorothy, **50**, **115**
The Rock and the River, **8–9**, 106–107
Rockwell, Anne, 72
Roessel, David, 66
Roll of Thunder, Hear My Cry, 41, **48**, 119
Rollins, Charlemae, **53**, **115**
Rosa, **66–67**
Ruffins, Reynold, **77**, **115**
Running the Road to ABC, **77**, **115**

S

Sadler, Sonia Lynn, **62–63**, **115–116**
Saint James, Synthia, **77**, **116**
San Souci, Robert, 78, 81, 82
Schroeder, Alan, 76

The Secret Olivia Told Me, **65**, 96
Seeds of Change, **62–63**, 116
17 Black Artists, **52**, 99
Shaffer, Terea, **79**, **116**
Shange, Ntozake, 67
Siegelson, Kim, 73
Simon, Tayna R., 7, **116**
The Singing Man, **79**, 116
The Skates of Uncle Richard, **44–45**, 100
The Skin I'm In, **26**
Slam! **28**
Smith, Charles R., Jr., **12**, 63, **116–117**
Smith, Hope Anita, **9–10**, **20**, **117**
Sojourner Truth: Ain't I a Woman? **33**
Soman, David, 34–35
Something on My Mind, **88**, 99
Somewhere in the Darkness, **33**, 110
Song of the Trees, 41, **49**, **118–119**
Soul Brothers and Sister Lou, 41, 104
Soul Looks Back in Wonder, **79**, 99
Southerland, Ellease, **44**, **117**
Southgate, Martha, **28**, **117**
Standing against the Wind, **14**, 105
Steptoe, Javaka, 62, 75, **117**
Steptoe, John, 83, 86, **117–118**
Stewart, Ruth Ann, **47**, **118**
Stolz, Mary, 83
Storm in the Night, **83**, 95
The Story of Stevie Wonder, **47–48**, 104
Strickland, Shadra, **64–65**, **118**
Sukey and the Mermaid, **81**
Sweet Whispers, Brother Rush, **40**, 103

T

The Tales of Uncle Remus: The Adventures of Brer Rabbit, **36–37**, 106
Talkin' About Bessie: The Story of Aviator Elizabeth Coleman, **20–21**, **70**, 103, 106
The Talking Eggs, **82**
Tar Beach, 52, 81, 115
Taylor, Mildred D., **22**, 34, 36, 41, 48, 49, **118–119**
Taylor, Theodore, III, **60**, **119**
Tears of a Tiger, **31**, 97
Temple, Herbert, 50
A Thief in the Village and Other Stories, **36**
This Life, **42**
This Strange New Feeling, **40–41**, 105–106

Thomas, Joyce Carol, **10**, **32**, **40**, 63–64, 74, 79, **119**
Thompson, John, 29–30
Thunder Rose, **69**, 111
Toning the Sweep, **31–32**, 105
Trouble's Child, **38**
Tucker, Demetria Renee, **119**, **120**
Twelve Rounds to Glory: The Story of Muhammad Ali, **12**, 116

U
Udry, Janice May, **56**
Unbought and Unbossed, **53–54**, 93
Uncle Jed's Barbershop, **80**, 114
Under the Sunday Tree, **83**, 100
Underground: Finding the Light to Freedom, **61**
Uptown, **72**, 94

V
Velasquez, Eric, **75**, **120**
Virgie Goes to School with Us Boys, **73**, 106
Visiting Langston, **70**, 94
The Voice of the Children, **55**, 105

W
Wahl, Jan, 80
Walter, Mildred Pitts, **33**, **37**, **38**, **40**, 85, **120**
The Watsons Go to Birmingham—1963, **29**, 95
The Way a Door Closes, **20**, 98, 117
We Are the Ship: The Story of Negro League Baseball, **9**, **64**, 111
Weatherford, Carole Boston, **10**, 64, 66, **120**
What a Morning! The Christmas Story in Black Spirituals, **83**
When I Am Old with You, **34–35**, 105
When the Beat Was Born: DJ Kool Herc and the Creation of Hip Hop, **60**, 119
Which Way Freedom? 103
Who Am I Without Him? Short Stories about Girls and the Boys in Their Lives, **17**, 100
Wiles, Deborah, 72
Williams, Mary, 67
Williams, Sherley Anne, 80
Williams-Garcia, Rita, **1**, **5–6**, **29**, **120**
Wilson, Kathleen Atkins, **80**, **121**
Wood, Michele, **74**, **121**
Woods, Brenda, **21**
Woodson, Jacqueline, **3**, **19**, **23**, **29**, **31**, **121–122**
Words with Wings, **2–3**
Working Cotton, **80**, 93
A Wreath for Emmett Till, **15–16**, 111

Y
Yarbrough, Camille, 87
The Young Landlords, **43**
Yummy: The Last Days of a Southside Shorty, **7**, 111–112

Z
Zaslavsky, Claudia, 87
Zora and Me, **7**, 91, 116